Real Estate Investing Made Simple

A Commonsense Approach to Building Wealth

M. Anthony Carr

American Management Association

New York • Atlanta • Brussels • Chicago • Mexico City • San Francisco
Shanghai • Tokyo • Toronto • Washington, D.C.

This publication is designed to provide accurate and authoritative information in regard to the subject matter covered. It is sold with the understanding that the publisher is not engaged in rendering legal, accounting, or other professional service. If legal advice or other expert assistance is required, the services of a competent professional person should be sought.

REALTOR® is a Registered collective membership mark that identifies a real estate professional who is a member of the National Association of REALTORS® and subscribes to its strict Code of Ethics. AMACOM uses these names throughout this book in initial capital letters or ALL CAPITAL letters for editorial purposes only, with no intention of trademark violation.

Library of Congress Cataloging-in-Publication Data

Carr, M. Anthony, 1961–
      Real estate investing made simple : a commonsense approach to building wealth / M. Anthony Carr.
            p.   cm.
      Includes index.
      ISBN 0-8144-7246-X (pbk.)
      1. Real estate investment.   2. Foreclosure.   3. Real property—Purchasing. 4. Real estate management.   5. Real estate investment—United States.   6. Foreclosure—United States.   7. Real property—Purchasing—United States.   8. Real estate management—United States.   I. Title.

      HD1382.5.C363   2005
      332.63'24—dc22   2004007436

Printing number

10   9   8   7   6   5   4   3   2

Contents

Find out why real estate has proven to be the best investment you can
make. How to get tax-free profit every two years, to build wealth with
phenomenal returns on your investment dollar, and to start building a
real estate portfolio with one personal residence after another.

Successful investors have a team of professionals working for them and
pay them well. Here's who you'll need and how to find the ones who
will work your way.

Here's where it all starts! Financing is everything. This chapter covers
the basics of the financing process, including how to get ready to finance
your first home and investor properties. This chapter discusses issues
such as buyers with less-than-perfect credit and what you can do about
these credit issues, as well as giving tips for budgeting and debt management.

Here's where we get into the nitty gritty of programs available in the
marketplace: from zero-down payment programs for first-time buyers
to jumbo loans for the well-to-do.

Continuing from Chapter 4, this chapter discusses the programs that are underwritten and provided by federal and state governments, as well as by nonprofit housing groups.

What it takes to win a contract—and it's not all about money! How to get put on the top of the contract pile, adding a personal touch, and strategies for the buyer with special needs.

Real estate investing isn't just about bricks and mortar. There are plenty of ways to invest in property. This chapter provides a brief description of various ways to get in the game. The following chapters get into deeper detail.

This is what most first-timers think they want to get involved in—and why not? Most true fixer-uppers need minimal repair, but can become cash generators for the savvy investor.

Here's where you start buying at wholesale and selling at retail. This chapter covers how to locate, purchase, finance, rehab, and sell or rent out foreclosures.

If you really want a high return on real estate investments, it's better to look for distressed sellers, instead of distressed properties. Here's how you can find them and how to approach them so they'll want to work with you instead of your competitors.

Getting the house ready to rent out, fixing up the property, and then looking for your renter and staying out of legal hot water by abiding by the Fair Housing Act.

When you start dealing in real estate, you practically have to become an expert on tracking paper trails. Contracts, deeds, trusts, and surveys are just a few of the documents you'll have to be familiar with. Here's what they are and what they mean for you.

For crying out loud, don't make a bunch of money and then give it all to Uncle Sam! Here's a resource chapter on what you can expect to pay in taxes, but also how you can expect to benefit from the tax code for doing your part in repairing and maintaining the national housing pool as a real estate investor.

By Brian Lee. Municipal jurisdictions around the country operate off real estate tax revenues. Thousands, if not millions, of homeowners become delinquent in paying their property taxes, thus creating a deficit in the city's budget. The municipality creates tax liens that are sold to investors at high returns—here's how to get in on the action.

Acknowledgments

No writing and production project can be completed alone. This book has been in the making for sixteen years and I've met a lot of great people along the way who have made it possible. Preeminent is my wonderful life partner, Corinne, who kept her hand on my back supporting me through more than just the writing of this book, but who never stopped believing in me. Thanks to Ann Nichols, my personal coach, for her mentoring and keeping me focused on the goals at hand (here's another one off my list!). Maria Stainer at the *Washington Times* deserves a lot of kudos, namely for giving me the opportunity she did at the Friday Home Guide. The good folks at RealtyTimes.com (Jody Lane, Peter Miller, and Christopher Lambert) put my column on the map with its extensive distribution.

Other real estate professionals who contributed to this book by sharing their knowledge and expertise over the years include: Phil Drew, investor and manager at Carteret Mortgage; Valerie Huffman, energetic leader and senior trainer at Weichert Realtors; David Hyatt, professional mentor and savvy political watchdog; Pat Jablonski, investor and 100-mile hiking pal; Henry Savage, mortgage professional and fellow columnist; and especially all the readers who kept me on my toes with even another new situation!

Finally, the crew at AMACOM Books are great. Particularly Christina "do-you-believe-in-fate" Parisi, the editor who first got this book going, and Erika Spelman, the editor who nursed this puppy to life. Thank y'all (that's Southern for "you guys") to the nicest New Yorkers I know (not to mention the only New Yorkers I know!).

Springfield, Virginia

CHAPTER 1

How to Make 500 to 1,000 Percent on Your Money

If you really want to sink your cash into a money-making venture—real estate is where it's at. *Real Estate Investing Made Simple* is your manual on what's available to you and your family in building wealth.

What you won't find here are unbelievable claims of overnight successes that will load up your bank account in just a few weeks (though there are plenty of fact-based stories about people who have done that). Rather, the chapters here provide you with a commonsense approach to begin your real estate investing trek. Whether you want to invest in brick and mortar or the paper that finances real estate, you'll find tips and steps to get you started.

This is not an all-inclusive book on how to invest in real estate—that would take several volumes. Plus, I don't want you sitting around reading all the time. The best teacher is a trustworthy mentor and a couple of transactions! "Doing" is the best way to learn, and that's what this book is about.

As a primer, let's take a look at how good an investment real estate can be. First—the figures. Over the last thirty years, real estate has proven to be the best investment option to the average American. As you can see in figure 1-1, the value of real estate has moved forward without a blip since 1968. In addition, the median price of

Figure 1-1. 1968–2002 national home price appreciation.

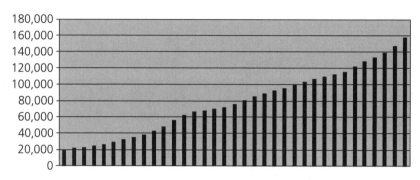

Source: U.S. Dept. Housing & Urban Development (www.hud.gov).

a home has increased by nearly 30 percent in the last five years, beating most stock investments hands down. (See figures 1-1 and 1-2.)

In 1998, the median price of a home across this great land was $128,400. At the end of 2003, it was around $167,000.

The Office of Federal Housing Enterprise Oversight (www

Figure 1-2. 1980–2003 Dow Jones Industrial.

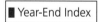

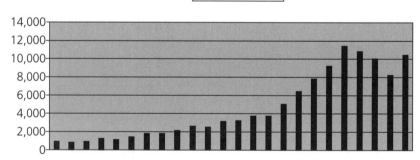

Source: EconStats.com.

.ofheo.gov) keeps up with how much your house is worth. Actually, it tracks single-family housing prices in more than two hundred metropolitan areas. Its resiliency and strength was clearly demonstrated during the last recession. Between 2002 and 2003, only one of these areas experienced a downturn in the pricing of houses. Since 1968, the national median price has soared by 735 percent. What that has meant to homeowners who actually bought and held a home since then is an astonishing return on their investment of roughly 3,675 percent. That's right. This is not a typo—three thousand six hundred seventy-five percent. How could that have happened?

Simply—your investment in real estate is and, for most buyers, will always be a leveraged investment. What you put into the purchase of the property is not its full value. To buy a home today, you need only a very small down payment—heck with zero-down financing, some of you won't even need a down payment!

To demonstrate this astounding possibility, let's say you put down 10 percent on a purchase of a house valued at $200,000. That's $20,000. Since your investment is leveraged, the increase in the value of the house now results in exponential growth on your initial down payment.

When that $200,000 increases in value by 5 percent (2003's average appreciation rate), the property jumps to $210,000. Well, 5 percent doesn't sound like a lot to get excited about, right? Surely you could find a conservative stock that will give you more than 5 percent. But that's the beauty of real estate—the 5 percent on the house ($10,000) is actually 50 percent for the money you have in the property. So now, your investment has grown from $20,000 to $30,000. Keep doing that for five years and your $20,000 investment will have grown by $55,000—that's a return of 276% in five years!

Now, in real estate, you can leverage that property with a lot less money than $20,000. In fact, there are now down payment programs of 5 percent, 3 percent, 1 percent, and even 0 percent. Let's look at what happens with a 3 percent loan:

Year 1 Home Price:	$200,000
Down Payment (3 percent):	$6,000
Year 5 Value of House:	$255,276
Total return on down payment	921 percent

Wow! No mutual fund can do that!

There are other ways to realize amazing returns on your money through real estate investments as well. If you're looking for more conservative but consistent returns, for instance, you may want to consider purchasing real estate tax liens or notes. I devote all of chapter 14 to tax liens; however, suffice it to say you can make consistent returns on these investments of 15 to 50 percent.

When renting out property, the return on your investment increases from the numbers above since you're also enjoying the monthly return of rental payments. Understanding the returns above from home appreciation, add to that the following scenario for the same house purchased with a down payment of 10 percent using investor financing:

Year 1 Home Price:	$200,000
Down Payment (10 percent):	$20,000
Note Amount:	$180,000
Year 5 Value of House:	$255,276
Total return on down payment:	276 percent

As you can see, the initial return on your down payment will be lower, however, let's key in the return on your down payment over the last five years from rental payments.

Note: These calculations use only the down payment and closing costs to determine a total return on investment. They do not take into account the monthly payments made to the lender to calculate the total return. The reason I've left out the monthly mortgage payment as a cost of investment is because most residents will have to pay on either a mortgage or rent, and thus the monthly payment on a mortgage is not an added expense compared to someone paying rent.

Here are the assumptions: You have a monthly payment of $1,226 with a 30-year fixed-rate mortgage and a 6.5 percent interest rate. We'll assume $250 per month for taxes and insurance, bringing your total payment to $1,476. If you are able to get $1,500 per month for the rental, your positive cash flow is going to be $24 per month. That's $288 positive cash flow for the first year—a return of 4.8 percent on the down payment. Though that doesn't sound like a lot, watch what happens as the money grows cumulatively. If your rent increases by 2 percent per year over the five years, then you will have a cumulative cash flow of $5,112—that's more than a 25 percent return on your money. As you can see by these simple calculations, the returns on investment for real estate can be tremendous.

Does this work in every market? No. Just like the stock market, you have to time your entry into the market and the exit. (And there's a section in this book on timing—chapter 7.) Long-term strategies will always work in your best financial interest.

When the stock market gets clobbered, like it did between 2000 and 2002, investors seek out safer havens for their dollars. Real estate, obviously, is at the top of the list. Unlike stocks, however, purchasing real estate is not as easy as clicking on a Web site and transferring your stocks from one fund to another.

Many differences abound between trading in stocks and real estate. If you are considering a change in your investment portfolio, keep in mind you're going to have some expenses in a real estate purchase that you don't have in a stock fund, but you will also enjoy some financial benefits a stock fund will never provide.

The good thing about stocks is that the price is the price. If a fund requires a deposit of $5,000, then you're in the fund for $5,000, less a few dollars for commissions or fees, depending on the fund. You hope and pray that it will grow to at least stay ahead of inflation these days, but in the past, 15 to 20 percent growth was not unusual. Thus a $5,000 investment that grew at 5 percent would be worth $5,250 in a year.

In real estate, it's not as simple. A $150,000 property isn't really going to cost you $150,000. It may cost you $15,000 by the time you fund the down payment, points, closing fees, and so on. However, the money you put into a real estate investment doesn't grow based on the amount of money you put into the transaction. A real estate investment grows based on the leveraged value.

The very nature of real estate enables you to earn much more per year than you could earn in a regular stock fund. The question usually follows immediately, "But what if the real estate market drops?"

Fair question, and I'll show you what happens through a condo I owned and sold two years ago, walking away with $11,000.

The initial purchase price was $66,000 in 1989, to which my down payment was $1,980, using a Federal Housing Administration (FHA) 3-percent-down program. With closing and other costs, the investment ended up being about $3,000. So my total investment was less than 5 percent of the value of the property.

Unfortunately, I bought at the height of the market and then the bottom fell out. In five years, condos like mine were selling for as low as $49,000, but I had already converted the unit into a rental by then.

The monthly payment for my loan was more than the rent coming in. With the condo fee, I was still paying out $75 per month more than what I was bringing in on the rent. As you can see, this was the equivalent of what we experienced on Wall Street around 2000 and 2001. However, with rentals, there are more benefits than just cash flow. Real estate comes with options, unlike its securities-based counterparts.

The tax benefits for the rental property saved me thousands of dollars over the years. The IRS allows me to depreciate the condo by 4 percent each year (based on the $66,000 purchase price), as well as deduct expenses for upkeep and real estate taxes on the property. By the end of each tax year, I may have flowed $900 into the property, but I was also receiving a deduction of more than $4,000 for depreciation, taxes, interest, and various expenses.

Although I made no money during the years I rented the property, by the time I sold, the market had turned, rents were up to where the positive cash flow would have been $200 per month, plus the condo had appreciated to a value of $75,000. My eventual return was more than 300 percent on the original down payment, but that's not even including all the tax savings throughout the rental years.

One of the biggest benefits about real estate is that even in a bust market, you have options to make money on the investment. In addition, real estate markets can stand separate from their counterparts in other jurisdictions. When the stock market falls, it takes just about everybody with it. When home values drop in Houston, it's not going to take down other jurisdictions, as well.

The Fast Way to Get Started

So how can you get into this type of investing and return?

Many investor-owners of residential real estate became landlords by default. These are the owners who couldn't sell a house in a slow market, were facing a transfer deadline, and ended up renting out the house instead of selling it.

If you're already in a house, before you sell it and move up, might I suggest you consider renting out your current home as a matter of financial planning? Sometimes renting out a house can make more financial sense in the long run than selling it. With the change in the home sale tax exemption passed in 1997, homeowners can now keep—tax free—the first $250,000 (for single sellers) or $500,000 (for married couple) of capital gain from a personal residence. Many homeowners find themselves with a wad of cash from the sale of their principal residence and end up using it to purchase their next house, then spend or invest the rest.

By changing the financial plan, a homeowner can make more

money in the long-term by renting out a principal residence than by selling it. If you can purchase another home without selling your current residence, then take a look at the financial and tax benefits you can take advantage of.

First of all, if there's a mortgage on the house and you rent it out to a tenant, someone else is now paying for the house. For our example, let's say someone bought a single family home in 1985 for $150,000 and took a 90 percent loan-to-value mortgage of $135,000 at 8 percent for 30 years. The monthly principal and interest payment would run $991. If taxes and insurance run roughly $200 per month, the total outlay is $1,191. After 16 years, the loan balance is down to under $100,000 and if the house appreciated 2 percent per year during that period of time, the value is now at $206,000. The investor's equity stands at $107,000.

Now that money looks mighty enticing—in the short-run. For the investor, however, it can be used for more than just moving up into one house or for taking vacations, paying off other consumer debt, buying cars and other luxuries. Instead, that equity can be used to purchase other investment houses. For the moment, let's just deal with the one house—yours.

For a monthly positive cash flow on our sample property, you will need to bring in more than $1,300 per month. If rental rates in your area are up to that level—great. Now you have a positive cash flow rental property that someone else is paying for. You're collecting the check, making the payments, and the value of your house is more than likely still moving up.

If the going rates are lower than that amount—say $1,000— then you might consider refinancing the balance of $100,000 over 30 years at 8 percent, bringing the principal, interest, taxes, and insurance (PITI) down to $756—now you have a positive cash flow, and someone else is still making the payments. (All rental income is taxable, but is reduced by rental expenses.)

As a landlord, you now have to keep the property up to code. It must be livable and have all housing systems in working order. This means you'll need to keep the heating and cooling systems in order, water flowing, electricity in working order, and so on. The renter should be taking care of regular maintenance, such as mowing the grass, trimming bushes, washing windows, and keeping the interior in shape. A blocked toilet, broken windows, and other incidental expenses may or may not be your responsibility, depending on what kind of limitations you have in your lease. I'll cover maintenance of property in chapter 11—this is just to give you an idea of what the whole investing scene is really about.

Other aspects of being a landlord include finding renters. I suggest working with a good rental agent in this regard. The agent will conduct background and financial checks on potential tenants—this is worth the agent's commission itself.

Other benefits of owning rental property are those carved out in the tax code for investors. Your expenses on upkeep are deductible, as are taxes, rental fees, legal and accounting expenses, and plenty of other items. There are limitations on deductions. For details check out the IRS Web site Digital Daily at www.irs.treas.gov.

Before making a final decision on renting a property rather than selling it, talk over the numbers with an accountant or financial planner and the how-to's with your real estate agent.

Another way to start investing in real estate without moving is to refinance your home and take the equity out to invest in real estate. Many first-time investors make this their first step.

Your Real Estate Business

But before you run out, refinance, and start hitting foreclosure auctions, you need to decide if you are ready to launch a new business. That's right—you are about to launch a real estate investment business.

What many potential real estate investors don't realize, it seems, is that real estate investing is not like investing in stocks and bonds where you simply place your money with a broker and hope for the best.

Real estate investing is an active investment (unless, of course, you're looking at real estate investment trusts (REITS), but that's a different story).

Many folks say: "I want to begin buying and selling real estate." Sounds pretty simple, doesn't it? Before you launch into the real estate investment world, first consider how the transaction went with your primary residence. The agent probably took care of many of the minute details, such as lining up contractors for inspection items and even getting the inspector. If you're going to start investing on a regular basis, then you'll want to develop relationships with these professionals yourself.

These are the steps you're going to have to take to get started in buying and selling real estate:

- Set up a limited liability corporation.

- Find a real estate agent who knows the marketplace in which you're interested in finding properties.

- Locate financing.

- Line up your contractors. If you're going to do it yourself, then you have to ask the following questions:

  - Do I have the expertise to handle tasks that require trade status, such as plumbing, electrical, HVAC?

  - Can I lay carpet?

  - Can I hang and repair drywall?

  - Can I fix dry rot and carry out other carpentry work?

  - Can I replace subflooring and deck work?

  - Can I repair the roof?

  - Do I have the proper permits and inspections needed to repair electrical and plumbing?

- Find a title company to check out titles of properties.

- Find a settlement or escrow company for closings.

- If you're holding onto the property short term, obtain a short-term insurance policy to cover the property until you sell it again.

■ And then here's the kicker—you have to do this every time you want to buy another house, fix it up, and sell it.

As you can see, this is another job when you're considering the refurbishing of property and selling. You CAN make a lot of money, and you're going to work hard to do it. The good part about it is that the returns are usually higher than what you'll find in any other business.

Before you get started, write down your financial goals together with your partner—usually your spouse. Find a real estate agent who can walk you through real estate investing as it pertains to your area and then talk with your accountant about tax liabilities and benefits—then, make your decision.

Can You Overdo It?

A reader of my weekly real estate column didn't think through the matter of timing, financing, tax liability, and other issues that come with real estate investing. In a matter of four years he had four properties and was at a crossroad, deciding whether to cash out his investments because he felt he may have overdone it—here's his question to me.

> **Question**: I own four new town houses. I have purchased each one over the last four years and then moved into the next one as my personal residence. I'm about to move next year to another house in a neighboring county. I am renting these out to good tenants, but I'm now worried because I put 10 to 20 percent down on each house. I have good equity and the rent covers all the mortgages. I even have a positive cash flow, but I have no other savings except my 401K and pension. I'm thirty-five years old and have a three-month-old baby.
>
> My wife is tired of moving every year and now she's scared that we could lose all our equity if the houses go

down in value. She's suggesting that we sell all the houses and pay off one to live in. Since we haven't lived in any of the houses for more than a year, we will be penalized if we sell now. Any suggestions?

Ibrahim
Northern Virginia

Answer: Your situation brings to the forefront all the elements of investing and how it can affect you personally. You've started investing the way most private investors do it—albeit in an accelerated progression.

Many investors I know purchase a home, rent it out, and move into another home. It's a good way to build your real estate portfolio. Getting four properties in four years is pretty aggressive.

Your wife is growing tired of living out of boxes, I am sure. And this is one of the factors you have to take into account with your investing—the personal toll it can take on your family if you're buying, selling, and moving each time you do it.

The answers to your questions pertain mostly to personal lifestyle choices and to the level of risk you're willing to take with your investments. You definitely are heavy on the real estate side, however, you are young (anyone under forty is young, in my mind).

You need to investigate the past performance of your local real estate market and then the future forecasts of the local economy to determine if now is the time to sell your investment properties. If you're in the real estate investment game for the long haul, then I would advise you to hang on to the real estate—someone else is making the payments for you, and if the economy is growing in your area, then the homes are gaining in equity, too.

It sounds like your wife needs a lot more numbers than what you're providing. Conduct due diligence on your financial situation, talk with the professionals you need to talk with, and then lay all the details out for her to see. Then make a decision that works for the both of you. Don't skimp on the details. If she asks a question and you don't have the details needed to answer it—then do the appropriate research, as likely you will need to know the answer, too.

On a side note: With a three-month-old baby, maybe you should stay up one night so she can get a full night of sleep before she weighs the above decisions. Sleep deprivation may be making her more nervous and less secure—besides facing another potential move.

Originally appeared in www.RealtyTimes.com

As you can see from the points in the above column, there's more to real estate investing than just cashing monthly rental checks. As you read *Real Estate Investing Made Simple*, I hope you start to understand that this is a business nearly anyone can do, but it means educating yourself and preparing for ups and downs. Nevertheless, I've seen lots of business opportunities and none has the security and potential for high returns like investing in real estate. Let's get started!

CHAPTER 2

Building Your Investment Team

The first rule of any successful real estate investor is to put together a team of professionals to guarantee a successful real estate investment business. As you move forward to build your real estate portfolio there are several people who must be on your team and others I suggest you consider.

Mentor

First and foremost is a mentor. Find someone in your marketplace who has gone down the road before you. Finding this person is not that difficult. Talk with your attorney, accountant, or Realtor. One of them will most likely know someone who owns several real estate investment properties.

A good mentor is a person who understands there is plenty of investment property to go around. You want to be careful you're not teaming up with someone who simply wants to use you as a scout for investment properties he can fold into his personal portfolio. A mentor should be a true investor and teacher—as well as someone who is respected by his or her peers. This is one of those times when it's okay to talk behind someone's back. You want to find out about this person's character and reputation in the real estate community.

The other three people I mentioned above should also be on your team: an attorney, an accountant, and a Realtor.

Attorney

Talk with an attorney to find out if you should set up a separate corporation to begin investing in real estate, whether you intend to hold the property as a rental or try to flip it in the case of a foreclosure. An attorney can look at your whole situation, including your liabilities as an investor and landlord, the way your title is written (joint tenants, tenants in common, and so on), how to protect yourself and your assets, as well as other issues of running a company and investing in real estate.

Accountant

The certified public accountant (CPA) is the person who will help you become profitable. He or she should know the ins and outs of real estate accounting practices. He or she can help you set up financially for receiving rents, paying mortgages and taxes, funding repairs, and, most important, keeping records. Now that you've started a business, some of your daily expenses are tax deductible—don't miss out by trying to do this yourself.

Realtor

A Realtor, of course, is the rubber-meets-the-road partner (as well as a good investment mortgage lender—but more about this person in a moment). You may want a couple of Realtors who deal regularly with investors. This is key. The person who helped you with your purchase of your personal residence may have done a great job getting you into your house, but if he doesn't know the nuances of investment real estate, it is in your best interest to find another Realtor (or two) who has done this more than a few times.

Just a note on the Realtor. Not all real estate licensees are Realtors, just like not all sodas are Pepsis. A Realtor is a member of the National Association of Realtors, as well as of the state and local Realtor associations. You must know at this point that I have worked for Realtor associations in the past and have developed a prejudice toward working with a licensee who is a Realtor over one who is not.

The Realtor association network provides me as an investor with another layer of ethics and accountability. All Realtors have vowed to uphold the Realtor Code of Ethics (which can be found at www.Realtor.com). In addition, if I have a grievance against a Realtor, I can take her before her peers for disciplinary action if the case warrants it.

Now, you may be thinking that taking her before her peers is a lost cause, because certainly the Realtors will protect their own—not necessarily. In a community with a strong Realtor association or board, you will find that the grievance committee wants to keep its members honest. One bad egg can ruin the reputation of the whole industry.

In addition, the Realtor association is usually the group that operates the local multiple listing service (MLS). This is a huge database of properties that are on the market. The association has spent hundreds of thousands, if not millions, of dollars to formulate this powerful tool. It's a pure database, meaning that the database is true. The listings are real listings—not ads—for property that is on the market. Most Web sites and lists of properties online are advertisements—meaning that once the house sells, it may still linger on this advertising database. If you go clicking through to these types of databases, you may waste a lot of time because the fixer-upper or preforeclosure may have sold months earlier.

With most MLS systems, the Realtors are fined if they let a listing linger that has already been sold! There are several other positives in working with Realtors that I'll not go into here—you can find more information about that by visiting www.Realtor.com and www.Realtor.org. I'll discuss the value of a good real estate agent in more depth at the end of this chapter.

Loan Officer

Next is the mortgage guy or gal. Maybe this is really the first contact you should make for the whole team, but nevertheless, you are going to quickly find out that this person makes or breaks every single deal that you are going to finance. (Eventually, you want to be creating enough cash flow that you are financing your own investments, but that's down the road a bit.)

The loan officer has to be creative and needs to demonstrate that he or she has access to various types of investors. Most likely, you're going to go with a mortgage broker, but if you have a good relationship with your bank or credit union, they may have programs available for real estate investors. Let them know what you're doing, what you want to do, and how you want to do it. Don't try to get a loan from them on false pretenses. In other words, if you're planning on buying low and selling high within sixty to ninety days—let them know that, so they can structure the best loan for you.

Contractor

As you purchase properties, you'll need a contractor or several tradespeople (plumbers, electricians, and so on) and service providers who can get your properties in shape. It's best to find a crew that can do all of the fix ups. Let them know ahead of time (about thirty days) that you're about to get a new property, so they can schedule time to help fix it up. The tradespeople you'll want to have a good relationship with include: an electrician, a plumber, a carpenter, a landscaper, a tree company, a roofer-siding-window contractor, a drywall installer, a masonry contractor, a heating and air conditioning company, a chimney sweep, a painter, a flooring outlet, an appliance outlet, and a pool maintenance company. One good contractor can create this network, but you may not want to be locked up with just one in case his schedule gets full, leaving you waiting in line or searching at the last minute for a fill-in.

Property Manager

Once you finally own the property you may want to consider hiring a professional property manager (unless you enjoy unclogging toilets, fixing leaky faucets, replacing light fixtures, and so on). While you can definitely save some money doing these tasks yourself—and it may be the way you need to go—a property manager removes this final headache of real estate investment from the equation.

The key to real estate investing is to make money going into the deal, make money on the rental, and make money when you sell. Your professional team of advisers will ensure you have a strong investment business instead of a money pit.

Insurance Agent

As you get into and out of properties, you'll need various types of insurance through the process. The mortgage insurance will be taken care of through the lender. You'll also want a homeowners insurance with good coverage for accidents during construction. Be sure to look for an insurance coverage certificate from all your contractors. This should cover accidents on the job and their materials in case of fire or theft.

Structural Engineer

For those who go after the real diamonds in the rough—abandoned and dilapidated properties—you will need a structural engineer. A house that looks like it is about to collapse may be a diamond in the rough, but safety first—have the structural engineer inspect the property to see if it can be rebuilt or if it just needs to be demolished and built from the ground up.

You're the Boss When Hiring an Agent

For novice real estate investors, I can't tell you how important it is to get a good Realtor on your team. For a commission, a Realtor carries out a lot of groundwork to get your business off the runway. There are several reasons why a relationship with a Realtor will help you while you're helping the Realtor develop her business:

- To steer new investors away from the many red-ink-filled pitfalls

- To find properties for investors, because the Realtor will make money when he or she writes acceptable contracts on these properties

- To develop investor clients for life, since investors buy more than just a personal residence

- To provide contacts with the above-mentioned team members

- To act as gateway to attorneys, settlement agents, workers, tradespeople, and others who can make your job a lot easier

So let's look a little deeper at how to find a Realtor who can become part of your team.

Build Your Team on the Internet

Have you looked up real estate on the Internet lately? Whoa . . . there's a bunch of stuff floating out in cyberspace. Not all of it actually has to do with buying or selling a house. What we'll deal with in this section are the aspects of getting the right person to work for you, including how to deal with personalities, business philosophies, services you should receive, and more.

When the Internet arrived on the real estate scene in the 1990s, Realtors rejoiced and cried. Some were fearful of its effects on their business, while those who understood the power of the World Wide Web knew they were about to experience a business boom. Most Realtors I work with see the Internet as a partner in business, not an adversary. If the ones you've worked with don't view it this way—take them off your list.

More than likely, buyers start their information gathering on the Internet. Buyers plod through dozens of sites to look at the houses on the market, maybe even calculating how much those houses cost with online mortgage calculators.

Offline, the prudent buyer wants to trek through houses in his price range to see if the Web pictures are revealing what they purport to reveal. Once a buyer sets foot in a house, it comes to life—unlike the two-dimensional pictures placed on the Web. The house actually tempts the senses.

This is where the Realtor comes in. Probably 99 percent of the houses advertised online are listed through Realtors. It is through their cooperative business efforts (and millions of dollars of investment) that the industry is able to bring together this huge database of houses for consumers to peruse. It's called the multiple listing system, and buyers get a small glimpse of it online through national Web sites like www.Realtor.com. To find your local association's Web site, go to Realtor.com and click on the link to local sites. Through those sites, you'll more than likely find the local database of homes online.

At the local Realtor association site, there will likely be a link to "Find A Realtor," which allows you to search by area, name, or even professional designation. For instance, a search at one of my local Realtor association sites—the Greater Capital Area Association of Realtors—in the Potomac, Maryland, area, produced results of 597 Realtors listed in alphabetical order with links to their information, including phone numbers, e-mail addresses, and Web sites.

With all the high-tech capabilities available to consumers, the king of the Realtor searching, however, is still the old standby of personal referral. Most top producers prefer this method of obtaining new business as well, since a referral is more apt to stay with the agent over one who responds to a postcard or calls into the front desk of the office.

Some home buyers work exclusively with a buyer's broker, specifically hired to represent them; some work with a seller's broker. In either case, choosing the right Realtor is a crucial first step in the home buying and real estate investing process. In making this important decision you should understand:

Just like searching for a doctor, an accountant, or a mechanic, most consumers trust the recommendation of a friend or family member over any other mode of selection. The same is true with a real estate professional.

Match Your Agent to Your Desired Investment

How you select an agent may also be determined by what type of home you want to purchase or where you want to buy. In most markets, Realtors work certain areas. It's wise to select a Realtor in the geographic area in which you want to buy. A nearby Realtor can get to your home of choice easier than someone from forty miles out during rush hour. In addition, a local Realtor is going to have a better handle on product knowledge.

Some buyers specifically want to purchase unique properties, such as condominiums, fixer-uppers, or investment properties. Realtors who do not have that particular expertise may even refer buyers out to another agent to help with their specific needs.

If you want to purchase a HUD or VA house, for instance (these are homes offered by two federal agencies—the U.S. Department of Housing and Urban Development and the U.S. Department of Veterans Affairs), then you must seek out agents who have gone through the HUD or VA courses, which certify them to sell these foreclosed properties.

Access to information is not everything. The knowledge of how to use information is more important—and that's what a professional agent provides to both buyers and sellers.

Once you get your list of agents down to two or three, you need to have a slate of requirements for the agent whom you will eventually hire as your representative in buying or selling your next house. An agent is bound by certain legal obligations. Traditionally, these common-law obligations are to:

- Put the client's interests above anyone else's.

- Keep the client's information confidential.

- Obey the client's lawful instructions.

- Report to the client anything that would be useful.

- Account to the client for any money involved.

You also want to make sure your agent has the proper experience. As you move forward to invest in real estate and tell your friends and family about your newfound interest in this business, you may find out that some of them have a real estate license. You'll be surprised, as never before had they mentioned this—but suddenly, with your past relationship, they want you to use them exclusively to find and buy investment properties.

Warning: Withhold your loyalties because of friendship and bloodline! In fact, unless you know a person has worked with inves-

TIP A Realtor is held to an even higher standard of conduct under the NAR's Code of Ethics. In recent years, state laws have been passed setting up various duties for different types of agents. As you start working with a Realtor, ask for a clear explanation of your state's current regulations, so that you will know where you stand on these important matters.

tors before—on a consistent basis—then pass. You need an agent with the experience necessary to carry out your real estate investing business goals.

Most agents help people buy a personal dwelling. The criteria for reaching such a goal is important, but it is a far cry from the criteria you have in growing a real estate investment business. The bottom line is the bottom line when it comes to investing. You don't care how nice a view a property has, what upgrades or amenities are included, or if it backs up to woods. You just want to know if this community is renting fast and for how much.

The job description for your investment agent may include:

- Has experience with investors (measured in number of transactions, rather than years)

- Understands desire for profitable cash flow

- Works full-time in the industry

- Boasts savvy negotiating skills capable of getting properties for the buyer with favorable price and terms

- Knows the targeted investment area like the back of her hand

- Possesses established network of contractors and professionals necessary to get houses fixed, listed, and sold in the quickest amount of time with highest profit margin

With all due respect—unless your friend or relative meets the above criteria—pass. It's your money, time, and risk—not theirs. I know hundreds of agents in my marketplace—but I've used only two or three of them in growing my business.

The Difference Between a Buyer's and a Seller's Broker

Suppose you sign an offer to buy a home for $150,000. You really want the property and there's a chance other offers are coming in, so you tell the broker that "I'll go up to $160,000 if we have to. But of course don't tell that to the seller."

If you're dealing with a seller's agent, he or she may be duty-bound by state law to tell the seller that important fact. In most states, the seller's agent doesn't have any duty of confidentiality toward you. Honest treatment may require the agent to warn you that "I must convey to the seller anything that would be useful, so don't tell me anything you wouldn't tell the seller."

 If you're dealing with seller's agents, it's a good idea to keep confidential information to yourself.

These days many homebuyers prefer instead to hire a buyer's broker, one who owes the full range of duties, including confidentiality and obedience, to the buyer. In most markets, the buyer's broker is paid by the proceeds from the sale (some would say, paid by the seller), rather than the buyer, thus using a buyer's broker—working for you—does not involve any extra cost as an investor.

How to Evaluate an Agent

There are certain questions you should ask when evaluating a potential agent.

The first question you should ask is whether the agent is a Realtor—and I discussed why that is important earlier. You should then ask:

- Does the agent have an active real estate license in good standing? (To find this information, you can check with your state's governing agency.)

- Does the agent belong to the multiple listing service (MLS) or a reliable online homebuyer's search service?

- Is real estate their full-time career?

- What real estate designations does the agent hold?

- Which party is he or she representing—you or the seller? The discussion is supposed to occur early on, at "first serious contact" with you. The agent should discuss your state's particular definitions of agency, so you know where you stand.

- In exchange for your commitment, how will the agent help you accomplish your goals?

Rules of Engagement with Agents

Question: I'm developing a business plan to purchase real estate as an investment. My plan is to buy single-family homes that will either be rehabilitated, flipped, or lease optioned. I have been in contact with a Realtor who wants me to sign an exclusive buyer's agreement. Is there a particular advantage or disadvantage in limiting myself to one Realtor?

If I do decide to work with this Realtor and restrict his fee to just the properties that are introduced by him, how do I handle a holdover period if we decide not to proceed with the agency at some future date. I want to be fair, but I'm uncomfortable with the concept of protecting his fee in perpetuity.
Reader, via e-mail

Answer: You bring up several good points about the real estate investment process. The fact that you're developing a business plan is very wise. Many would-be investors I've met begin their investments in real estate by just showing up at the courthouse steps at a foreclosure sale with a blank check in their hands. The fact that you're planning out your steps is to be commended.

When it comes to purchasing your private residence, it makes complete sense to sign an exclusive buyer's agreement to guarantee you're represented in the homebuying process. Some buyers are misguided in believing they can somehow get a better deal on a home purchase by working with just one agent—the listing or seller's agent. This could not be further from the truth. When you have a buyer's agent in your corner, you know that agent is going to negotiate on your behalf, let you know what it takes to make a good offer, and help you line up the financing necessary to be successful.

For investing in real estate, it's probably even more important to have a buyer's agent working for you since you're going to be doing this type of transaction again and again. A Realtor who understands the goals and pitfalls of investing in real estate is invaluable. You definitely want an investment Realtor on your team. Exclusive? I'm not so sure.

Unlike the scenario of buying a personal residence, where you'll find pretty much everything in the multiple listing service, investment properties, many times, are not in the MLS. A Realtor who works with investors consistently knows they may not get all the deals from one investor. Some transactions are going to be through the courts, others through corporations, and then there are the investment properties that come through the traditional avenues—the MLS and a Realtor's network.

I would sign an exclusive buyer's agreement with an agent to represent me on a particular deal, rather than for a prolonged, open-ended contract. When it comes to investment properties, one Realtor can't have his ear to the ground as well as three or four can. Be upfront with your Realtors and let them know you're working with several others who understand investment real estate—as they get good properties, they should contact you. THEN, as you're moving in to buy a particular property—sign an agreement.

Again, I would not recommend this nonexclusive arrangement for purchasing your private residence. In the investment scenario, however, you're the investor with the money. You're going to buy property with or without this Realtor. You're the engine—see if he or she wants to get on board. Work out a LONG-TERM arrangement to show that you're not going away after just one deal, but that you have to have a broader net to maximize your bottom line. A Realtor who doesn't understand this part of your business plan should not be on your team.

Trust Your Realtor to Refer You to the Right Services

Only in stabilized real estate markets do consumers and commentators on the market want to maintain commonsense purchasing and selling practices, such as getting a buyer's agent to purchase a house, requesting home inspections, and getting referrals from Realtors on the residual services needed to buy or sell a home.

When the market heats up, buyers are willing to forgo the protection they need to complete a purchase. Home inspections are the first to go, it seems, to both the buyers' and sellers' dismay. Buyers usually find something glaringly dysfunctional in the house when they finally move in and sue the seller. Ouch . . . but so goes the throwing away of good advice.

One standard practice I've seen attacked in many markets during the last few years is the use of referrals from the Realtor for residual services. The Realtor, in essence, is the center of the transaction. He or she is the one who puts the seller's house on the market and starts the selling and buying process by placing it in the MLS.

Once a buyer places a contract on the house, the residual services kick in—some of them even before a contract is presented. Buyers and sellers on average go through this process about once every seven to ten years. So it is in their best interest to ask the Realtor for a referral in the business to fulfill the necessary tasks that must be completed. These residual services include the mortgage provider, appraiser, home inspector, pest inspector, environmental inspector, title company (with homeowners insurance), contractors for repairs, and others.

Some of my cohorts in the media encourage buyers and sellers to take a real hard look at the list of referrals they receive from their Realtor, arguing that they may be in cahoots together just to get the transaction through. They're not so concerned about your needs, you see, and just want to get their money. (Let's forget that most agents I know want your business for life and understand full well that they are in heated competition with their colleagues and want you to remember them in seven years for a job well done.) But in the minds of many in the real estate media, that's beside the point.

They encourage you to go find your own lender, inspector, appraiser, home inspector, and so on, because then you know they're not trying to pull the wool over your eyes. Poppycock! Since the transaction begins with the Realtor, this is where your first referral should start. Ask around for a good Realtor. Talk with your friends who just sold or bought a house. It's really not that hard. If you decide on a Realtor the same way you decide what fast-food restaurant to eat lunch at (who can get it to me hottest, fastest, and for the cheapest), then you're probably asking for nothing more than a quick fix, followed by a prolonged case of indigestion.

Ask around. Then trust the agent for the referrals. If the agent is top notch, he has been through transactions scores of times and has developed professional relationships with the residual service providers who get the job done, when they say they'll get it done, for the price they say they'll get it done for.

You'll be faced with two types of referrals, usually—the one where the agent's company owns the residual service company and the second where it's an agent's personal sphere of professionals he does business with.

Ask the agent up front if he has ever used the particular referral in a business transaction before. How did it go for his past clients and how many times did a deal get messed up with that person? (And trust me, there's always a deal that gets messed up—it's just part of the industry.) Very important is the fact that he has built his referral network through professionalism and not family, religious, political, or other ties. You don't want to use a referral solely because he's the Realtor's brother or a fellow Moose club member.

I'm not saying that all referrals guarantee a bump-free transaction. However, successful Realtors don't let a lot of people in their sphere unless they are professional and can get the job done.

Do-It-Yourselfers Take Heed

Finally, I would like to talk about why it's important to have a group of Realtors on your team. Many home sellers have a difficult time paying someone a commission for a sales job that seemed effortless. Is it worth it to go alone and save the commission dollar? To answer that question simply, yes, you can sell your property without an agent. Many have done it and done it well (16 percent of all sales, according to the National Association of Realtors).

Once you're done reworking a property all you have to do is draw a contract or two and voila, money in the bank, right? If you picked up my book, you probably have property to sell or are looking for those investment properties that will fill your pockets with cold hard cash—why turn over some of it to an agent? I can't argue with that logic, but you may find that a real estate professional is worth more than you pay her in terms of the headaches you'll miss and the laws you won't violate by having her on your team.

There is a good reason I advise people who want to get into real estate investing to develop a professional real estate investment team, one that includes a lender-investor, an attorney, a construction crew, a list of vendors (such as home inspectors, pest control professionals, painters, roofers, and so on), and a savvy, professional, ethical real estate agent.

Keep in mind, the agent has undergone between 80 and 120 hours of state-required course work (that's more than some college requirements). In addition, if you get an experienced Realtor, more than likely he's learned a lot more outside the class than inside. It is this expertise and knowledge for which you are paying.

Selling real estate is like writing—it looks easy to those who have never done it. A sign goes up in the yard, and a few weeks later (or months, sometimes) the sign goes down. How hard can that be? There's a lot more to the job than this. Here's what a typical agent will do to close a deal.

She will analyze the value of your house to come up with a salable price. This entails researching the market through the local multiple listing system and court records to find what has sold that matches your property. Then she will determine a price either as a cost per square foot or model type, taking into account the amenities and features of the house. She will consult with the owner to get the house in shape, and have the gall to tell the seller that the mauve walls just won't work and to paint them all cream. She'll replace the carpet and rent a storage unit and take 25 to 50 percent of the household items out of the house to make it presentable. She will construct a marketing campaign to get your house in front of enough people to attract offers from qualified buyers, and pay for the marketing up front with her own money. Agents spend thousands of dollars a year marketing real estate—some up to 25 or 35 percent of their revenue—on newspapers, real estate publications, Web sites (and usually not just one), pagers, handheld devices, cell phone expenses (and forget the family plan, this is usually about a $300 + bill per month), and a plethora of other expenses.

Now she's going to show the property at the convenience of the buyer, not the agent's schedule or the seller's schedule. If you're working full-time and trying to sell your house, when will you take off to show the property to potential buyers? And how will you know if they are really qualified to purchase the house without asking a lot of personal questions that, frankly, they should not be answering.

Let's say you get a contract; now the agent is going to negotiate this multipage document, loaded with a lot of legal requirements (statutory and regulatory—by the way, does the contract you're considering meet the legal requirements of your area?). Besides making sure that no laws are broken and that the appropriate contract and state-required addenda are connected to it, she's also going to get the price you want for your property with acceptable terms.

Once the contract is signed off on, the real work begins. Now the fulfillment of the contract has to happen. This means monitoring the terms: Is the loan on track for the buyer? Did the work crew get the inspection items fixed? Did the termite inspection pass? Oh, it didn't? Then can the termite guy get out here and treat the house before settlement? And so on. . . .

Until you have several investment properties creating enough cash flow so that you can seek out investment opportunities fulltime, you need a full-time professional agent on your side. Suffice it to say, I have agents in several markets looking for houses for me. I'm not going to worry how much they get paid—just if the deal meets my financial goals.

While you may be excited to start making money on real estate investments as soon as possible, get your foundation set first. Get the team in order. Start with a Realtor or loan officer who has worked with investors. These two professionals can direct you to other investors and investor groups where you can start learning from someone who's been down the road a few bends more than you. Now, let's look at the glue that holds everything together—financing.

CHAPTER 3

Getting Ready for the Big Game!

In this chapter, we'll cover the basics of financing, including such processes as qualifying for a loan, getting credit scores and reports, and budgeting and debt reduction. Then I'll review the various loan programs available to personal buyers and investors, discuss the ins and outs of these programs, and show you how to use them to increase your wealth. At the end, we'll go over some creative financing for those who want to get more out of a house with less out of their pocket.

The first thing anyone investing in real estate must learn about is financing. What does it take to get a house when you're buying one to live in, buying one to rent out, buying one to flip, buying one to live in for the short-term or for the long-term—even buying one when you're retiring?

Financing is the name of the game. It affects every aspect of the investment. If you're buying to rent out, you may need two loans—one to purchase and one to fix up. Do you know where you'll get those two types of loans? Or maybe you want to get in the house for just a little money out of your pocket. If not, you may be one of these folks who wants a big down payment to lower your monthly outgo. All of these questions must be dealt with right up front.

If you don't get the financing down, you'll never own a house or be able to build wealth in real estate. Once you've overcome the financing part of the formula, you're more than halfway there. So you want to invest in foreclosures and make a ton of money? First, invest in the best house you can invest in—the one you call home.

Financing Basics

Before I go much further into financing, let's review some basics so we all understand what the heck I'm talking about in this section.

■ Most Americans use a mortgage to purchase a property. Homebuyers must save enough money for a down payment on a house, anywhere from 3 to 20 percent. For buyers with excellent credit and strong incomes, zero-percent-down programs are available. The down payment amount, along with your credit rating and other financial parameters, will play an important part in determining your interest rate. The loan is amortized (spread over a number of years), with the most basic type being for 30 years; however, 10-, 15-, 20-, and 40-year programs also exist, usually with a fixed rate of mortgage—in this book, we'll give examples between 7 and 9 percent. Once you qualify for a mortgage, the note is then either serviced by the company from which you obtained the mortgage or sold to a group of investors. Thus, if you obtain a mortgage from ABC Mortgage, you may find that you'll end up sending payments to Acme Loan Services by the time all is said and done.

■ The mortgage payment is made up of four parts: principal, interest, taxes, and insurance, referred to in the industry as PITI. The principal and interest go to the mortgage company. The amounts for taxes and insurance are usually collected by the mortgage company and held in escrow. When the taxes and insurance are due, the mortgage company makes the payments on the borrower's behalf.

1. **Principal**. This is the amount the buyer borrows. If the house is priced at $200,000 and the buyer purchases the

home with a 10 percent down payment ($20,000), the principal amount is $180,000. This also means the mortgage is a 90 percent loan-to-value (LTV) mortgage since 90 percent of the value of the house is being financed.

2. **Interest**. The eventual owner of the note earns money on the note through the interest charged on the principal amount. Home mortgage interest is a deductible expense from your income. As the mortgage payments begin, you will pay more on interest than on the principal. For instance, with the above loan, a 7 percent interest rate will provide you with a monthly principal and interest payment of $1,197.54. During the first year, the interest part of the payment will linger around $1,045 and the principal portion will be around $150 per month. By the thirtieth year, those numbers will flip—your interest portion will be only about $50 while the principal will rocket to more than $1,000 per month. Thus your deductions for interest payments are greater in the first several years of the mortgage and fall during the latter years.

3. **Taxes**. Once a mortgage is paid off, taxes will continue. While you have a mortgage, the mortgage company will collect these taxes from you and forward them to your local tax office. The annual amount is spread over the year in each payment that is sent in with your mortgage. Each community has a different tax requirement, so you can't even look at taxes on a state level to determine your average property tax bill. For instance, my property taxes in northern Virginia are more than $300 per month, but my father's in northeast Alabama stand at $70 per year. This portion of your bill is also tax deductible. Your annual payment for this line item will be listed on Form 1098 (Mortgage Interest Statement), which is sent out at the beginning of each year from your mortgage service provider. If you are using owner financing, then the owner-financier must fill this out for you and send it to you.

4. **Insurance**: The mortgage company requires you to pay for a hazard insurance policy to protect the mortgage company in case the house burns down or is destroyed by a natural or man-made disaster. This premium is also spread over the year in payments to your mortgage service provider. Insurance payments are not tax deductible.

■ The numbers and figures used in this book are for illustration purposes only. A $200,000 loan in Fairfax, Virginia, will not cost the same as it does in Wheaton, Illinois, because the taxes are so different. Examples here will use a modest tax structure, but you will need to talk with a Realtor or loan officer in your area to get the bottom line on a monthly payment in your area.

■ As mentioned earlier, the interest and taxes are expenses deductible from your income; however, they are fluid numbers. If you have a fixed-rate mortgage, the monthly principal and interest will remain the same throughout the term of the loan. However, because property tax assessments fluctuate, how much the mortgage company must put into its escrow fund will also fluctuate. Thus, your PITI payment for $1,100 this year could be $1,200 next year and $1,098 the next year. It just depends on what's happening with property assessments in your jurisdiction.

With these basics out of the way, lets get back to the importance of financing.

The federal tax code provides us with the best way to build wealth through our own dwelling place. If you're renting, you're making a major mistake in growing your personal wealth. Unless you just have to rent, because of your job situation or you've totally blown your credit so that you can't get a mortgage on a house, then you should invest in a property for yourself, first.

Renters are building wealth for the landlord or conglomerate that owns their apartment or house. Their money is being used to pay off someone else's mortgage instead of their own and helping those folks build wealth.

Now, this doesn't mean that by owning your own home you're making money on your first investment. Actually, as Robert Kiyosaki so succinctly points out in his book, *Cash Flow Quadrant,* a house is a liability. You have to put money into it all the time. You're paying the PITI each month, as well as the upkeep, utilities, and everything else that comes with owning a home.

The property does not pay you anything in return on a regular basis. Until that dwelling place is converted into a rental and is bringing money to your bank account, it's not an investment. Nevertheless, for most people, it's one of the best places to start building wealth for the long-term, but it's going to cost you money—and lots of it. But, hey, you have to pay to live somewhere, so you might as well pay yourself. When you join the growing ranks of homeowners and real estate investors, you'll find there are many benefits to this form of investment that no other investment provides:

■ The monthly payment helps increase your equity in the property, which hopefully is also growing by way of appreciation.

■ The tax and interest payments are then turning around and lowering your income tax bill, as well. These two items are tax deductible (as described above). Depending on your tax bracket, these two deductions can save you hundreds, if not thousands, of dollars in taxes each year. Jeff Schnepper, author of *How to Pay Zero Taxes,* reports that nearly 36 million taxpayers took this deduction in 2001—about $9,100 per taxpayer. For a taxpayer in the 28 percent tax bracket, that's a savings of more than $2,500 per year.[1]

■ Renting a dwelling instead of owning real estate costs you more, because it doesn't allow the small down payment you make when buying a house to grow on the basis of a much larger amount of money. If you used 10 percent as a down payment, your money (let's say $10,000) is growing on the basis of the value of the house ($100,000), not the down payment. Thus, if the house grows by 5 percent ($5,000), your actual investment of $10,000 has grown by 50 percent in just the first year! So, in the long run, your first home is a great way to start investing in real estate.

To cash in on all these benefits, you must first qualify for a loan.

Home Shopping Starts with a Lender

We'll first talk about qualifying for your first property, then your first rental, then what it takes to get into rental properties on a more advanced basis . . . but first the basics. Most homebuyers don't have a boat load of money to get into a piece of real estate. Let's face it, the average home price in mid-year 2003 was $176,500, which was up 7.7 percent from the same period a year earlier. The median household income nationwide in 2002 (the latest statistics available) was at $42,409, according to the U.S. Census Bureau. With these two averages, you can see that the common man or woman would have to save a long time to get the average price into an account to pay cash. Enter financing.

You may want to get into that house with 3 bedrooms, 2.5 baths, and the half-acre lot, but first you have to see just how much you can actually qualify to buy. Before you get into the car with your favorite Realtor, track down a good loan officer. You may need to go through a Realtor to find a lender who can get the best mortgage for you.

There are mortgage bankers and mortgage brokers. Both have their advantages and disadvantages. The banker is able to create unique products to meet a buyer's needs, but is pretty much limited to his own products. Bank of America is not going to sell Wachovia or SunTrust products. However, a broker can work through all three to help you find the mortgage that works best for you. If a banker cannot create a loan for a buyer with less-than-perfect credit, a broker can usually find it through another venue.

The Mortgage Process Requires Paperwork

To qualify, the lender is going to have to see your financials. Get out your bank statement, your latest pay stub, all your moonlighting income, investment statements, and so on, to substantiate how much you make. He wants to see your monthly income. Next, he wants to see how much you're spending on debts. I'm talking about installment loans, like car loans, student loans, credit card payments, and other such debt. I'm not talking about your living expenses, such as electricity, groceries, or gas for your car.

Most lenders also use programs that will look at a debt-to-income ratio of 28/36. (There are a growing number of programs that allow larger ratios.) This means that 28 percent of your income will go toward your housing payment, which will include principal, interest, taxes, and insurance—all paid to the mortgage company. Then, the rest of your monthly installments combined with this mortgage payment cannot exceed 36 percent. These ratios are not set in stone, but they are good averages to follow.

For example, say your income is $5,000 per month. This means your household payment cannot exceed $1,400 per month. Your monthly debts outside your mortgage can't exceed $400. As you can see, one expensive car payment can dump you out of the housing market real quick. (For a really good selection of online mortgage calculators, visit the Mortgage Professor at www.Mtg Professor.com. The site is operated by Jack M. Guttentag, professor of finance emeritus at the Wharton School of the University of Pennsylvania, and chairman of GHR Systems, Inc., a mortgage technology company.) The reason I prefer these calculators is because they are not trying to sell you a loan—just information about your financing capabilities.

But let's say you have the above-mentioned income and want to go for the house. Great! That means with a thirty-year mortgage with a fixed interest rate of 7.5 percent, and monthly taxes/insurance payments of $200, you can qualify for $181,621—and that's if you have $10,000 to go in on the deal. Excellent! You're into your first house, right?

Not so fast. Qualifying, unfortunately, is more than just making enough money. How you manage your money and pay your bills also comes into play. Lenders aren't going to hand over $180,000-plus to you without knowing you're going to pay it back, rather than take cruises, buy expensive cars, go on shopping sprees, and ruin any chance of honoring your commitment to them. So they want to find out your creditworthiness.

Enter the credit report and credit score.

Your Credit Report Decides Your Future

For years, we've been hearing about credit scores, but no one was quite sure how it worked. Fair Isaac and Co. in California is the group that created the concept of credit scores and put in place a formula to determine them.

Also for years, no one but the mortgage practitioners were allowed access to these secretive numbers. In 2000, that all changed. An outcry from the public and online mortgage service providers forced Fair Isaac (FICO) to release its hidden formulas and explain to the public how the credit scores were tabulated.

TIP For detailed information, glide by www.myfico.com and follow the links to "Consumer Info and Credit Scores." The company has done a fine job of explaining what consumers should watch for in their credit habits to keep their scores as high as possible.

Your credit score is a snapshot of your credit risk picture at a particular point in time. Lenders use the score to determine if your credit habits are low risk enough for them to lend you money.

The descriptions below of how FICO determines credit scores seem pretty reasonable at first glance, so why all the secrecy? Well, the folks at FICO have always held that if the consumer knew how the score was tabulated, then the consumer could manipulate the score by changing habits, thus reflecting an untrue score.

How Others Determine Your Credit Score

Now that they've released the secret code, time should tell if their fears were founded on reality. And now, the mystery is unveiled—how is your score determined?

1. Payment History. FICO first looks at how you pay off your debts. This information accounts for 35 percent of the credit score. It looks at:

- Account payment information on specific types of accounts (credit cards, retail accounts, installment loans, finance company accounts, mortgages, and so on).
- Presence of adverse public records (bankruptcy, judgments, suits, liens, wage attachments, and so on), collection items, and delinquency (past due items).
- Severity of delinquency (how long past due).
- Amount past due on delinquent accounts or collection items.
- Time since (recency of) past due items (delinquency), adverse public records (if any), or collection items (if any).
- Number of past due items on file.
- Number of accounts paid as agreed.

2. Amount of Credit Owed. Next, outstanding debt is considered and makes up about 30 percent of the credit score. Variables considered include:

- Amount owed on specific types of accounts.
- Lack of a specific type of balance, in some cases.
- Number of accounts with balances.
- Proportion of credit lines used (proportion of balances to total credit limits on certain types of revolving accounts).
- Proportion of installment loan amounts still owed (proportion of balance-to-original loan amount on certain types of installment loans).

3. Length of Time Credit Established. How long you've actually had credit makes up about 15 percent of your credit score and includes:

- Time since accounts opened.
- Time since accounts opened, by specific type of account.
- Time since account activity.

4. Search for and Acquisition of New Credit. New credit also affects your credit score. This accounts for about 10 percent of your score.

- Number of recently opened accounts, and proportion of accounts that are recently opened, by type of account.
- Number of recent credit inquiries. (If you're seeking financing for a home, such inquiries are weighed in the calculation and are understood to be an infrequent inquiry. Inquiries for credit card accounts, store cards, retail purchases, auto loans, and so on will lower your score.)
- Time since recent account opening(s), by type of account.
- Time since credit inquiry(s).
- Reestablishment of positive credit history following past payment problems.

5. Types of Credit Established. Finally, FICO considers the type of credit you hold; this accounts for about 10 percent of your credit score.

- Number of (presence, prevalence, and recent information on) various types of accounts (credit cards, retail accounts, installment loans, mortgage, consumer finance accounts, and so on).

Basically, the FICO score reflects how much debt you have (is it too much compared to your income?); whether you make payments on time; how many accounts you have open; and, if you've run into credit problems, how long it took you to get it fixed and how you did it. Pretty much, the mystery isn't so mysterious. Controlling your debt level, limiting the number of accounts and making payments on time, and so on, has always been the sound advice of financial planners and credit counselors.

Along with the FICO, they review your credit report, which is put out by three credit rating agencies.

- Equifax, P.O. Box 740241, Atlanta, GA, 30374-0241; (800) 685-1111

- Experian, P.O. Box 2002, Allen, TX, 75013; (888) EXPERIAN (397-3742)

- Trans Union, P.O. Box 1000, Chester, PA, 19022; (800) 916-8800

Keeping Your Credit Clean

As with all computer-based operations, junk in equals junk out. Never has this been more true than with your credit report. If you've never conducted a credit check, rush over to www.True Credit.com or to various other credit report Web sites to purchase a 3-in-1 credit report. The all-inclusive report pulls together all the information in your credit file from the above three agencies. You'll know within a few minutes how creditors look at your financial history. Most important, you'll find any erroneous information on your report. Most recently, I found four erroneous mailing addresses on my report—all four were in cities in which I've never lived.

If you find incorrect information, you'll want to remove it as soon as possible. The Federal Trade Commission has easy-to-follow steps on how to do this in the tip "Checking Out Your Credit" on page 46.

Credit Score Can Limit Traditional Investor Financing

As you begin acquiring more than one property, these financial events will begin showing up on your credit report, as well. As one of my readers found out, building wealth can actually have an adverse affect on your credit rating:

Question: I recently acquired a rental home in addition to my primary residence. I am now in the middle of acquiring another rental. I noticed my Experian score dropped thirteen points when the real estate debt showed up on my credit report. Even though the rental generates income, my score takes a hit. How do the lenders view this? Do they consider a healthy bureau report (no negative information) with a point drop due to real estate acquisition as a positive or a negative?

Answer: Your credit score is a fluid number. It's not like a grade given to you at graduation that follows you the rest of your life. Today, your score might be 750. Next year it could edge up to 760 and later turn down to 695. There are variables that determine your score on any given day depending on what's happening in your credit life at the moment.

Experian's Web site explains: "Scores used by individual lenders may use such elements as income, occupation, and type of residence in determining their own custom credit score."[2] As your debt level increases and decreases, you will experience fluctuations in your score, as well. However, debt level is only one of the factors that determine your score.

As an investor, acquiring property after property will eventually beat up on your score if you're not careful. This is why you'll see a lot of investor courses out there talking about zero-down, owner financing.

The reason an owner may be interested in financing the sale of a property is twofold: 1) He will benefit from all the equity that has built up on the house over the years;

and 2) now that equity is turned into a note, he is receiving a guaranteed interest return.

Just to digress a moment, let's look at such a scenario. If an investor purchased a property for $50,000 and fifteen years later it sells for $150,000, that's a 200 percent gain on the value of the property. The property has already created a lot of cash flow over the years through rental payments, but now he sells and holds the loan for $150,000 (if it's zero-down financing). With a zero-down-payment option, the investor is obviously going to charge a higher interest rate than what the traditional money market demands—say 2 percentage points more.

A $150,000 mortgage at 8 percent today will result in a mortgage payment of $1,100.65. If the investor had originally financed the property fifteen years earlier at 6 percent, his payment on $50,000 would have been $299.78—a spread of $801.87 per month if he holds onto the old note; that's more than $9,000 per year in income from the property.

The investor holding the note now has a couple of options—hold onto the note for a passive cash flow over the next several years or sell it at a discount and take his cash and run.

This is obviously not traditional financing. When an investor goes through traditional channels to obtain financing for purchases, those banks and lenders are going to report the investor's debt load to the credit reporting agencies. As your debt load increases, it will affect your credit score—even if the properties being held are creating a cash flow. You may have a cash flow, but the reality still remains that the house maintains a mortgage from Bank A or B. Those mortgage amounts will affect your credit score.

When you use owner financing, as described above, most likely a private owner is not going to report to anyone, except maybe the courthouse, that you have a loan from him. It's a personal deal between the investor and the note holder, who is probably an investor just like the purchaser. An investor could hold millions of dollars in mortgages on investor properties from personal note holders and never have it show up on his credit report. It just depends on whether the notes are recorded with the agencies. At settlement, the attorneys or escrow agents will report any income from the transaction to the IRS.

Most investors are at least going to record the note at the courthouse to protect their interests and give them the legal hold on the property needed to foreclose if the new owner defaults.

As far as your cash flow is concerned, this will be looked on as income, but the loan officer may also write in a vacancy factor. Most likely, you will experience periods of vacancy, and the loan officer will compensate for that against the cash flow.

As we move through the chapters of this book, all the financing we are discussing will eventually affect your ability to get loans through traditional means; that's why I talk about wrapping loans, holding seconds, using owner financing, and the like. Eventually, as your properties become self-sustaining (no debt and income only), all the income will bode well for your credit report. Before you worry too much about this, however, let's get you into your first investment property!

Getting Your Credit Report

If you've been denied credit, insurance, or employment because of information supplied by a consumer reporting agency (CRA), the

TIP **Checking Out Your Credit.** Your credit report—a type of consumer report—contains information about where you work and live and how you pay your bills. It also may show whether you've been sued or arrested or have filed for bankruptcy. Companies called consumer reporting agencies (CRAs) or credit bureaus compile and sell your credit report to businesses. Because businesses use this information to evaluate your applications for credit, insurance, employment, and other purposes allowed by the Fair Credit Reporting Act (FCRA), it's important that the information in your report is complete and accurate.

Some financial advisers suggest that you periodically review your credit report for inaccuracies or omissions. This can be especially important if you're considering making a major purchase, such as buying a home. Checking in advance on the accuracy of information in your credit file can speed the credit-granting process.

Fair Credit Reporting Act (FCRA) says the company you applied to must give you the CRA's name, address, and telephone number. If you contact the agency for a copy of your report within sixty days of receiving a denial notice, the report is free. In addition, you're entitled to one free copy of your report a year if you certify in writing that (1) you're unemployed and plan to look for a job within sixty days, (2) you're on welfare, or (3) your report is inaccurate because of fraud. Otherwise, a CRA may charge you up to $9 for a copy of your report. If you simply want a copy of your report, call the CRAs listed in the Yellow Pages under "credit" or "credit rating and reporting." Call each credit bureau listed since more than one agency may have a file on you, some with different information.

Correcting Errors

Under the FCRA, both the CRA and the organization that provided the information to the CRA, such as a bank or credit card company, have responsibilities for correcting inaccurate or incomplete information in your report. To protect all your rights under the law, contact both the CRA and the information provider.

First, tell the CRA in writing what information you believe is inaccurate. Include copies (NOT originals) of documents that support your position. In addition to providing your complete name and address, your letter should clearly identify each item you dispute, state the facts and explain why you dispute the information, and request deletion or correction. You may want to enclose a copy of your report with circles around the items in question. Your letter may look something like the sample on page 49.

Send your letter by certified mail, return receipt requested, so you can document what the CRA received. Keep copies of your dispute letter and enclosures. CRAs must reinvestigate the items in question—usually within thirty days—unless they consider your dispute frivolous. They also must forward all relevant data you provide about the dispute to the information provider.

After the information provider receives notice of a dispute from the CRA, it must investigate, review all relevant information provided by the CRA, and report the results to the CRA. If the information provider finds the disputed information to be inaccurate, it must notify all nationwide CRAs so they can correct this information in your file. Disputed information that cannot be verified must be deleted from your file.

- If your report contains erroneous information, the CRA must correct it.

- If an item is incomplete, the CRA must complete it. For example, if your file showed that you were late making payments, but failed to show that you were no longer delinquent, the CRA must show that you're current.

- If your file shows an account that belongs only to another person, the CRA must delete it.

When the reinvestigation is complete, the CRA must give you the written results, and if the dispute results in a change, a free copy of your report. If an item is changed or removed, the CRA cannot put the disputed information back in your file unless the information provider verifies its accuracy and completeness, and the CRA gives you a written notice that includes the name, address, and phone number of the provider.

Also, if you request, the CRA must send notices of corrections to anyone who received your report in the past six months. Job applicants can have a corrected copy of their report sent to anyone who received a copy during the past two years for employment purposes. If a reinvestigation does not resolve your dispute, ask the CRA to include your statement of the dispute in your file and in future reports.

Second, in addition to writing to the CRA, tell the creditor or other information provider in writing that you dispute an item. Again, include copies (NOT originals) of documents that support your position. Many providers specify an address for disputes. If the provider then reports the item to any CRA, it must include a notice of your dispute. In addition, if you are correct—that is, if the disputed information is not accurate—the information provider may not use it again. If you find accurate negative information, only the passage of time can assure its removal. Accurate negative information (late payments, judgments, bankruptcy, and so on) can generally stay on your report for seven years. There are certain exceptions:

- Information about criminal convictions may be reported without any time limitation.
- Bankruptcy information may be reported for ten years.
- Credit information reported in response to an application for a job with a salary of more than $75,000 has no time limit.
- Credit information reported because of an application for more than $150,000 worth of credit or life insurance has no time limit.

■ Information about a lawsuit or an unpaid judgment against you can be reported for seven years or until the statute of limitations runs out, whichever is longer. Criminal convictions can be reported without any time limit.

Adding Accounts to Your File

Your credit file may not reflect all your credit accounts. Although most national department store and all-purpose bank credit card accounts will be included in your file, not all creditors supply information to CRAs: Some travel, entertainment, and gasoline card companies, as well as local retailers and credit unions are among those creditors that don't. If you've been told you were denied credit because of an "insufficient credit file" or "no credit file" and you have accounts with creditors that don't appear in your credit file, ask the CRA to add this information to future reports. Although they are not required to do so, many CRAs will add verifiable accounts for a fee. You should, however, understand that if these creditors do not report to the CRA on a regular basis, these added items will not be updated in your file.

Sample Dispute Letter

Date
Your Name
Your Address
Your City, State, Zip Code

Complaint Department
Name of Credit Reporting Agency
Address
City, State, Zip Code

Dear Sir or Madam:

I am writing to dispute the following information in my file. The items I dispute are also encircled on the attached copy of the report I received. (Identify item(s) disputed by name of source, such as creditors or tax court, and identify type of item, such as credit account, judgment, and so on.)

This item is (inaccurate or incomplete) because (describe what is inaccurate or incomplete and why). I am requesting that the item be deleted (or request another specific change) to correct the information.

Enclosed are copies of (use this sentence if applicable and describe any enclosed documentation, such as payment records, court documents) supporting my position. Please reinvestigate this (these) matter(s) and (delete or correct) the disputed item(s) as soon as possible.

Sincerely,
Your name

Enclosures: (List what you are enclosing)

Source: Federal Trade Commission (www.ftc.gov)

Increasing Buying Power by Reducing Debt

Once you've gone through the mortgage broker's excruciating process called prequalification (not to be confused with preapproval, which means you have a mortgage ready to go and just need a property), you may find that you can purchase a house, but your dream home has just been placed beyond your grasp because of that nice, brand new Chevy sitting in your driveway. Well, the question comes begging: Should you pay off all your debt before investing in real estate for yourself and for your future?

The answer always depends on several factors, but as a general rule—no. If you're looking to purchase a house soon, like most people in the United States, then you need cash for down payment (unless you're looking at a zero-down program), closing costs, and then reserves.

The down payment can range from 1 percent up. Let's say you had $4,000 in credit card debt. If you have that much cash and use it to pay off your credit card, you just lost the ability to use it for closing costs. If you spend all your extra cash to pay off that amount, then you are at ground zero again and have to start saving up for the above-mentioned expenses. Besides, the traditional debt-to-income ratio calculation allows buyers to have consumer debt when qualifying for the loan.

For example: A person who wants to purchase a $200,000 property with a 10 percent down payment must qualify for a $180,000 loan. At 7 percent on a 30-year fixed rate, the estimated principal-interest-taxes-insurance payment will be about $1,400 per month (depending on your local property tax rate). That payment is 28 percent of $5,000, which means our buyer has to make $60,000 annually to qualify for the loan described above.

In addition, the borrower can have another 8 percent in debt—bringing his or her total debt payments to $1,800 per month. As you can see, if you pay off a loan balance for $4,000, but it only gives you another $75 to $100 in monthly cash flow, it's not going to positively affect your buying power. It just eats up the cash you would have had without paying off the debt.

(This is a good time to show how interest rates will affect your buying power. A buyer with a salary of $49,971 could also afford to buy the above house if she found a mortgage with an interest rate of only 5 percent. The payment would drop down to roughly $1,166, allowing more buying power with less income.)

Granted, there are some loan programs that allow higher ratios, but you are more than likely going to pay higher interest rates and points to use that type program.

Keep in mind, I adhere to the G.O.O.D. Principle—Get Out Of Debt—just as a matter of smart money management. But it's not always the best move to pay off all your debt while you're trying to save money for the purchase of your house. Owning a home is always a lot better than renting and if paying off your consumer debt first keeps you out of the housing market it may be better to maintain the debt, get into a house, and start enjoying tax savings, which could enable you to pay off the debt quicker.

This is especially true if you live in an area that is experiencing good appreciation in home values. If nothing else, you can refinance your house in a few months or years and pay off the debt with cash from your equity.

If the $200,000 property above is appreciating at 5 percent (just below the national average in 2001 of 5.5 percent, according to the National Association of Realtors), then in one year, that house will be worth $210,000. The next year it will be worth $220,500—which gives you more than $40,000 of equity to dip into to pay off consumer debt if you want. (The $40,000 comes from subtracting your loan amount—$180,000—from the current value of your house—$220,500.)

With a bit of patience and budgeting, you've now started building wealth by leveraging your money. The $20,000 down payment has more than doubled, you now have equity to pay off debt, and you're taking home more of your paycheck because you can deduct all that interest each year from your income, thus lowering your tax bill.

If you have saved no money at all for buying a home, don't worry. Sit down and set up a plan to save for your down payment and closing costs $1 at a time.

Twenty-First-Century Americans: The Unsaving Generation

The number one barrier to owning a home for most consumers is the down payment. Even people with good-paying jobs find this challenge hard to overcome. For a large number of these potential homebuyers, they cannot save enough money simply because at the end of the month, there is no more money to save. Easy credit has captured their paycheck, leaving little, if any, spare change to put away for that house. A few years ago at the Choose to Save Forum in Washington, D.C., former U.S. Treasury secretary Lawrence H.

Summers made some disturbing remarks about Americans (the wealthiest people on the planet) and their savings habits:

- Half of American families on the brink of retirement had financial assets valued at less than $40,000 in 1998. And for those "not as close" to "further from" retirement, their financial assets were even lower.

- Only half of American workers are currently participating in any kind of employer-provided pension plan, and more than 75 million Americans and their spouses are not covered by such a plan. Indeed, more than 50 million Americans had no retirement saving whatsoever.

- In spite of America's economic performance, the level of household debt rose by nearly 10 percent in 1999 and personal bankruptcies have risen by 60 percent since 1994. Household debt service is now at its highest share of disposable income since the late 1980s.

Mr. Summers left the forum with positive remarks, however. "Saving in a way that makes for genuine wealth accumulation and will make a real difference to life in retirement is within the reach of almost every American family," he said.[3]

The exclamation point of his remarks came in a poignant example of what it really takes to save:

"An individual who saved $15 a week—today's price of two movie tickets—for the past ten years would have accumulated $22,000 by investing in the stock market," he said. "This rises to $120,000 if he had started twenty years ago and almost $400,000 if he started thirty years ago." Even with the corrections in the stock market in the beginning of this decade, it stands to reason: Saving is better than not saving.

"So how do I get started," you may ask. I did some scrounging around on the net, talked with some planners, and pulled from personal experience to come up with some practical strategies for debt reduction and saving.

Analyze Your Debt

Let's start with where you are financially. Take a budget inventory. Quicken.com has a "Debt Reduction Planner" on its Web site to help guide consumers through this tricky analysis. Searching online for "debt reduction plan" will provide you with plenty of programs, charts, and worksheets to set up a debt reduction plan. When I was paying off my debt, I used a simple chart program with Word-Perfect (Microsoft Word has the same capability) to create a bar chart for each account I was paying off. Then I keep up with it each month—plugging in the balance of each credit account as it dropped.

Many advisers suggest paying off the card with the highest interest rate first, then taking those payments and adding them to the account with the second highest interest rate, and so forth. I found that psychologically it was very encouraging to eliminate my debt by the lowest balance and move up. It was very empowering to see accounts disappear one after the other from my credit roles!

Here are some online resources with self-help tools:

Free Debt Help and Debt Consolidation www.free-debt-help-and-debt-consolidation.com/self.html

Debt Reduction Calculator http://money.cnn.com/tools

Kiplinger.com www.kiplinger.com (Click on Your Finances link)

www.DaveRamsey.com

www.MyVesta.org

About.com's Debt Free Area: http://frugalliving.about.com/cs/debtfree/

Cut Spending

Even if Congress can't get its spending under control, you can. Start eliminating items you really don't need. I began a debt reduction plan years ago, starting with canceling several monthly amenities. Cable TV ($35), mobile phone ($60), voicemail/pager ($8), and other items added up to a couple hundred dollars per month. While canceling each item may not seem like a lot, added together it can save you hundreds of dollars between paychecks, totaling thousands of dollars per year.

Meanwhile, here are some steps you can take to get debt free!

- **Get Started**. Put all your debt down on paper. Find out where you really stand. You may be surprised (but don't get depressed).

- **Stop Charging**. Remove credit cards from your wallet and place them in a spot where it takes a concerted mental decision to pull them out to use. My spot was the top of my home office desk drawer. Removing them from your wallet keeps you from impulsive buying and peer pressure purchases.

- **Track Spending and Cut Expenses**. Whether you organize your spending by categories, dates, or amounts, at least organize them. Without knowing where the money is being spent, you'll never get a grip on reducing the financial bloodletting.

- **Keep Going**. Start reducing one account at a time and keep it going. Don't stop too long to celebrate. When you pay off one debt, take that monthly payment and add it to the other payments to remove your debt even quicker. Start paying off high-interest loans first.

- **Start Saving**. This may sound tougher than it really is. But saving doesn't take as much as you may think. At least by saving a little each week, you can have some cash ready for holiday gift buying without pulling out the plastic. Just $20 per week saves more than $1,000 for purchases in a year.

Taking inventory of your finances, moving on action items to reduce debt, and then saving consistently is what it takes to get you on your way to owning your own home. The best time to start is now.

Need Cash? Down Payment Assistance Available More Than Ever

Down payment assistance programs are one of the most overlooked benefits in the homebuyer's toolbox. For many homebuyers, the number one obstacle to buying a house is the down payment—not the ability to qualify for the monthly payment. With the appropriate down payment of 5 to 10 percent, many homebuyers can qualify for the purchase of their dream home. Following years of forming creative home financing, governments on all levels and nonprofits realized one of the missing elements was the down payment. Now, more than ever, down payment assistance programs are readily available to homebuyers.

Sellers competing for buyers can benefit from these programs as well. Neighborhood Gold is such a program that requires the seller's participation before granting the down payment funds to the buyer. NeighborhoodGold.com reports that "the seller gets full asking price for her home and agrees to pay a seller's service fee to Neighborhood Gold. The fee equals the grant amount plus 1 percent of the cost of the home (not to exceed $1,000)." The program can be used on any lender program that allows a gift from a nonprofit group.

The six-step process in using the program may create problems for buyers in a hot sellers' market, however, as the Neighborhood Gold nonprofit must be involved in the settlement process—and that slows down the closing process, which may scare some sellers.

If you're well on your way to saving up for a down payment

but would like some help in making those dollars grow, then you may consider an Individual Development Account.

"Individual Development Accounts are, in essence, 401k plans for low-income families and individuals who probably do not have access to such a savings plan through their employment," according to IDANetwork.org. IDAs are generally available through nonprofit groups, as well as through credit unions.

Here's how they work. The individual or family commits to a set amount of monthly savings over a period of time, one to two years, for instance. Once the future homebuyers have met their savings goals, the nonprofit matches these savings through the IDA program. Section 8 participants interested in homeownership should consider enrolling in a local IDA program. Not every city has an IDA geared towards homeownership. For state by state IDA information, visit www.IDANetwork.org and click "State Pages."

Another down payment assistance program may be as close as the human resources department where you work. More and more employers are implementing employer-assisted housing (EAH) programs to hang on to valued employees.

Fannie Mae has a great online brochure at its site, www.efannie mae.com, about how an EAH program works, but the brochure is pretty well hidden from the front page. Punch in efanniemae.com, click "Single Family" under the Affordable Housing and Community Development section, then click "Employee-Assisted Housing" under Initiatives and Partnerships. If your employer doesn't have an EAH program, this brochure can direct them on how to get one established.

Probably the leader of the pack in down payment assistance programs is the Nehemiah Program (www.getdownpayment.com or call toll free 877-NEHEMIAH). This program provides grants to homebuyers from 1 to 6 percent of the selling price of the home. Since 1997, the program has funded more than 120,000 grants to families seeking homeownership.

These are just a small example of what's available in the area of down payment assistance programs—and not all of the programs out there have income limits. Many of these programs are administered on the local and state level. Visit your favorite search engine and type in "down payment assistance" and then the state name for regional programs.

When Escrows Rise—What Then?

Once you get into your first house and start making the payment, you may feel like you have finally taken control of your monthly housing expenses. Your monthly payments of principal, interest, taxes, and insurance (PITI) are, for the most part, a guesstimate of what you'll need to keep your taxes and insurance payments current. The mortgage company forwards the insurance and taxes to the appropriate agencies. You're going to find that each year the mortgage company analyzes your escrow balances—the taxes and insurance. This amount will most likely fluctuate year after year. I had one reader tell me that after the second year of purchase her lender dropped her payment approximately $30. The third year into the loan, the lender sent her a letter advising her they had made an error and raised her payment $230 per month. What are the rules governing escrow management?

It's unusual for a mortgage service provider to "miscalculate" the amount needed each month for escrows. It is not unusual, however, for escrows to fluctuate throughout the life of the loan. Escrows are the funds paid each month by a borrower to cover the lump sum payments due throughout the year for taxes and hazard insurance. To protect its secured loan, a lender obviously wants to be assured that the taxes are paid when they are due. If not, the house can be sold out from underneath the homeowner to pay taxes and the lender will be put at risk of losing the collateral for the loan he has provided the homeowner.

Some critics of this system point out that the lenders are also gaining quite a bit of interest money from the funds that are held in escrow throughout the year. Since lenders are not required to pay the borrower any interest earned on the money, they can hold the funds in interest-bearing accounts—obviously making a skim on the side . . . but that's another story.

For escrow payments to jump so much in one year, as it did for this borrower, it appears that the lender was having to do two things at once—make up for the insufficient funds he didn't collect last year and, more than likely, jack up the amount to cover the increase in taxes and insurance for this next year.

If you ever believe the lender is mishandling your escrow funds or collections, you can file a complaint to a couple of groups. The Real Estate Settlement Procedures Act (RESPA) is the legislation that regulates the collection and handling of escrow funds. The enforcement of this law falls under the U.S. Department of Housing and Urban Development. Go to www.hud.gov, search for RESPA, and you'll find all you need to file a complaint.

The Mortgage Bankers Association of America launched a self-policing arm several years ago. Check out www.mbaa.org for details. Keep in mind that even though you file a complaint, the wheels of justice (as well as investigations and enforcement) roll along very slowly. When it comes to your mortgage payments, keep making them, even though you may disagree with what's happening on the lender's end. The wheels of foreclosure and courthouse steps' sales move at a much quicker pace.

As far as your escrow payments fluctuating—this is normal. The number one reason for increasing or decreasing escrow amounts is your local taxes. When homeowners are ecstatic about appreciating home values, they tend to forget that they're going to get bit on the back end. If the fair market value goes up, so does the tax assessment. If your local jurisdiction doesn't adjust its tax rate, then your bill is about to jump.

That's what happened to me in my monthly mortgage payment. My taxes have increased by upwards of $122 per month. (Thank you, Fairfax County Board of Supervisors.) It's a hard pill to swallow, and it is a surprise to many new homeowners who purchased a house, in part, to get away from rent increases. A side benefit is that the tax increases are 100 percent tax deductible on my federal return.

Combining Buying Power Results in Fulfilled Dreams

Finally, I want to point out one other creative way of beefing up your credit and financing so you can buy a home. For single buyers, this can be a very important financial strategy.

Many buyers operate under the belief that they have to make a huge salary, have perfect credit, and save up for a 20 percent down payment before they can buy a house for themselves. In the old days—you know, back when I was in grade school—this was the case.

There's something crazy about old business myths: They don't die gracefully. They linger, painfully deluding everyone around them and costing people money. Never was this more true than with real estate. Many of the traditional methods of buying a home remain. But new methods are helping more renters become home-owners.

For instance, take the idea that only a spouse or a parent can help someone buy a house. Actually, any warm body with a good job and some credit can help another person buy a house.

The most common means of assistance is in the form of cash. Plenty of parents, trying desperately to cut the apron strings, will use their personal savings to do it. But if money isn't enough to satisfy the lender, they could also offer to cosign the loan. This way, the kids get into a house, begin building their own credit, and the parents can share in the equity.

Parents aren't the only cosigners available, however. Friends have purchased property together, as well. All a lender is looking for is a good loan application. Investors purchase property with co-owners all the time. Most single buyers usually don't consider purchasing a home using this strategy.

(Single parents living on a fixed income may consider linking up with another single-parent family. Using this method of purchasing, both of them would increase their purchasing power, get back into the wealth-building game, and, at the same time, get a housing partner to help with raising the children.)

Another way of purchasing a house with multiple buyers is soliciting help from a seller who is willing to remain on the loan and title when the house is sold to the purchaser.

I saw this strategy used once where two friends agreed to purchase their first home together. The loan application revealed, however, that one of the buyers' credit was so bad at the time that it would be a hindrance, rather than a help, for her to be placed on the loan. Instead, the seller, who was moving cross-country, agreed to cosign with the buyer whose credit was good and remain on the title. Once the house was sold (about ten years later), the original owner then shared in the profit.

As a single buyer, you don't have to go this road alone. Linking up with a second buyer—though not a relative—can help both of you attain your housing goals.

Let the Games Begin

You've now seen how getting ready to invest in real estate is more than just pulling out the classifieds and visiting open houses. Getting your financial house in order creates a strong investment foundation from which you can build your personal wealth. Let's review:

1. Your first investment is your own residence. If you're renting, get into a home of your choice.

2. Meet with a loan officer to determine your buying power.

3. Check out your credit history to determine your financial health.

4. Lose the debt!

5. Start saving.

6. If you can't buy on your own, get help with community groups or co-buyers.

I hope you now have more knowledge on how the real estate financing system works and what you need to move into your first investment property. Now let's take a look at all the mortgage programs available to you as a real estate investor!

Notes

1 Jeff Schnepper, ''The Basics,'' http://moneycentral.msn.com/, Nov. 11, 2003.

2 Experian, www.experian.com, 2004.

3 Lawrence Summers, U.S. Secretary of the Treasury, Choose to Save Forum, Washington D.C., April 4, 2000.

CHAPTER 4

All the Programs You'll Ever Need–Conventional Programs

Usually, I catch first-time buyers speculating on money. They're poring over the mortgage section of a newspaper, looking for the lowest rate. Consumers are always in search of the ever-illusive lower rate, hoping to figure out what economic indicator to watch as a sign that rates will drop even more.

"What you don't want to do is be an interest rate speculator," says Doug Duncan, chief economist for the Mortgage Bankers Association of America. "Because you can see what the results are for a pro is that sometimes he makes money, sometimes he loses money."[1]

Despite this advice, many homebuyers spend their time online and thumbing through real estate sections searching out the lowest rate and for how many points. (Points are equal to 1 percent of the loan amount and are used to prepay interest or "buy-down" an interest rate.) In addition, borrowers wonder why the mortgage interest rates don't drop when the Federal Reserve lowers its short-term interest rates.

"The Fed is trying to understand what is an appropriate level of liquidity in the economy that will allow a sustainable, noninflationary level of growth," Mr. Duncan says. "Its number one priority is the prevention of inflation," not necessarily to make mortgage interest rates cheaper.[2]

To monitor mortgage interest rates, ignore the Fed and look at the ten-year Treasury Bond.

"While mortgage rates aren't set directly in the Treasury market (they are actually priced in the so-called "swaps" market), changes in yields on ten-year Treasury notes give a pretty good indication of the direction of movement (and the order of magnitude) for fixed-rate mortgages," says Fannie Mae Chief Economist David Berson. "If the market anticipates that economic growth is going to accelerate or inflation is going to rise, we could see Treasury rates increase—which suggests that mortgage rates could climb as well."[3]

(Yahoo.com has all the bond charting you'll ever need at http://bonds.yahoo.com/. Go to it and bookmark it so you can keep up with this important indicator.)

The Fed moving up or down does not necessarily affect mortgage interest rates, says Lawrence Yun, chief economic forecaster for the National Association of Realtors. Referring to a time when economists expected the Fed to drop rates, but didn't, Yun notes, "the short-term adjustable rates fell, but the thirty-year rates did not move."[4] Thus, the economic turns of the Fed don't necessarily mean all the other indexes will follow suit.

Mr. Duncan of MBAA says "Trying to time a bottom is like trying to time a top in the stock market. It can't be done with certainty. If the participants in bond markets feel that inflation will go up, then the rates for mortgages could go up." He says mortgage rates are generally made on the ten-year Treasury Bond. Sometimes mortgage interest rates are a little more than the Treasury Bond. A typical thirty-year loan doesn't last thirty years; this causes a problem for consumers speculating on the interest rates. It's possible the Fed cuts its rate and the market says "we're not expecting that cut," and therefore doesn't respond by dropping bond rates, thus keeping mortgage rates unmoved.

So who is "the market?" Since "the market" holds so much

control on mortgage interest rates, it's nice to know it's not one person or group of people.

Dr. Berson explains that the market is made up of "thousands and thousands of individual bond traders and institutions who are buying and selling bonds every day. The biggest bond market is the U.S. Treasury market and it affects all other interest rates because it is viewed as having no credit risk, since we know the federal government is not going to default on its obligations."

"The Federal Reserve controls short-term rates. How long rates respond to that action is what the mortgage investment community looks at to see what kind of inflationary expectations will come from that move," says Mr. Yun. "Obviously, to just crank out the money would cause interest increases. When the Fed is cutting rates, if people perceive the economy is continuing to weaken, then the inflation rate problem is not a future concern; therefore, the thirty-year mortgage rate would correspond to that decline.

"However if the bond market perceives that with a cut, the economy is turning the corner and going back on track, say a few quarters down the line, as the economy picks up, inflation would pick up with it," Mr. Yun says. "Then they may feel the economy is back on track and if they perceive too much is being pumped into the market and could cause inflation, the thirty-year rate would go the opposite way. Short-term rates would definitely go down but it's not certain long-term rates would go down."

In reality, when you see low rates on the market today for mortgage loans they were actually in the making months earlier. Getting into the borrowing game when interest rates do hit lows can save homebuyers and investors more money than just prospecting.

Mr. Duncan concurs, saying astute consumers will be "well informed on their housing needs and what their financial characteristics are. Are they a good risk? Have they saved money, paid bills on time?" and issues such as these, he says, will have a larger effect on the consumer's personal interest rate than the Fed dropping rates. Consider, instead, "What kind of credit quality do you represent to a lender. Once you know what kind of risk you present then you can go about assessing" interest rates, he says.

Mortgage Players

Before we get into the actual mortgage types, let's take a look at the big players in the mortgage game you've entered.

Where does all this money come from anyway? In 2002, more than $2.41 trillion was financed for the purchase and refinancing of homes ($1.4 trillion for refinances, $1.01 trillion for home purchases). One would think, "Well, the bank, where else?" Plenty of other investors have money to lend to you for buying a house and they aren't even connected with a bank.

Two of the largest providers of money for real estate loans are Fannie Mae (www.fanniemae.com) and Freddie Mac (www .freddiemac.com). These two companies were chartered by the federal government many years ago and are called government-sponsored enterprises (GSEs). They provide thousands of lenders across the country with money to lend out to buyers. Neither of them lend money directly to borrowers. Instead, they loan millions of dollars to a financial institution, which then loans it to borrowers. All these loans are then packaged into securities and sold on Wall Street to investors like you and me.

Conventional vs. Unconventional

Both GSEs offer loans that are considered "conventional," meaning the loans meet certain criteria before being approved. Since they meet this standardization of financing, that's how they can be packaged into securities and sold on the stock market.

Conventional loans won't exceed a certain loan amount (at this writing, $322,700—but this tends to change each year as inflation moves the average home price up), and the buyers meet criteria as well—they must have a good credit score, must have their debt ratios in order, and must earn enough money to pay back the loan.

In addition, the property meets a certain type as well—single-family homes, townhouses, and condos in residential neighborhoods. It would be difficult to purchase a farm, for instance, with a Fannie Mae or Freddie Mac loan.

Loans that don't meet these criteria are considered "unconventional." An unconventional loan can be called so for many reasons. The borrower may have bad credit or high debt-to-income ratios. Or it may be the loan is outside the "conventional" parameters: secured by a nontraditional property (vacant land, farm, apartment building), the loan exceeds $322,700, and so on.

Unconventional doesn't mean the house or borrower can't get a loan to purchase a house, it just means the loan is going to be a unique product—usually with higher points and interest rates. Unconventional loans have to be serviced (meaning, payments collected, taxes and insurance paid) by the lender or investor who is providing the money, rather than being able to be sold as a security. The lender or investor can, however, sell it on the discounted market to a service provider (yet another means of investing in notes—chapter 7). Owner financing is considered unconventional—and that's an important kind of financing available to investors.

Some of the above players lend money to companies who will lend money to you. Others don't lend money, but rather insure the loans borrowers receive from lenders.

Lenders

The best place to go for money is where they know you the best. It may be your bank, credit union, or mortgage broker. Lenders range from major conglomerate banks to individual investors. For our purposes here, we'll talk about the mainline players.

Banks are an obvious source of purchasing money. Check with your bank to see the type of programs it offers for account holders (those with checking and savings accounts). But don't make a decision on giving your business to the bank right away. Shop around with other mortgage providers as well.

If you belong to a credit union, find out if it offers mortgages for real estate purchases. Finally, there are mortgage brokers who can shop your mortgage needs around to several companies that have dozens, if not hundreds, of programs to fit your particular situation.

Keep in mind that there's going to be a lot of in-house lingo being thrown around when you start investing in real estate. As far as financing goes, all these financing names can be divided into two camps: products and programs.

Products include the following:

Fixed Loans
30-year
20-year
15-year
10/20
7/balloons
5/balloons

Adjustable-Rate Mortgages
1-year (adjust each year)
3/1 (fixed-rate for 3 years, adjusts annually year 4 and beyond)
3/3 (fixed-rate for 3 years, then adjusts every 3 years)
5/1
7/1
10/1
LIBOR (based on the London Interbank Offering Rate)
COFI (Cost of Funds Index)
COSI (Cost of Savings Index)
CODI (Certificates of Deposit Index)

Prime Rate

Interest-Only Loans

Government Loans
Federal Housing Administration

Veterans Affairs
Rural Housing Loan Program

2nd Trusts

Home Equity Loans

Closed End 2nds

Home Equity Line of Credit

Below is a list of basic programs through which you can get the above products, but this list is by no means exhaustive. The monthly payments do not include your local taxes or insurance payments. The assumed purchase price is $150,000.

Thirty-Year Fixed-Rate Mortgage

This is the most common mortgage. It is amortized over thirty years with a fixed interest rate and requires a 5, 10, 15, or 20 percent down payment. With a 5 percent down payment, this loan at 8 percent, amortized over 30 years, will require a monthly payment of $1045.61.

Fifteen-Year Fixed-Rate Mortgage

If you can pull off this mortgage, go for it. Since the loan is amortized over fifteen years, the payment is higher than a thirty-year fixed rate; however, the interest savings are tremendous. With 5 percent down ($7,500), the monthly payment at 8 percent is $1361.80.

Thirty-Year Adjustable-Rate Mortgage

An adjustable rate is exactly as it sounds. The interest rate changes throughout the life of the loan, rather than holding steady over the years. The rate is based on some sort of index, such as a U.S. thirty-year Treasury bond. The interest rate provided to investors changes daily, but the adjustable-rate mortgage (ARM) adjusts once per year—wherever the Treasury bond is at the time. Now this can be good and bad. In a stable market, the buyer has an interest rate below the market rate of a fixed mortgage—say, about 2 percent (depending on how many points are paid by the buyer). However, if the bond rate starts escalating, the buyer's interest rate will also go up, as will the monthly payment. ARMs usually come with two caps—the first is on how much an interest rate can go up at one time and the second is how much it can increase for the life of the loan.

Therefore, an ARM that starts at 6 percent with a 2 percent cap per year and a 6 percent cap on the life of the loan means the first year, it can go up to only 8 percent, but for the life of the loan (if it's thirty years) it can go up to 12 percent maximum. Thus an ARM starting at 6 percent with a 5 percent down payment will be $854.36. If it went up the next year at the maximum rate (which may or may not happen) the payment would increase to $1045.61. If at any point over the life of the loan it reaches its maximum rate of 12 percent, the monthly payment will be $1,465.77.

ARMs adjust at different times, depending on the program. A 1/1 ARM is one that starts with a lower interest rate for one year, then adjusts every year after that. A 3/1 ARM has a low rate for three years, then adjusts every year thereafter. Some adjustable rate loans have adjust dates every three or six years, as well—thus they are called 3/3 and 6/6 loans accordingly—three years at one rate, then adjusting every three years.

Hybrid Mortgage

The hybrid mortgage is an interesting animal indeed. It is called a hybrid because it includes the features of both a fixed- and an adjustable-rate mortgage. With these loans, you start at a lower rate, then either move to an even lower rate or jump to a higher one, depending on where the market is heading. For instance, the loan may be set at a rate of 5.75 percent for the first seven years, then adjust upward to a higher rate and be re-amortized over twenty-three years. This is referred to as a 7/23 ARM.

Is the 2 Percent Mortgage Too Good to Be True?

How does a 2 percent loan sound? Great, doesn't it? Well, there's always a catch and here's just the minimal information consumers should understand about these ARMs, the COFI, the COSI, and the CODI, which plenty of buyers and investors use to provide lower monthly payments. The interest rates on these three programs are super low. The index as of July 1, 2003, was 2.130 percent for the COFI, 2.140 percent for the COSI, and 1.419 percent for the CODI.

The total index includes the above mentioned rates coupled with the "margin," which is added onto the index rate to provide the total interest rate. When added, the "fully indexed" payment comes to about 3 to 5 percent, depending on the margin, at the latest index quoted above.

There's a possible bite when using these indexed loans, and I'll tell you about that in a moment. First a brief description of each.

The COFI historically has been the slowest moving index in the United States and Europe. Each month, it allows borrowers to select from one of several payment amounts: a super low minimum payment, much like a credit card; an interest-only payment; a fully indexed loan, as described earlier; a payment equal to a fifteen-year term payment; or a payment amount determined by the borrower that is above the minimum payment.

It can be a complex loan to understand, and that's why a lot of buyers avoid it. Many of my investor friends like it, however, when purchasing rental properties or properties they want to fix up and sell quickly. The payments are very low, which preserves their cash flow for the short term while they're refurbishing the property.

The COSI program is tied to the average interest rate paid out to consumers, known as the "cost of savings." In lay terms, the lender borrows money from consumers in the form of deposits, such as certificates of deposit (CDs) or checking and savings accounts, and turns around to lend the money to homebuyers and owners as mortgages. Again, the rate is very low and a margin is placed on top of the index.

Have you seen what you're getting in your interest-bearing

checking account lately? The eleventh district takes all of its banks' interest payments on such accounts and determines an average cost of savings—through a weighted annualized rate on these deposit accounts as of the last day of each month. And now you know why a lot of people don't know about this loan—it's just so darned complicated.

Nevertheless, historically, the COSI's fluctuation has moved a lot less rapidly than indexes based on the prime rate (the rate you hear about every month from Federal Reserve Board Chairman Alan Greenspan); the Federal Reserve discount rate; or the Treasury bill rate (the most popular one-year ARM index quoted by the general media).

I would like to explain to you why the COSI Index moves so slowly, but the good editors I work with limit how much I'm allowed to write. Suffice it to say, bean counters who graduated a lot higher in class than I did came up with a formula to determine the index and margins that provide consumers with a really low rate from which to choose.

Trying to understand it before using it is like trying to understand electricity before flipping on the light switch. I encourage you to conduct due diligence on this index before deciding to use it for your home purchase.

Finally, the CODI Index. This one is based on the rates banks pay on three-month certificates of deposits. This index is based on the average of the most recently published monthly yields on three-month certificates of deposit for the twelve most recent calendar months as published by the Federal Reserve Board.

The formula involves something like annual percentage averages, divided by twelve and rounded to the nearest 1,000th—so, again, you can imagine the complexity of how these interest rates are determined and why they are not commonly used loans. Because of its smaller pool of money to loan out, the CODI program's margins are slightly higher than the COFI or COSI indexes.

Now—here's the bite. If you take the minimum payments allowed with these loans, a borrower can find himself in a negative amortization situation. That's the official of way of saying your loan amount grows instead of shrinks. Some loan officers will tell you it's not negative amortization—just deferred interest. Call it what you will, you run the risk of owing more at the end of the loan than what you signed up for.

It works just like a credit card would if you paid only the minimum amount—except this time, the interest rate keeps changing each month. In a worst-case scenario you could wind up not even paying the interest payment and yet your balance has grown. Your only hope, if you hang onto the loan for long, is that the appreciation on your home has outpaced the ebb and flow of the COFI, COSI, or CODI's index and margins.

I've had a COFI loan before and it allowed me more purchasing power. I held it for more than five years and I'm not the poorer for it. Before applying for one of these loans, however, be sure to get a handle on what it means for your financial standing. For more information, talk with your loan officer or visit the Federal Reserve Bank Web site at www.FederalReserve.gov.

Private Investors and Owner Financing

Don't overlook private investors and owner financing to purchase your personal or investment property. "Private investors" is just a fancy title for a family member or friend who has a lot of money to loan out for a long-term return. By writing a promissory note, the private investor then fronts the money to the seller, and you start making payments to that investor instead of to the bank. Please be advised to work with a real estate attorney to set this up between you and the investor.

If you come across a deal where the owner is willing to put up financing, this doesn't mean you can forgo the advice of traditional advisers, such as a real estate agent or a mortgage broker. In fact, you may need them more than ever, as they may have dealt with this type of scenario before.

Be sure the owner is actually the owner by having an attorney conduct a title search. Hiring a real estate agent would also be a smart move, as the process of selling a house is just a bit more difficult than selling your car.

Like the example with a private investor, the seller and buyer work out a financial agreement on how much the loan will be, the interest rate, the terms, and so on. Again, use an attorney to work out the details so that all parties are protected.

One of the most exciting things about buying a house is that there are very many loan programs to meet your needs. There are loans for people with plenty of cash for a down payment and loans for those who have no cash for a down payment. Mortgages abound for folks with great credit and bad credit alike. You just have to know what you're looking for and then move from one lender to the next till you find it. Knowing what to look for is the first step. So here are some definitions of loan types you can consider as you march toward buying your next house.

Zero-Down Loans

Marketers tell us the best way to get the masses to respond to an advertisement or mailing is to offer something free. In the world of real estate, free, unfortunately, is not an option. However, we have our own response mechanism in real estate marketing—it's called "zero-down financing."

Generally most zero-down programs require two things: good income and excellent credit. If you don't possess these two credentials, then read on if you wish, but only for future planning. Lenders have developed various zero-down programs, making them almost as common as conventional loans.

Loan Assumption with an Owner-Held Second Loan

Many loans are assumable, meaning the owner can let the buyer assume the loan as long as the buyer can qualify for the loan. Usually, there is added equity in the process, which could be held as a second trust by the owner. For instance, say a house priced at

$250,000 has a mortgage amount of $200,000. The borrower can assume the $200,000 loan and take over payments, then take out a second loan with the owner for $50,000, thus creating a zero-down mortgage. I'll talk more about assuming a mortgage in the next section.

C.R.A. (Community Reinvestment Act) Loans

Federal regulations require banks to originate mortgages in the markets where they have a retail banking presence. Buyers who meet certain financial criteria—income, credit (including scores), and first-time home buyer status—can qualify for so called "give-away loans." The benefits of this loan include below-market interest rates, a nominal or no down payment, and no private mortgage insurance.

Freddie Mac Alt 97

Using this 97 loan-to-value (LTV) program, borrowers can make it a 100 percent loan by using Freddie Mac's liberal version of its original First Timer's program—Freddie Mac Gold. The buyer receives a credit card then takes an immediate cash advance to be used for the 3 percent down payment and closing costs. Voila, zero-down financing.

Just a couple of notes on zero-down financing. As a general rule, zero-down does not necessarily mean no money out of your pocket. There are still closing costs, origination fees, commissions, and other expenses to consider, which can add up to several thousand dollars. However, the down payment, which is usually the largest expense in buying a home, is nil.

Assuming Loans Can Save Money

If you find yourself in a housing market with interest rates edging upward, don't sign the bottom line on a high interest–rate loan before looking around for a low-rate assumable mortgage. I'm referring to assumable loans available from homeowners who either refinanced or purchased homes in a low-interest period. Next time your real estate agent pulls multiple listing sheets for you, be sure to look over the current mortgage information. Was it acquired during the low-interest years? Is it assumable? If you can answer yes to both of these, you may have found your low-interest loan. Keep in mind, the buyer will be assuming the loan amount, which means he or she will then have to come up with enough cash to pay for the difference between the loan amount and the market value.

For instance, say the loan amount is for $185,000, but the market value of the house is $235,000—the buyer will have to produce $50,000 to assume the loan (plus closing costs). If you have done well in other investments, this may not be a problem, but review the possibilities with your agent or financial planner, nonetheless.

Before running out and signing up to take over payments from a seller, make sure you understand some nuances about loan assumptions. There are "freely assumable loans" and "qualified assumptions." In a freely assumable loan, the lender allows a new borrower to take over the mortgage payments without first getting the lender's approval or even qualifying for the loan. Sounds great, doesn't it? That's why there aren't too many of these left. There are a number of older loan programs that feature freely assumable mortgages, such as FHA (Federal Housing Administration–insured) loans originated prior to December 1, 1986, for any buyer, and before December 15, 1989, for owner-occupant purchasers. With VA (Veterans Affairs–insured) mortgages, search for loans made before March 1, 1988. These programs are discussed in more detail in the next chapter on government and nonprofit mortgage programs.

Most of the assumable loans you'll find in today's market are "qualified assumptions." For these loans, the lender must first approve the new buyer for the loan before it will allow the assumption. The tricky part here for the seller is that some of these assumptions still leave the seller liable for the loan if the new buyer defaults. Both buyer and seller should read the fine print on the assumption agreement on this matter.

Sometimes you'll see an offer to purchase a property "subject to" the mortgage. This is kind of like an assumption in that the lender lets the new buyer take over the loan. However, the lender will first pursue the new borrower if he defaults—then the original borrower. The lender protects itself from default either way.

Many loans specifically prohibit an assumption. With a "due-on-sale" clause, the lender may require complete payment of the mortgage when the property sells. If the seller's mortgage papers include a due-on-sale clause (or acceleration clause) then it effectively prohibits the mortgage from being assumed by another borrower.

Jumbo Loans: Loans for the Well-to-Do

Since the number one barrier to homeownership is coming up with the down payment, lenders have spent plenty of time creating programs that will allow homebuyers to purchase a house with very little or no money up front. These loans are higher-risk loans, since the buyers don't have as much financial risk in the loan as the lender. But what about the borrowers who don't have a cash problem or are purchasing a higher-priced house than the majority of buyers in the real estate market? In other words, what you might call the well-to-do buyer, the one who was able to cash-in on the stock market during the 1990s, use an inheritance to purchase a house, or use the equity from one house to buy another.

Those with cash to purchase houses above the conventional loan ceiling find themselves using jumbo loan programs. Since you're talking higher-priced houses and, therefore, higher-income purchasers, these programs provide different benefits than the conventional route of programs.

Jumbo Loans

Mortgages in 2004 for $333,700 and less are considered conventional or conforming loans. Loans above that figure are considered jumbo or nonconforming loans. The limits on conforming loans are determined by Fannie Mae, one of the two government-sponsored enterprises established years ago to promote homeownership across the country. Since jumbo loans aren't "conforming," there's no one set of rules that govern how they can be created. Your best place to research the individual programs would be with the loan providers themselves. RealtyTimes.com's columnists have several articles on this type of loan, and you can find limited information at www .Realtor.com.

Interest rates are higher for jumbo loans. For the latest interest rates reported nationwide, check out www.jumboloansnationwide .com. You'll find that interest rates for the higher-priced loans run from 0.50 to 1.50 basis points higher than the average conforming loan rate.

No-Income Verification Loans

One of the ways buyers with plenty of cash purchase houses with nonconforming loans is to use a no-income verification loan. This type of loan is designed for self-employed borrowers who after taking all their deductions may not show enough net income to qualify for a mortgage. A no-income verification loan allows the lender to bypass using a borrower's income on the loan application. In addition, it allows the lender to eliminate the use of tax returns, W-2's, or pay stubs. Interest rates and down payments will vary for this kind of loan program (usually a down payment of more than 20 percent is required). The borrower must show an excellent credit history, since his or her income will not be verified.

One of the best explanations of how low-documentation and no-documentation loan programs work comes from MortgageX .com (http://www.mortgagex.com/). Because of the risk associated with low- or no-documentation loans, the loan-to-value on them is limited to 70 to 75 percent, though some lenders allow a 90 percent LTV. (Loan-to-value represents the percentage amount a loan is made on the value of a house. For instance, a $70,000 loan on a $100,000 home would be a 70 percent LTV loan.)

"Credit standards are generally a little higher for Easy/No Doc loans," according to the group's site. "Borrowers must have maintained a good repayment history within the last two years. Additionally, some lenders will require borrowers to maintain higher bank balances than typical applicants usually must have." In addition, borrowers using these loans will probably receive higher interest rates and be assessed higher fees.

"Expect the interest rate to be about one-half to one percent more than the rate on a fully documented loan. Consequently, easy- and no-documentation loans should only be used when necessary, not simply to avoid the paperwork requirements of a full-documentation loan."

Employer-Assisted Housing Programs

Employers are always looking for a way to build employee loyalty with new perks or benefits. One way some are doing this is through employer-assisted housing benefits. These benefits may include offering money for a down payment, cosigning on a loan, even offering financing. By giving employees these type of benefits, employers find themselves with a pool of workers who don't want to leave.

Employer-assisted housing (EAH) is a very useful tool in a first-time or low-income buyer's purchasing toolbox. The employer provides a housing benefit to its employee "in the form of a forgivable, deferred, or repayable second loan; a grant; a matched savings plan; or a home-buyer education that helps the employee achieve homeownership," according to Fannie Mae's employer-assisted housing publication.

Though Fannie Mae (www.fanniemae.com) began its form of EAH in the 1990s, it took a tight labor pool across the country for it to become common knowledge to business owners. Fannie Mae has a program for its own employees that offers a forgivable loan. Since its inception, thousands of its employees have used the program. Eligible employees must work ninety-one days for Fannie Mae and remain at the company an additional five years to receive the full forgiveness on the EAH loan.

Company spokesperson H. Beth Marcus, director of community-based lending, says when the program started about 6 percent of eligible employees took advantage of it each year, but that number edged up year after year. She says the program has helped tremendously in the company's ability to retain good employees. "We did an analysis for the program over the last ten years. Those who took advantage of the program had a 25 percent lower turnover rate than those who didn't."

Ms. Marcus says employers can find assistance on Fannie Mae's Web site about the EAH program, including a questionnaire to help them decide which program best suits their needs. The following options are available to companies setting up such a program:

■ **Grant.** A one-time, lump sum of money given to the employee. It may have to be repaid if the employee leaves the company within a specified time period.

■ **Forgivable Loan.** The employer provides the employee with a second loan at the same time the first-trust loan is provided from a lender, which can facilitate the employer's loan to the employee. Some or all of the principal of the loan is forgiven during a specified period of time (usually years) that the employee remains with the company.

■ **Deferred or Repayable Loan.** This type of loan operates much like the forgivable loan, but there is a repayment feature at some time in the future, such as when the home is sold or the employee switches companies.

■ **Matched Savings.** In much the same way that employers match an employees' contributions to a retirement plan, the employer matches savings by an employee for the down payment money. The employer can either accrue the dollar amount on the company's books for an obligation to provide a grant at closing or cash deposits (dedicated for the home purchase) are made into an employee's account.

■ **Homebuyer Education.** While this program may not involve actual money changing hands, just offering employees the knowledge of how to purchase a house could be all the employees need to acquire a home. Such programs can help eliminate the mystery of the homebuying process and instruct potential buyers on what they need to do to improve credit, save for a down payment, and get approved for a loan.

Various industries have worked with Fannie Mae to set up EAH programs, from the healthcare industry to school district and municipal employees. Over the past 10 years, more than 250 groups have established EAH programs. Employers should keep in mind, however, that there are several tax issues associated with housing benefit plans.

"Typically, housing benefits are taxable to the employee and result in a commensurate tax reduction for the employer," according to Fannie Mae. "Specific treatment will vary with the employer's location and type of business, as well as the specifics of the EAH plan."

Reverse Mortgages

If you're nearing retirement age and have a lot of equity in your home, you can tap that equity and receive a monthly payment much like an annuity or you can pull out a lump sum. This is called a reverse mortgage, and since the initial Baby Boomers began retiring, this kind of mortgage has grown rapidly. If you are considering a reverse mortgage, be sure to read the fine print. For retirees, especially those considering investing in real estate during their golden years, this kind of mortgage lends some very interesting twists that others do not.

I have coached and trained many a senior who has cut out of

the rat race and taken up real estate as a second career. It's a great scenario—you're retired, plenty of time on your hands, and if you invested wisely, you already have an income, and real estate provides a great second income. For the retiree who desires to begin investing in real estate, the reverse mortgage can be the way to do so by tapping into equity. Here's another great aspect of this program—the borrower doesn't pay back the loan until the house sells or the owner dies.

A reverse mortgage is for homeowners sixty-two years of age and older and uses the equity in their home to receive monthly payments from a lender. The lender is paid from the proceeds of the sale, but the loan amount can never exceed the value of the house.

A report by Consumers Union, the nonprofit publisher of *Consumer Reports* magazine, states that "the right reverse mortgage can enable a senior to maintain financial independence and an adequate standard of living by converting a home's equity into tax-free cash." If used with wise council, the reverse mortgage can also provide investment money. On the other hand, for some senior borrowers, such a program can have the following hazards:

- High cost, leading homeowners to often owe dramatically more than they borrowed

- Complex contract terms that are confusing, are often not fully disclosed, and serve to increase overall costs

- Numerous fees that drive up the costs, including origination fees, points, mortgage insurance premiums, closing costs, servicing fees, shared equity or "maturity" fees, and shared appreciation fees

- Financial counseling often inconsistent and not independent of the lender

■ Adverse impacts on government benefits

■ "Estate planning" fee scams

Both the National Center for Home Equity Conversion (NCHEC) and Consumers Union offer some tips to help you make the best decision about reverse mortgages:

■ Determine if a reverse mortgage is really for you. Instead of slowly losing equity in your home, there may be another way to secure the money for your current and long-term financial needs.

■ Make an appointment with a HUD-approved reverse mortgage counselor—free of charge.

■ Take your mother's advice and shop around. Not all reverse mortgages come with the same terms and requirements.

■ If you are receiving monthly public benefits, ask if receiving funds from a reverse mortgage will affect your qualifications for these benefits. For example, if you are receiving "need-based" benefits, such as Medicaid or Supplemental Social Security Income (SSI), payments from a reverse mortgage will definitely affect your qualifications. For instance, if you choose monthly payments from a reverse mortgage and don't spend all the money each month, that is considered income and may reduce your eligibility for public assistance.

■ One of the most important items to consider is the cost of the loan. Most lenders can give you the amount of money you need, based on the value of your house; however, make sure you understand how much that money is going to cost you. Check out up-front fees, administrative fees, shared-equity arrangements, any amount of money the lender is going to receive. After interviewing several lenders, place their fees side by side and compare.

As with any other loan product, you want to ask specific questions. Don't ASSUME anything about how the loan works. Here are a few questions to ask the loan officer:

- Do I still own my home with the program?

- Must I sell my house before I die to pay off the reverse mortgage?

- What happens if my spouse dies? Will he or she have to pay off the loan immediately?

- How will this loan affect my heirs when I die?

- Are there any prepayment penalties on the loan?

- Who pays taxes, insurance, and property maintenance?

For more detailed information on reverse mortgages, check out these two independent organizations online:

Consumers Union: www.consumersunion.org

National Center for Home Equity Conversion: www.reverse.org

Bridge Loans: Torn Between Two Closings

The process of buying and selling a house is much like the domino effect. Everything gets lined up perfectly and when it's time to get things going, you just flip a switch and watch all the pieces fall into place.

But as we all know, not everything falls into place perfectly. In most cases, a seller puts his house on the market, sells it, and then goes into the market to buy a replacement home. This usually takes a couple of weeks; then an offer is made and settlements are arranged to coincide with one another. The first home settles, from which the seller-turned-buyer has plenty of cash to settle on the new house. Settlement happens again, followed by moving vans that arrive at the old house one day and deliver all the stuff to the new house the next week.

Sometimes, these timelines are not so perfect. A buyer may sell a house and settlement stares him in the face before he has found a home of choice. Worse yet, he has sold his house, has everything packed, and his own home of choice can't go to settlement because the folks he bought it from were just told that the house they bought won't settle because the house he bought won't settle because the people he bought it from can't settle because. . . .

I think you get the picture. What to do when you're torn between two settlements?

Let's take it a deal at a time.

The best scenario for all of the following examples is that the parties involved renegotiate settlement dates so that the domino effect goes off without a hitch. If not, here are some tips on what to do:

Scenario #1: You've sold a house and bought a house, but for some reason the settlements don't coincide.

If you've already settled on your old house, and you can't settle for a couple weeks (or months) then you need two things— actually, three—1) a place to stay during the time period; 2) storage space for your belongings; 3) a really big aspirin. (You will find that number 3 is a common theme with all these problems.)

You're really only up against logistics here. Find a friend or family member who can put you up for a while or possibly look for temporary housing if you're moving into a completely new neighborhood. You might even consider asking around at some worship centers to find out if they have housing where they can let you stay for a few days while you await settlement.

Scenario #2: Let's say you've sold your house and bought a new one, but the buyers of your home can't settle until after you're scheduled to close on your new home. Your obvious problem is that you won't have the money to get into your new home without the closing.

This one is tough. First, see if you can postpone your second settlement. If that doesn't work, then talk with your loan officer about constructing a bridge loan to get you through the two transactions.

A bridge loan, otherwise known as a "swing" loan, is secured by the borrower's present house. Its obvious use is to provide the borrower with enough funds to close on a new house before settling on his existing home. According to the *Realty Bluebook*—the Bible of real estate—a bridge loan is acceptable, if:

- "[T]he purchaser has the ability to carry the payment on the new home, the payment on the other obligations, the payment on the current home, and the payment on the bridge loan; and

- "[T]he bridge loan is not cross-collateralized against the new property." (This means, the bridge loan is not secured by the new house—just the home trying to be sold.)

Scenario #3: This is a bad scenario. No one can settle on time and you find yourself in a gridlock. What happens next will depend on the reasons behind the houses not going to settlement. Either the buyer and seller have a friendly, albeit frustrating, release of contract or they exchange harsh words followed by threats of lawsuits. This scenario is rare, but it happens occasionally.

Being torn between two closings can be avoided by secure financing, careful planning, and surrounding yourself with able professionals. Don't leave home without one.

Second Trusts: Eliminate PMI, Help with Cash Flow, Lower Payments

If you're looking for financing with a low down payment, be sure to look over multilayered loans that help reduce your monthly payment and increase your buying power.

Lenders have created financial programs to allow the cash-strapped borrower to purchase a house with two loans. A first-trust loan for 80 percent is provided by the primary lender, then a secondary lender, coupled with the buyer's down payment money, takes care of the other 20 percent. For instance, such a loan structured as described may be referred to as an 80/15/5 loan. The first trust finances 80 percent of the purchase price, the second trust finances 15 percent, and the borrower puts up 5 percent cash.

This strategy increases the purchaser's buying power since the money that would have been spent each month for private mortgage insurance is now part of the payment that goes to principal and interest.

Private mortgage insurance (PMI) is a policy taken out by a borrower for the benefit of the lender. Statistics show that buyers who take out a home mortgage for more than 80 percent of the value of the home run a higher risk of defaulting on the loan than similar buyers who place a down payment of 20 percent or higher. Because of this higher risk on the lender's part, the company requires the borrower to take out an insurance policy to protect the lender in case the borrower defaults.

For FHA, VA, and other kinds of loans insured by government agencies, the PMI is a common expense on the borrowing side. Many VA loans are for more than 100 percent of the value of the house, since Uncle Sam also allows military veterans to finance closing costs. FHA allows loans up to 97 percent of the value of the house, while other conventional loans are also available for less than a 20 percent down payment, thus requiring private mortgage insurance.

If you're looking at purchasing a house with a second trust, there are a couple of nuances about a second mortgage of which you should be aware. First, the interest rate is going to seem a bit higher than what you will be quoted for a regular mortgage. For instance, if you're paying 8 percent on the first trust, don't be surprised to see the second mortgage interest rate in the double digits—10 to 15 percent. Shop and compare, but your primary lender should be able to set up the whole transaction.

The interest rate is going to run higher for at least a couple of reasons:

- The lender/investor stands second in line to get his money if the buyer defaults. In case of a default, the first trust holder may foreclose to receive payment on the loan—the second mortgage holder doesn't get a cent until the first trust holder is paid completely.

- In addition, the amount of the loan is so small that the lender/investor must charge a higher interest rate to receive ample compensation.

Another characteristic of a second trust is that it is usually loaned out for a much shorter term than the first trust. A typical first mortgage term is thirty years. A second mortgage can run as long as fifteen years or as short as five years.

If you've owned a home for any amount of time, you've received offers for home equity loans. In essence, these are also second trusts. As you make payments on your current mortgage and as your home appreciates in value, your equity in the house will grow; many homeowners use this equity to finance various projects. Debt consolidation is one of the many reasons a person will borrow money against his equity, to reduce the monthly payment and interest rates of credit cards and other consumer debts.

A home equity loan, however, is different from a home equity line of credit. A loan expires after a certain time period, whereas a home equity line of credit operates like a cash advance on your credit card. As the homeowner needs the cash, he or she pulls that amount out of the home's equity and then begins making payments back on a prearranged schedule.

Nontraditional Loans: Think Outside of the Box for House Financing

Hopefully, you've learned throughout this chapter that the key to any real estate transaction is financing. If you can qualify for the loan and the risks are within the lender's limits, you're in.

Most potential buyers look at real estate and see only the traditional means of buying a home. Creative financing is more than just a phrase in the real estate vernacular. It really does exist. If you want to break out of the box, consider seller financing in a hot sellers' market. If your marketplace is experiencing appreciating prices, some homeowners may consider financing the home loan themselves, if they are looking for a regular cash flow. It works like this:

Buyer Jones agrees to purchase the house for $150,000 with a $7,500 down payment (5 percent). Seller Smith provides a note for $142,500 at 8 percent and buyer Jones sends payments ($1,041 per month) to seller Smith, who then continues to make payments ($665/month) to his original lender, holding a note valued at $80,000. (NOTE: Some lenders do not allow this type of arrangement. The seller must check for a "due-on-sale" clause in the original mortgage to see if the note is due upon sale of the property.)

Mr. Smith has wrapped this new loan around his personal loan. In essence, he's making money to the tune of $376 on the property each month, based on today's prices. (Consult with a real estate or mortgage professional before attempting this yourself—we don't want anyone falling down and losing an eye at this point.) You will have to work out the details on who will pay for the hazard insurance and property taxes, when they will be paid, and to whom—held in escrow or paid by the buyer.

It can be a bit complicated, but it's another way of financing that is a tad nontraditional, and it works for thousands of buyers and sellers in today's market. Plus it introduces another way to make money by selling, buying, and holding real estate notes, which I'll deal with in chapter 7.

Do you have a rich uncle or another relative who wants to make money on his money? Consider having this relative finance the purchase of your next house instead of the traditional banking institutions. A good real estate attorney can help with the paperwork to make sure all the i's are dotted and t's crossed.

Finally, here are a few more outside-of-the-box ideas on financing, some of which I'll detail in a separate chapter:

■ **Cosigner.** Many first-time buyers use this type of arrangement with a relative who acts as a second party who signs a promissory note and takes responsibility for the debt.

■ **Shared-Appreciation Mortgage.** This is a loan that allows a lender or other party to share in the borrower's profits when the home is sold. Usually, the lender or other party puts up part or all of the down payment. It's more popular in an up market, when houses are appreciating in value.

■ **Shared-Equity Transaction.** Similar to the shared-appreciation mortgage, the shared-equity involves a transaction in which two buyers purchase a property, one as a resident co-owner and the other as an investor co-owner. The difference is one shares in PROFIT, the other shares in EQUITY (whether or not there is profit).

■ **Lease Option.** If you're a renter and you're not sure you want to buy a house outright, or you like the house you're renting but don't have cash for a down payment, the lease option gives the renter the right to purchase the property for a specific price within a certain time frame. Many times the renter pays more than market price for the rent, say $100 more per month, and that money is placed in escrow to use as a down payment at a later time.

Creative financing can enable many cash-poor buyers to purchase the home of their dreams . . . whether a first-time buyer or a former president of a major world power.

Case Study: The President Bill Clinton Loan Program

While President and Mrs. Bill Clinton were in the process of exiting the White House, they put together a creative financing package for their home purchase in New York in 2001. Democratic Party fundraiser Terence McAuliffe agreed to guarantee the Clintons' $1.3 million mortgage by placing that same amount of his own funds in a Bankers Trust bank account.

Even though the Office of Government Ethics ruled that the assistance does not constitute a gift under federal law, naysayers were concerned the arrangement was at least gray, since Mr. McAuliffe also heads up fund-raising for the Clintons with all of their political debts. The Clintons claimed it was "a legitimate business arrangement." And folks, from where I sit . . . they were exactly right.

What they did was nothing unusual or unavailable to every potential homebuyer in this country. It's called a "guarantee mortgage," which is simply a loan guaranteed by a third party, such as a government institution or well-financed uncle.

Have you ever heard a loan officer talk about how she can get you into a house with some "creative financing"? Well, this is one of those forms of creative financing. When you think about it, all Mr. McAuliffe did was act as an insurance policy for the Clintons in case they defaulted on the loan. A large portion of borrowers in this country have this type of guarantor—it's called the Federal Housing Administration (FHA).

You know all those HUD (Housing and Urban Development) properties you see advertised in the foreclosure section of the newspaper? These are properties with loans guaranteed by the federal government—HUD, in this case. When the borrowers defaulted, HUD took over the properties and then resold them to get its money back.

If the Clintons default, not only will they lose their five-bedroom, $1.7 million house, but Mr. McAuliffe's funds will be used to pay Bankers Trust for the loan. Creative financing works on all levels of real estate—from first-time buyers to retired presidents.

Paying Off Mortgage Early More of a Security Question

As you start making that monthly payment on your dream home, the question will always arise—"Should I pay off the mortgage or keep it for the tax benefits?" Well, I don't know if it's the economy or if people suddenly see the benefit of being debt-free, but there seems to be a lot of press and cyber print on paying off a mortgage early. Is this a good idea or not? There are two schools of thought on this question.

For me, having been down the "barely making it" trail, I'm all for being debt free. Pay off that bugger as fast as you can—but within financial reason. Don't make yourself so cash poor that you don't have any money to maintain the house, save for your retirement, or enjoy your life. Even though it may be a drawn-out plan, a thirty-year mortgage is a financial plan for owning your home.

Some financial planners encourage you to have a mortgage—even a big one (www.ricedelman.com), while others give you plenty of ideas on how to get rid of it as soon as possible (www.crown.org). It comes down to what you can do financially. Financial planner Ric Edelman makes a compelling argument for hanging onto the mortgage and using the extra money to invest in your emergency fund or other investments. He plays out two fictitious homeowners: One wants to get completely out of debt and uses all of his savings to lower his mortgage amount and then throws his extra money toward the principal. The second character takes on a higher mortgage with a longer term and smaller monthly payment.

The difference between the two is revealed with an example of both of them losing their jobs. Obviously the buyer with the higher savings account is able to weather the downturn. Another question to consider is how much money you can make from the extra payment you're sending to your lender. With some online savings calculators (http://www.financenterinc.com/products/savings.html) and mortgage calculators (www.decisionaide.com), I think you'll be able to determine whether the early payoff eventually results in a big payoff financially.

For a home priced at $154,000, assuming a 5 percent down payment, thirty-year fixed rate mortgage at 7 percent, along with a savings investment averaging 8 percent per year, here are some calculations on both scenarios. The monthly principal and interest payment is $973.34.

First, let's look at taking that extra money and placing it in a savings program instead of reducing your mortgage. Most people think about just adding an extra $100 to the payment, so let's use that amount as both the investment amount and the debt-reduction amount.

With the Finance Center Inc. savings calculator, $100 saved per month in an investment yielding 8 percent would result in savings of $60,608 in a taxable investment and $81,020 in a tax-deferred or tax-exempt investment after thirty years. At the end of thirty years this same homeowner will have paid out $204,098 in interest, as well as the $146,300 principal amount of the loan.

Now, let's take that $100 per month and plop it onto the principal of the loan, resulting in a monthly payment of $1,073.34. Here's what happens: the term of the loan is cut by 7.25 years, saving the homeowner $57,860 in interest payments. Here's the second step of that scenario. Now take the monthly payment amount—take that $1,073.34 payment and start placing it in an investment plan just like we did earlier with the $100—except the model here is only going to save for the remaining 7.25 years left from the original loan.

By saving $1,073.34 per month at 8 percent over 7.25 years a homeowner would have $101,008 in a taxable investment or $107,117 in a tax-deferred or tax-exempt investment. This doesn't include the interest payment savings of $57,860 (which is actually a paper savings).

Keep in mind that by cutting out the interest payments, the homeowner also loses tax deductions in that same amount, which can result in a new tax bill over those 7.25 years of $15,912 (at roughly 28 percent). But the owner still has a plus of $11,000 or so over that period by not paying out the larger amount of interest. As with any tax deduction, you have to spend the money to get the deduction. Why spend $1,000 to get a savings of $280? Sometimes it just doesn't make sense.

These are pretty impressive numbers. However, I must point out that the average homeowner chooses to move every five to seven years instead of staying in the same house and allowing these numbers to come to fruition. So, should you pay off your mortgage and go for the gold debt-free ring? The real question is, will you?

We've covered various methods of financing your home and investment properties. As you can see, the days of the mandated 20 percent down payment program are gone! We've learned how the right mortgage program can be dictated by your credit score, income, debt ratios, and payment habits. The programs above are available through thousands of loan officers in your area. Now, let's look at some other programs that make it easier for buyers with credit problems or little cash or income to buy their own home or invest in properties.

Notes

1 M. Anthony Carr, "Speculating Can Cost You Money," *The Washington Times,* May 4, 2001.

2 Ibid.

3 Ibid.

4 Ibid.

CHAPTER 5

All the Programs You'll Ever Need–Government and Nonprofit

I've had many readers write me with questions about investing, only to find out they've never purchased a house and they could barely qualify to purchase a primary dwelling, much less an investment property. Government and nonprofit programs give low- and moderate-income buyers the buying power to purchase their first home. If you have never purchased a home, then such a move should be the first step in your plans to invest in real estate. This chapter covers programs to help you do just that.

While the mortgage players discussed in the previous chapter offer the actual cash to buy a home, the way the money is handed over to buyers differs from buyer to buyer. A home purchaser with a great job, excellent credit, and a hefty down payment can qualify for just about any darn loan he or she wants.

Many buyers don't fit this category. For one reason or another, they are a greater risk to the lender than someone with A1 credit. It may not be that they have bad credit, but maybe they don't have enough credit. If they don't have a large enough down payment, that also makes them a higher risk. Mortgage history has revealed that people with large down payments are a lot less likely to default on a loan than are those who make small down payments. With a

95

lot more of her own money at stake, a borrower who puts down $20,000 won't be as likely to walk away from the house as one who puts down $3,000.

FHA-Guaranteed Loans

For buyers who represent a greater credit risk, there are government programs to help them get into a house. The FHA loan is the most widely used government program. FHA stands for Federal Housing Agency, which is operated out of the U.S. Department of Housing and Urban Development (HUD—online at www.hud .gov).

The FHA loan is insured by HUD, which is NOT providing the funds for the loan. Uncle Sam is in essence saying to the mortgage provider, "If this yahoo goes belly up and quits paying back the money he owes you, Uncle Sam will take over the property and pay back your mortgage." Thus, you may have heard the phrase "HUD Properties."

FHA produces regulations that guide Fannie Mae, Freddie Mac, and other program providers on how to create the criteria for their programs. FHA may dictate how low of a credit score the program can take, how much money the seller can contribute to the buyer's closing costs, and other particulars such as this.

Community housing associations use FHA programs quite a bit in constructing their own programs. The key for all of them is that if the buyer defaults, the lender is covered with the insurance from FHA. The risk is about double for foreclosure on FHAs over conventional mortgages—about 4 percent of all FHA borrowers will default on the mortgage.

Graduated Payments

HUD has several programs that enable buyers to purchase a house with graduated payment mortgage insurance. This program is much like a conventional 2–1 buy-down program. The program still relies on the FHA borrower limitations, which allow a purchaser who is somewhat higher risk to buy a house.

The graduated payment mortgage program allows a buyer to purchase a house with a lower-than-normal interest rate, but then raises the interest rate each year for the first few years, thus enabling the buyer to ease into the higher loan amount. Referred to as Section 245 loans, the program has five plans for homebuyers. Three of the five plans permit mortgage payments to increase at a rate of 2.5, 5, or 7.5 percent during the first five years of the loan. The other two plans permit payments to increase 2 and 3 percent annually over ten years. Starting at the sixth year of the five-year plans and the eleventh-year of the ten-year plans, payments will stay the same for the remaining term of the mortgage. The greater the rate of increase and the longer the period of increase, the lower the mortgage payments in the early years.

Another HUD program comes under Section 223(e), which provides mortgage insurance for a home or project that may be otherwise difficult to finance because it is located in an older, declining urban area. The program is also open to sponsors of multifamily housing located in older, declining urban areas.

Keep in mind that what HUD is offering is mortgage insurance to lenders who will make loans such as the ones described above. HUD does not originate loans, but it protects lenders from possible default. HUD has several little-known, yet vibrant programs to help potential buyers purchase a home of their own. The key to these insurance programs is that they reduce the down payment and other stringent requirements to make homeownership easier for low- and moderate-income borrowers.

As you move toward investing in real estate, talk with your banker about HUD's Section 207 mortgage insurance. This program may be used for new construction, repair or rehabilitation, or manufactured home parks. To be eligible, the properties must consist of five or more units of detached, semidetached, walkup, or elevator-style rental housing. Generally, a project is eligible for project mortgage insurance if the sponsors can demonstrate that there is a definite market demand, that the project is economically self-sufficient, and that project financing is secure.

One final note on HUD-based programs, and that is the organization's 203k program, where a purchaser can buy a fixer-upper home and get a loan that also covers the refurbishing of the property as well as its original purchase. This program even allows for the purchase of a lot and for moving another home onto it. For more information about any of these programs, go to http://www.hud.gov and see the "Home Improvement" or "Other Funds" sections.

Veterans Affairs Loans

Another government insurance provider is the Department of Veterans Affairs or VA (www.va.gov). These are mortgages, again, underwritten by a government agency rather than loaned out by a government agency. The VA program is a very powerful program for military veterans or active military. This program enables our men and women in uniform to borrow money with no down payment—actually with no money out of their pockets whatsoever, as they are also allowed to finance all closing costs. Thus, a VA loan will go up to 106 percent of the value of the loan (100 percent for the loan, 6 percent for closing costs).

VA loans are notorious for paperwork. I have yet to see a real estate contract folder that is less than a couple of inches thick. While the sales contract may run from only one to a dozen pages, plenty of trees are required for disclosure forms, the mortgage application, addenda, notification forms, and so on.

If you are applying for a government-insured loan, such as an FHA, FmHA (Farmers Home Administration), or VA—then the file gets even thicker. Nevertheless, much of the paperwork can save you money.

Before even applying for a VA loan, a borrower must first prove to the lender that he or she is eligible for such a loan by supplying a Certificate of Eligibility. This certificate is available through the VA. To start the process, veterans or active military personnel must fill out VA Form 26-1880 ("Request for a Certificate of Eligibility for Home Loan Benefits") and submit it to one of the VA's eligibility centers. The office in Los Angeles serves the west side of the United States and Winston-Salem, North Carolina, serves the east. For the dividing lines, visit http://www.homeloans.va.gov/elig.htm.

Part of the eligibility process is to provide acceptable proof of military service, which involves several other forms, depending on when you were discharged. Keep in mind, the VA loan stays with the property. If a buyer assumes a VA loan, then the original borrower may not obtain another VA loan until that original loan is paid off or if the new borrower is also a veteran and willing to substitute his or her available eligibility for that of the original veteran. If a veteran pays off a loan, and hangs onto the property, and attempts to purchase another property with another VA loan, eligibility for the VA benefit may be restored once only. Just provide proof that the first VA loan has been retired to prevent delays in the new financing.

One final note. The surviving spouse of a veteran who died on active duty or as the result of a service-related disability is eligible to use the VA loan benefit so long as he or she has not remarried. If the surviving spouse obtained the loan with the veteran prior to the veteran's death, the spouse may qualify for a VA-guaranteed, interest rate-reduction refinance loan. Contact one of the eligibility centers for details.

State and Local Housing Authorities

Housing authorities are agencies set up by states and local jurisdictions to help revitalize dilapidated areas and to help low- to moderate-income buyers. They do this by issuing bonds to raise money for loans or by partnering with Fannie Mae, Freddie Mac, and other investors to provide money for these types of loans, usually with a below-market interest rate. The loans customarily have limitations, such as income and size of household. For the housing authority that serves your area, search online by typing in "[your state] housing authority," or contact your county government.

There are a plethora of private, nonprofit housing agencies to help people get into a home of their own. The appendix contains a list of the Web sites for the housing agencies in every state, which is a valuable resource to find financing assistance from such groups in your local area. Housing agencies offer homebuying education, money for down payments, and low-interest loans, if you qualify. See the appendix for a complete list of state housing authorities.

Special Financing Available for Low-Income Buyers

I regularly receive e-mails from readers who desperately want to buy a house but just seem to be in dire straits financially. Beyond that, they are dismayed at the ever-increasing price of their rent and housing in general. In addition, they just can't seem to make more money. They are in industries that do not offer them more opportunity than what they now have.

One writer shared with me that his salary was at $15,000 and though there are houses priced about $50,000, his debt-to-salary ratio knocks him out of the buying arena at this time. He can't see homeownership as a part of his future. For this person, I say, don't give up hope. Someone making $15,000 can purchase a house in several markets with today's interest rates. The traditional percentage of a person's salary allowed by lenders for housing costs and credit debt is 36 percent, though higher for many programs today. Therefore, a person making $15,000 with no credit debts will have $450 for a monthly mortgage payment (36 percent of $1,250 in monthly income). This amount could borrow roughly $65,000 to $70,000, depending on the interest rate and taxes.

While that won't buy a single-family house in most markets, it will buy a property of some sort that provides a lower-income borrower with a home of his own. That's the bottom line. The details may be a little more complex. Those in lower-income brackets may have to make some tough decisions in order to raise the savings and cash flow needed to own a home. The best advice I can give is to talk with a mortgage or real estate professional to see where you stand financially. Here are some quick directions on heading toward homeownership when price is an issue:

■ **Increase your cash flow.** This may mean getting into another line of work, taking on a part-time job, or getting the skills (going to school) to prepare yourself for a higher salary. It may be as involved as pursuing a college degree or getting into a trade, such as plumbing, carpentry, or electrical work, which takes less training but pays higher than unskilled labor.

■ **Move.** If you are in a very expensive metropolitan area and the above step isn't going to work, then find a job elsewhere in a cheaper housing market. The minimum wage is the minimum wage whether in expensive New York City or rural Turtletown, Tennessee. Obviously, you'll have more purchasing power in Turtletown (yes, a real town—the hometown of my grandparents).

■ **Get Out of Debt (GOOD).** Frankly, being debt free gives you more housing options (and a lot less stress) than anything else you can do.

■ **Look to low- to medium-income housing assistance programs.** Below are various organizations across the country that can help buyers with down payments, closing costs, and debt reduction. These are national groups; however, there are plenty of state-based organizations available as well. Search for them online using your search engine of choice by plugging in "housing assistance" and your state name.

■ Housing Assistance Corporation (http://www.housing assistance.com/) is a Nevada-based nonprofit corporation that operates "Home Grants," a special down payment assistance program providing nonrepayable grants and gifts to individuals and families nationwide. Phone: 702/385-3973.

■ Housing Assistance Council (http://www.ruralhome.org/) helps local organizations build affordable houses in rural America. It provides help in developing both single- and multi-family houses and assists low-income rural buyers through a self-help "sweat-equity" construction program. The Housing Assistance Council maintains a focus on high-need groups and regions: Indian country, the Mississippi Delta, farm workers, the Southwest border region, and Appalachia. Housing Assistance Council, 1025 Vermont Ave., NW, Suite 606, Washington, D.C. 20005, Phone: 202/842-8600.

- Community Housing Assistance Program, Inc. (http:// www.chapausa.org/) was founded in 1991 and services predominantly California, Oregon, and Washington. The nonprofit organization is a managing partner for forty-two tax credit partnerships with more than 5,500 units of affordable housing. Community Housing Assistance Program, 3803 E. Casselle Ave., Orange, California 92869, Phone: 714/744-6252.

- USDA Rural Development. (http://www.rurdev.usda.gov/) This is the only government agency I've included in this list because of its unique programs, which support loans to businesses through banks and community-managed lending pools. Plus, the largest demographic of its client base are single moms, who usually need plenty of help in the search for affordable housing. Rural Housing Service National Office, U.S. Department of Agriculture, Room 5037, South Building, 14th Street and Independence Avenue, S.W., Washington, D.C. 20250, Phone: 202/720-4323.

- The Nehemiah Program (http://www.nehemiahprogram .org/) provides gift funds for down payment and closing costs (of any resale or new property) to qualified buyers using an eligible loan program, such as an FHA loan. Gift funds of 1 to 6 percent of the contract sales price can be requested, depending on the particular needs of the buyer. Homebuyers often move into their new home with as little as 1 percent of the sales price in reserves. No repayment, geographical restrictions, or income or asset requirements. Nehemiah Program: Phone: 877/634-3642.

- The Housing Action Resource Trust (http://www.hart program.com/) operates its Down Payment Assistance Program. It assists with down payment costs for buyers who qualify for a first mortgage loan. The organization is supported through various builders and sellers and other businesses. The gift amount is limited to $15,000, which can be used for closing costs, prepaids, rate buy-downs, and debts or collections (as mandated by the loan underwriter). Phone: 909/945-1574.

Rural Loans: Homeownership Outside the City Grows

Residents in the boonies may appreciate homeownership more than city slickers. The U.S. Department of Agriculture reports that while America overall celebrated an all-time high 67 percent homeownership rate in 2002, throughout rural America, it stands at a whopping 75 percent.

USDA operates the Rural Development loan and grant programs (Section 502), which assist seniors and lower-income families with home repair financing and home loans through its Rural Housing Service (RHS) programs. Formerly referred to as FmHA loans, the RHS mortgage comes in several shapes and sizes.

They have the same attributes as the more popular and widely used FHA (Federal Housing Administration, operated by the U.S. Department of Housing and Urban Development) and VA (U.S. Department of Veterans Affairs) programs in being guaranteed by a government agency. If the borrower defaults, Uncle Sam pays the lender to get out of the loan, and this is how they differ. USDA actually lends money through its direct loan programs and uses a network of 2,400 lenders for its guaranteed programs. Through this option, some homeowners can get loans with an interest rate as low as 1 percent.

The program allows 100 percent loan-to-value with no private mortgage insurance, which helps buyers arrive at a much better debt-to-income ratio since there is no PMI. The direct program is low-income (80 percent of median) based. In some cases the program is partnered with state FHA and borrowers receive a below-market interest rate. About 30 percent of the families in the guarantee program are 80 percent or below median income.

One of the largest beneficiaries of the RHS mortgage are single mothers, who made up 31.8 percent of mortgagees in 1998 (the latest figures available). USDA also reports that married couples with children make up nearly 40 percent of the home purchasers.

The loan limits are based on the Housing and Urban Development limits, which flow through a range of prices depending on where the house is located and how expensive or inexpensive the market. Searching for "FHA loan limits" on your favorite search engine is the easiest way to see the latest loan limits for this program.

The loan limits are only one of the restrictions on the RHS mortgage. There are income limits and population limits as well. The property must be located in a rural area (town), defined as having a population of 25,000 or less. There is a way around this population limit near larger metropolitan areas, however. Towns near New York City or Dallas, for instance, have to have a population under 10,000 before an RHS mortgage can be used there. While these loans are generally considered rural loans, RHS representatives tell me buyers in commuter towns around metropolitan areas can also qualify for the program.

As far as income limits are concerned, buyers cannot make more than 115 percent of the county median income level for the guaranteed loan program. Income limits for the direct program, however, are 80 percent of median income for low–income buyers and 50 percent of the median income for very low–income borrowers.

When you consider that some of the Section 502 program allows for 100 percent loan to value and 1 percent mortgage rates, you can see why it's a thriving program with plenty of room to grow. For more information about the RHS/Section 502 programs and a list of field offices around the country, potential borrowers would do best to visit the Rural Development Web site at http://www.rurdev.usda.gov/recd_map.html. Once there, click the desired state for its Web site.

As-Is Condition Not Good Enough for Some Loan Programs

Keep in mind that with all the financing available out there, just because a house is a house, doesn't mean all those programs are available to finance it. At times a seller is not as interested in getting the maximum amount on the sale of a property as he is in just getting out of a property. Investors who have depreciated a rental unit to the max, homeowners who face an emergency move, or distressed property owners may be motivated by time, rather than the bottom line.

These scenarios bring into play the sale of a property in "as-is" condition. Buyers can pick up good deals on these type of houses. An "as-is" house could be a handyman special in need of paint, afflicted by termite infestation, with dry rot on the deck, and a leaking roof that needs replacement.

The problem with these houses is that many loan programs cannot be used to purchase them. For both conforming and non-conforming loans, lenders want a house to meet a certain standard before putting their money on the line to help a buyer purchase it. If a house is a complete disaster, a lender may be more interested in helping a buyer acquire the land, but not the house on the land.

Mortgages insured by the Federal Housing Administration (which operates under the U.S. Department of Housing and Urban Development), require that houses come under a minimal condition standard. In the absence of local or state codes, the guidelines come from HUD's Section 8 department, which generally regulates the rental programs. These guidelines are known as the Housing Quality Standard (HQS).

Houses being bought with HUD-insured loans must be inspected by a HUD representative (this can be an appraiser or a representative from the lender). HUD rules stipulate the required repairs necessary to preserve the continued marketability of the property and to protect the health and safety of the occupants. These are known as the three S's:

1. Salability—preserve the continued marketability of the property

2. Safety—protect the health and safety of the occupants

3. Security—protect the security of the property (security for the FHA-insured mortgage)

The general requirements include these thirteen points:

1. Sanitary facilities

2. Food preparation and refuse disposal

3. Space and security

4. Thermal environment

5. Illumination and electricity

6. Structure and materials

7. Interior air quality

8. Water supply

9. Lead-based paint

10. Access

11. Site and neighborhood

12. Sanitary condition

13. Smoke detectors

Here's where the confusion begins. There are no published standards on how these points are to be met or enforced. In fact, HUD advises those in the field who have to determine the fitness of the property that, pretty much, it's a subjective process.

"Public Housing Authorities should strive to ensure consistency among staff in areas requiring judgment. Not all areas of HQS are exactly defined, while acceptability criteria specifically state the minimum standards necessary to meet HQS. Inspector judgment or tenant preference may also need to be considered in determining whether the unit meets minimum standards or are desirable."[1]

In other words, what is acceptable in one locality may fail miserably in another. In fact, HUD isn't even leaving it up to the professionals, since "tenant preference" can also be considered in the equation of whether the property meets the standard. Lord help those with an overly picky tenant.

Once you have found a fixer-upper, be sure the loan program you're looking to use for the purchase of such a diamond-in-the-rough will actually cover all the problems you find. If a property is in such disrepair that the lender won't approve the loan to purchase it in its as-is condition, you may consider a rehabilitation loan along with the acquisition loan. Rehabilitation loans are offered to buyers who are looking to buy a dilapidated property in order to fix it up. Talk this over with your lender to see if it will work for your particular situation.

DOE Programs: Good Loans for Good Insulation

Once you're in a property, you must dedicate resources and money from your budget to take care of the property. Your home is your largest investment in life and letting it deteriorate is not an option. The Department of Energy offers loans to homeowners (and renters) who qualify to make their house warmer or cooler and keep their utility bills down.

The Department of Energy reports that while middle- to high-income families spend only 3.5 percent of their annual income on energy costs, low-income families spend an average of 14 percent to heat and cool their dwellings. Until reform hits in the utilities industry, you can't really shop around for a better price on energy. The only thing you can do is cut back use or take energy-saving measures around the house, like adding insulation, sealing windows, and caulking around doors.

To help reduce the burden of these costs, DOE has developed the Weatherization Assistance Program. The Weatherization Assistance Program (WAP) reduces the heating and cooling costs for low-income families—particularly for the elderly and persons with disabilities or children. The program has weatherized more than 5 million homes since its inception in 1976.

WAP works pretty simply. States receive DOE grants and then award grants to local agencies, usually community-action agencies or other nonprofit or government organizations, to perform the actual weatherization services. The process is simple as well. After an application has been made, a professional team conducts a computerized energy audit, using advanced diagnostic equipment to identify energy-saving measures that are cost-effective or essential for health and safety. Then a crew arrives to weatherize the dwelling.

The energy-saving measures may include installing insulation and ventilation fans, tuning up heating and cooling units, and modifying and replacing heating or cooling units to ensure energy efficiency and safety. An education program is also used to inform clients about the proper use and maintenance of installed weatherization measures. These services are available for single-family homes, multifamily dwellings, and mobile homes, whether the client owns or rents the structure. DOE reports the energy cost savings per household is often between 25 and 30 percent.

The funding for the WAP outreach is a mixture of government and private monies. Federal funds come from DOE's appropriation and the Low-Income Home Energy Assistance Program (LIHEAP) block grant. The remainder of the funds come from utility companies, the states, and other sources.

Qualified applicants must fit in one of the two following financial categories: Any household at or below the higher of (1) the federal poverty level or (2) 60 percent of the state median income. The DOE Web site provides information on eligibility for the program:

"Whether you own or rent, live in a single-family home, multifamily housing complex, or a mobile home, you can apply for assistance. If you rent, you must get written permission from your landlord before weatherization services can be performed. Preference is given to persons over sixty, persons with disabilities, and, in some cases, children. If you receive Supplemental Security Income (SSI) and/or Aid to Families with Dependent Children (AFDC), you are automatically eligible. You may also be eligible for assistance if your income falls within the federally established income guidelines."

The financial guidelines are based on size of family and income range.

Size	Income
1	$9,863–$11,835
2	$13,263–$15,915
3	$16,663–$19,995
4	$20,063–$24,075
5	$23,463–$28,155
6	$26,863–$32,235
7	$30,263–$36,315
8	$33,663–$40,395

For more information, go to the Department of Energy's Web site for Energy Efficiency and Renewable Energy Network. Unfortunately, the program is well hidden on the site, so here's the unabridged link to the program: http://www.eere.energy.gov/weatherization/.

Note

1 U.S. Department of Housing and Urban Development, http://www.hud.gov/renting/phprog.cfm, 2004.

CHAPTER 6

Negotiating–The Win-Win Gets You More

Once you have the financing ironed out, you're ready to search for a property. I'm not going to talk here about what you're looking for, making your wish list, and so on. Your real estate professional will do all of that. What I will do is go through some strategies that can save you a headache later regarding your contract.

Unfortunately—or maybe fortunately—purchasing a property is not as simple as buying a car. The right to own land in America is one of the freedoms that separates us from most other countries. It is what we call the American Dream. Owning property makes you a little more of an active part of the community at large. It also gives you new ways of building wealth with those monthly rent payments. If you decide to start investing in real estate, you'll soon find out why this type of investing has built more millionaires in this country than any other type of product. More than stocks, bonds, even businesses. So let's get started with the world of contracts, negotiations, and creative ways to buy property.

What you know here can determine whether you pay a lot of money or get a great deal. In most resale markets, Realtors possess the most comprehensive contracts available when it comes to local sales. Many for sale by owner groups and investment groups will talk about having an attorney draft contracts for you and using a software program to construct a contract. The problem with this is that real estate transactions are directed by local and state regulations and laws; therefore, the contract used in San Francisco most likely won't work in Atlanta. And the contract in Atlanta may not even work in Calhoun, Georgia, a town right up the street from Atlanta!

A contract must take into account federal, state, county, and town or city laws. The local laws usually regulate disclosures and fair housing laws. For instance, Montgomery County, Maryland, has an airport disclosure requirement in the contract. In Washington, D.C., you cannot discriminate to whom you sell a house based on the federally protected classes of race, color, creed, national origin, sex, religion, and familial status, the same as everywhere else. Based on the city's fair housing ordinance, D.C. sellers also cannot discriminate based on political affiliation (Democrat, Republican, and so on), matriculation (students), and even ancestry (you can't discriminate against the child of an infamous murderer, for instance).

Thus, get to know your local contract.

"What Is 'Is'" and Other Contract Verbiage

The question, "What is 'is'?" may have elicited some guffaws when talking about a presidential impeachment investigation, but it's no laughing matter when it comes to a real estate transaction—especially the sales contract.

Most transactions involving a Realtor will default to using a contract devised by the local Realtor association. (Keep in mind, not all real estate agents are Realtors, just as not every tissue is a Kleenex.) While consumers can draft their own contract, local and state Realtor associations have devoted hundreds of thousands, if not millions, of dollars to develop their forms to keep buyers, sellers, and themselves out of legal hot water.

The Washington, D.C., regional sales contract is five pages, and there are forty-nine other forms related to it. Realtors are allowed to write these contracts in this region, meaning, fill in the blanks on a standard form and institute handwritten changes as directed by the client. But many other jurisdictions require that lawyers write the contracts. Nevertheless, there is no standard contract for real estate. Realtor associations on both the state and local levels maintain their contracts. Builders write and require consumers to use their own version of contracts. Lawyers, obviously, can write residential sales contracts for a fee, and there are programs and Web sites available where consumers can pay a small fee for a contract. (My word on these is if you need to sell a car or other property with a contract—go for it. However, since real estate contracts have so many laws, rules, and regulations that can cause buyers and sellers a plethora of headaches later if something goes wrong, stay away from the Web versions.)

Gone are the days of a handshake and word of honor between buyers and sellers. In fact, the contract can't really stand alone given the required disclosures, addenda, and contingencies that crop up in a real estate transaction.

The real estate sales contract and all the residual forms are only the beginning of the transaction. Then there are the loan papers, which are usually completed before settlement day (and add about another inch of paperwork).

Despite all the pages and pages of information a buyer or seller must go through, there are the tricky phrases and paragraphs that must be maneuvered to keep from falling into a legal quandary or money pit. What is "is," really does matter.

For instance, when a contract says the property is sold "as is," what does that really mean? Some contracts go further to say the property is sold as is, "except as otherwise provided herein," and then list a bunch of items that must be in working order according to the contract. These items may include a list of appliances, plumbing, electricity, etc.

But "as is" can mean different things to different people. To a Virginia judge recently, a homebuyer had to swallow termite damage repair because of a handwritten note on the contract. There was substantial termite damage on the property and the contract checked off the fact that the house was "free of termites." However, a handwritten note on the contract stated that the buyer agreed to buy the house "as is" and that the seller was a nonresident owner who had no knowledge of the condition of the property.

Just because a contract is printed one way, doesn't ensure it will always mean what it says in the end. In fact, during the offer/counteroffer stage of a contract, once either party writes a change on the contract, the original offer is null and void.

If a consumer, seeking to save legal or commission fees, writes his own contract, he better understand what the law requires on such a document. What does the law require for agency or property disclosure, fair housing, and a myriad of other topics? Are you using the correct font size in the contract? That's right, there is a law in one state that stipulates the font size required in a particular paragraph dealing with the selection of the title company. Put in the wrong font size with the bold button turned off, and you could be violating state law.

Real estate contract law continues to change year after year. Every time the state legislatures in this country meet, there's a change in real estate law and practices and that means it's even more important to work with professionals who know what t's to cross, what i's to dot, and what "is" is.

Rules of Buying a House Keep Changing

In the 1990s, a buyers' market presented sellers with declining prices after years of real estate inflation (in some areas more than 20 percent some years). The first plan of action for Realtors was laying down the marketing law for the seller (and you prayed you were the third Realtor hired to sell the house, as the seller fired the first two agents, before reducing the price to a realistic level and being willing to negotiate with buyers).

Although those who worked in the daily real estate market understood the 1980s period of escalating home prices was passé, it took a while for the sellers to come on board. Homeowners were also facing the harsh reality of having purchased the house in a peak market and needing to sell in a down market.

While a house lingered on the market, Realtors would set up a promotion plan that included price reductions; would buy plenty of advertising in newspapers and magazines, and on cable television; and place the house on the latest tool in a Realtor's pocket—something called the Internet.

Sellers would offer closing costs, as much as the loan program would allow. The usual assistance from the seller would include: a reduction in price (on average, about 5 to 6 percent), points, closing costs, paying buyers' debt, and more. Sometimes the seller contribution would even include real property, such as gas grills, furniture, exotic vacations, and automobiles—anything to attract an offer. All of this added up to thousands of dollars from the seller to the buyer.

Some Realtors would even encourage sellers to offer to make mortgage payments for the buyer for six months if the purchaser was willing to come to the table with a full-price contract. This was a good strategy for the seller to bring less money to the table for closing (since many of them were upside down in their mortgages—owing more than the house was worth). It also gave cash-poor buyers more money for the transaction.

In a buyers' market another problem was low appraisals. With declining values, the seller and buyer would finally agree to a price, but when the bank appraised the property, many times the house came in lower than the agreed-upon sales price. This meant either the buyer had to come up with more cash to purchase the house or the seller had to lower the sales price so the buyer could qualify for the loan. Many times the two would split the difference.

Home inspections ruled in a buyers' market, as well. Pretty much, whatever was found during the home inspection, the seller agreed to fix. If the buyer felt the seller wasn't giving enough, he or she would simply move along—after all there were plenty of houses from which to choose and plenty of time to shop.

Fast forward a mere five years and the market had changed altogether—again.

··

Rules Change with the Markets

The rules for buying a house changed through the 1990s and into the 2000s. If you're looking to buy in a fast-paced market, here are some steps to take and some suggestions as to what you should and shouldn't do.

1. Get preapproved. This means, if you need a loan to purchase a house, have it ready to go before you walk into the first property. It just makes sense that if you've decided to buy a house in a hot market, go ahead and get ready for it.

2. If you want to kick tires, do it on the Internet. The worst thing to do in a hot market is to hop in a car with an agent who gets paid only when you buy a house. Why should you expect her to be your taxi driver and get you into hard-to-find properties that you have no intention of buying, just so you can "get a feel" for the market? Instead, if you're at the information-gathering stage (and you should do this) visit open houses, click around on the Web, and request to be placed on your favorite Realtor's mailing list.

3. Once you start seriously looking at houses, have your checkbook with you. When you have finally narrowed down where you want to live, be ready to move quickly. I've heard several buyers tell me that they should have listened to their agent about writing a contract now, about making up their mind now. The agent wasn't trying to force these buyers into a quick decision just to write a contract, the Realtor, instead, knew from experience that the house simply was not going to be there next week—or even later this week, for that matter.

4. Start your home search in a neighborhood where prices are less than your maximum purchasing power. In a hot market, if you qualify for $250,000, then you need to look at houses priced

less than that amount, say from $200,000 to $235,000—and be ready to pay $250,000 for them. While Realtors are trying to price according to the market, as soon as they think they have it at the "ceiling" price, another buyer comes in and raises the ante even more.

Negotiating Away Protections Is Not a Good Idea

With the above tips taken into account, in a competitive contract situation, I see buyers willing to give away many of the traditional protections they enjoy in a normal market environment. If a buyer finds himself in a bidding war, the collective wisdom is to price the contract as high as possible and with as few contingencies as allowed.

In a heated contract competition buyers are willing to let go of many contingencies, including home inspection, sale of a current home, and appraisal. While this strategy sounds good in theory—and many homes have been sold and bought using it—buyers must prepare themselves for a plethora of problems to face once they move into a house without the protections these requirements provide.

Home Inspection

Giving away the home inspection, for instance, means the buyer is giving up the ability to discover defects in the house before she moves in. Most buyers say, at the outset, "That's okay. If I leave the home inspection requirement in the contract, I might not get the house."

If that's your strategy, then okay. Go with it. But be very aware of what you're giving up and what you may be receiving. If the roof needs replacing, you're now the one to pay the $5,000 to $15,000 it will take to do it. If there's rot in the framing, it's your responsibility; if the toilets leak or don't flush, you've got to take care of them. Leaky basement? Your problem.

The house for which you may have just overpaid now includes defects that will cost even more to fix with money you don't have.

Sale of Home

If you have a house to sell before you can buy a new one—sell it first. Unless you're paying all cash for your next home without the funds from your current home, then you will face having to qualify for two mortgages to purchase your new home if you cannot sell your current home (see bridge loans in chapter 4). Since you just removed that Sale of Home contingency, your new contract can't fall out because you haven't sold your old home.

Plus, once you're up against a deadline to meet with the settling of your new home, you may be forced to accept a much lower sales price than you would otherwise. Selling your home first is not a bad thing. You're not going to be left homeless as long as you have friends, family, or a smart agent who includes a "Home of Choice" clause in the contract you have with your buyer. Remember, in a sellers' market, the seller is in control and can dictate more of the terms.

Appraisal

I am most amazed at buyers willing to write that the sale of the home is not contingent on an acceptable appraisal. Okay, folks, just hand them your checkbook with your name signed on each check! This strategy is ONLY for people with lots of money. Here's how it works. Buyer A qualifies for a purchase price of $225,000. He shops for homes in his price range and finds himself in a bidding war on a $200,000 sticker price that winds up at $225,000. He's excited and hands over his $5,000 earnest money deposit, which is part of his down payment money. Sounds okay, right? But wait, during the appraisal that MUST be conducted by the bank, but which is not a contingency in the contract, the house appraises for only $205,000. Oops—we're $20,000 short of the asking price.

The bank will loan only $184,500 on the property (90 percent loan to value) and our buyer must come up with the difference—

$40,500. He has to come up with that because he struck out the appraisal clause in the contract. It doesn't matter that the house is worth only $205,000—he's agreed to pay $225,000—no matter if it is actually worth that amount. Can he get out of the contract? Sure, but the seller can keep the buyer's $5,000 earnest money deposit.

To give up on contingencies is also dangerous for sellers and agents in some cases. In California, during one of its awful home appreciation periods where houses worth no more than $200,000 were selling for $1 million plus, a buyer sued her agent because she overpaid for a house. Once she moved in, she lost her job and became angered by what she had done to herself financially— bought an overpriced house. Who better to blame than her agent, right?

A seller was also sued by another buyer because of all the defects found in the house once the buyer moved in. Just because a buyer is willing to buy a house without a home inspection, doesn't mean he can't sue the seller later if major defects are discovered. Even if the seller wins, he is going to be out thousands of dollars in legal fees or in repair bills.

Be careful about what you're willing to do without when it comes to buying your home. There are risks involved, and the astute buyer will weigh them before making a final decision. If the market is so hot that it's just not making good financial sense personally, there's nothing wrong with waiting.

Look at the local economic forecasts. Do they look good? Is business growing—and are companies profitable? Is the population on an upswing? All of these can point to a sustained economic upward curve, meaning the prices that are escalating now may never come down. There are some markets that have had that happen.

Negotiating Inspection Items Unpredictable

With every house I've purchased, I've required a home inspection. While I always advise buyers to request a home inspection, the findings should not be the only determining factor of whether or not to purchase the house.

The home inspection report should also be weighed against the buyer's desire for the house, how much cash the buyer or seller has to fix the defects, and the agent's ability to negotiate away the defects from her client's bottom line.

With a newly built house, buyers should expect pretty much every piece of the house to be, well, new. No spots on the carpet, no rot around the door frames, no settling of the foundation, no banging pipes—just a property in pristine condition.

When a resale house comes onto the market in new-home condition, it doesn't last long—regardless of the temperature of the marketplace. There are several reasons why many buyers prefer resales: They are readily available to be moved into, there are no preconceptions about what you expect to receive (what you see is what you get), and the house has a history to it—established amenities, landscaping, and schools.

New home developments usually lack these elements of mature communities; however, they are brand new. So a home inspection of the dwelling takes on a different flavor than the inspection of a resale property.

A creak in the floor does not add "character" to the house—it's just a loose board, and the buyer will most likely want it fixed. A resale house, on the other hand, is going to come with a list of defects. The key for buyers is to understand they are, in essence, buying a "previously owned" dwelling and therefore some natural wear and tear is expected.

An inspection will "review the condition of the home's heating system, central air-conditioning system (temperature permitting), interior plumbing, and electrical systems; the roof, attic, and visible insulation; walls, ceilings, floors, windows, and doors; the foundation, basement, and visible structure," according to the American Society of Home Inspectors' Web site (www.ashi.com).[1]

As a buyer, you have a right to expect many of these systems to be running without defect. In fact, most sales contracts will include language that states the purchaser accepts the property in as-is condition, particularly in states that operate on a caveat emptor, "buyer beware," basis.

It is this "as-is condition" paragraph that prompts the overwhelming majority of written contracts to include a home inspection contingency clause, meaning the contract is not ratified until the buyers obtain a satisfactory home inspection.

When that report comes back, however, keep in mind that every jot and tittle you add to or subtract from the contract equals a brand new contract. As a buyer, my original contract is what is being considered by the seller—including the home inspection contingency. But if I then write a counteroffer to an original contract, the counteroffer (the second) becomes the contract on the table, not the first one.

So when the report comes back from the home inspector that there are thirteen defects in the house, if you decide to ask the seller to fix even one item, you've killed the first contract. If the seller says "no" to fixing the one item you request, he or she has no obligation to revert back to accepting the original contract you wrote, even if you want to use it.

At the same time, a seller who doesn't want to fix the items shouldn't expect a buyer to counter his counter. Even if the seller agrees to all but one of the items, he has now written a new contract and slipped it across the table to the buyer.

Sometimes sellers may be willing to give the buyers money to fix the items once they move in, hoping to save themselves the hassle of calling in contractors to repair inspection items before settlement day. But buyers like houses that are in "move-in" condition. Many times, a home inspection can shock a buyer into thinking the house is about to fall apart, when in reality, the house's current condition represents a home that has been lived in and enjoyed by the current owners.

When you are in the middle of a home inspection, keep in mind that just because the seller of your friends' house was willing to fix all the items on a list, doesn't mean your seller will do the same.

On the other hand, sellers, just because you've been willing to live with the loose siding above the garage door, doesn't mean your buyer is going to be okay with it as well.

Each home inspection is as different as the inspector and the buyer. When you receive your list of defects (and you will) consider which items you absolutely want fixed and the ones you think could blow a deal. Sometimes home inspections are all about give and take. The goal for both parties is to sell and buy the house.

Contingencies That Can Make or Break Your Contract

The home inspection is one of the most common contingency clauses on a contract. Below, I've listed other common contingencies that you can add or that you may come across as you try to sell your home.

- **Financing Contingency**. This makes a contract contingent upon the buyer getting approved for a loan to purchase the house.

- **Sell House Contingency**. This makes a contract contingent upon a buyer selling his or her house. This clause is more prevalent in a buyers' market than in a sellers' market.

- **Find Home of Choice Contingency**. Usually written by the seller, this contingency keeps a seller from being kicked out of his house without being able to find a new home into which to move. This clause is more prevalent in a sellers' market.

- **Appraisal Contingency**. This protects the buyer from paying too much for a house and not being able to get financing for it. Lenders will loan only a certain percentage of the sales price to a buyer. This is called loan to value (LTV). If the house is a 90 percent LTV, this means the lender will loan only $90,000 for every $100,000 of the sales price, thus, a $150,000 sales price will warrant only a $135,000 loan.

The appraisal determines how much a lender will loan on a house. If the appraisal doesn't meet the sales price, then the buyer will have to make up the difference—unless the buyer has an appraisal contingency. For instance, if an appraisal for the above-mentioned sales price came up to only $145,000, then the buyer would have to come up with the additional $5,000 or the seller would have to drop the price by that amount—or the deal doesn't go through.

With all the aforementioned contingencies in mind, a ratified contract is usually the term we use in the industry to relay to our buyers and sellers that they've sold or bought their house. In technical terms, that's correct. However, at the point a contract is ratified—meaning all parties have signed it and agreed to its terms—the house still isn't sold if there are certain contingencies to fulfill. In layman's terms, "ratified" means all parties to the contract have agreed to the terms of the contract—whether or not contingencies have been removed. You might say it's a launch date. Once the contract is ratified the sellers must fulfill their end of the agreement, such as bringing the house up to standard per a particular paragraph (that is, major systems must be operating), and the buyers must start on their quest to obtain satisfactory financing, and so on.

Ratified does not mean the house will necessarily go to settlement. There are several ways a contract, once signed off on by everyone, can still fall apart. One way is if the sellers don't deliver the homeowner association documents in a timely manner per the contract. If they have delivered the documents, the buyers have a certain amount of time to look them over (depending on what state you're in). If for any reason at all the buyers don't like what they read (no bright-colored doors allowed, no bikes allowed on the balcony, and so on), they can bail on the contract.

The same is true with the inspection. If the buyers cannot get a satisfactory response from the sellers regarding items found in the home inspection, this is the time they can request a release from the contract.

Buyers Still Have Negotiation Options

In a sellers' market, many buyers believe all they can do to compete is bid higher than their competitors, remove all contingencies, and just write a large check to the seller for an earnest deposit.

Not true. Buyers still have a few strategies and rights in a sellers' market they shouldn't forget. For instance, in a hot market the first contingency to be sliced away is the home inspection. With plenty of buyers beating down the doors to purchase a house, conventional wisdom dictates buyers shouldn't reduce their chances of winning the house by throwing in a home inspection. While this may be a good negotiation strategy, it's not a good homebuying one.

Buyers can still request a home inspection without it being a contingency. Even though buyers may be willing to move into the house as is doesn't mean they shouldn't know what problems and defects will greet them at the door. A noncontingent home inspection can help alleviate anxiety for the buyer who wants to know what other expenses there will be once settlement occurs.

A contingency that plays well in the buyers' hands and one that cannot be waived is the homeowners documents contingency. Most jurisdictions require a period of a few days for buyers to review the governance documents of a homeowners association (HOA). Buyers should read over these documents carefully to determine if they want to live in the dwelling under the HOA restrictions. If the buyer finds concerns in the HOA documents, this is reason enough to pull out of the contract.

If you're a buyer who needs financial assistance from the seller to get into a house, one strategy is to go ahead and request the assistance, but make sure the rest of your contract is rock solid. For instance, get preapproved (the next step after prequalified) to ensure no financial contingencies, offer enough over the asking price to help the seller give back what you need in the transaction, and apply for a mortgage program that allows the seller to give you a lot of assistance (upwards of 6 percent with some programs).

Just because a buyer needs financial aid from the seller to make the deal work doesn't mean the buyer is out of luck. If prices are appreciating at a good clip, you can take the chance of moving the price upward to give the seller the funds to help you out. For example, if you need 6 percent assistance on a $200,000 loan ($12,000), then offer that much more in the asking price, requesting the difference back from the seller in the form of closing costs, points on the loan, and so on.

Where you might run into trouble is if the house doesn't appraise for the contract price. If you offer $212,000 for the above-mentioned property, but the lender's appraisal comes in at $207,000—somebody has to move up or down. The buyer must come up with another $5,000 or the seller must bring down the price. This is a good time to have an experienced Realtor with excellent negotiating skills on your side.

If you're facing a sellers' market, keep in mind there are ways other than just outbidding your competitors to come out the winner.

Personal Touch Gets to the Heart of the Matter

If you add contingencies to your contract, it can be enough to put the contract on the "back up" pile, as the seller looks for a contract that doesn't have anything in it to make it fall through. However, in the world of real estate, the rules don't always flow the same way.

I've seen weaker contracts win in a competitive situation, believe it or not. For instance, on a house I was helping to sell, the two buyers were comparable. It appeared my seller was going to do what most sellers do and see which one came down with the most money.

By going with Contract A, the seller would walk away with a couple thousand dollars more. However, Mrs. Seller looked at a handwritten note under conveyances—this buyer wanted her refrigerator. And who wouldn't? It was one of those new models with the water and ice dispenser in the door. Press one button and you have cubes of ice, yet another and you have crushed ice, just like at the burger joint!

Mrs. Seller had purchased it just a few months earlier and really liked it. Actually, she liked it so much, that she turned down the higher-priced contract just so she could pack up the new refrigerator and move it to Texas from Virginia.

The highest price doesn't always win, is what I'm saying. If you find yourself in a competitive situation, submit the strongest contract possible, then personalize the contract with a personal note or a contract gift.

A personal letter about why you picked this property over all the others you visited can do wonders. Put a picture of you and your family, and tell the seller why you liked his or her decorating, landscaping, choice of colors, or how the neighborhood schools will enable you to walk your kids to school—whatever works.

For you—you're buying a home. For the sellers, at this point, they are selling a house, a commodity. However, they still take pride in having planted that thirty-foot tree in the front yard when their son was born. The fact that you can't wait to let your kids swing from the swing they have tied on the lower limb is going to make them, well, like you. It would appear that not everything they have worked on over the years is going to be changed by the new owners. Sellers like to know that all their work on the house may actually outlive them!

Meeting a home seller heart to heart is a strategy, but also a relationship angle, to winning a contract war. Many home sellers don't care that they received $5,000 more from one buyer over another. That they feel good about the people buying their house can be a selling point.

One family wrote a letter to the seller explaining how this home was perfect for their handicapped child and how it would meet the family's needs so well they hoped the seller would consider their offer. After it was verified that the family indeed had a handicapped child, the seller was touched deeply that the house he had worked on for so many years would serve this family perfectly. The contract won.

Letters to the seller are a nice touch, but keep in mind this is not a time to give the seller a biography on the family, providing a dissertation on what each child likes about the property. Just explain how the house fulfills your dreams or needs and what particularly drew you to the house. I would definitely compliment the seller on their upgrades, color selections, additions, and so on. If you don't really believe this about the house, then don't write it. This is not a time for unadulterated kissing up, but a time to explain why you want the house, not just that you can afford it.

Now, if the personal letter angle has been overused in your market area, it might not work anymore (especially if the competing buyer did the same thing!). But try something to make your offer stand out—offer to buy the sellers a weekend at a resort or a short cruise—both of which can be done for about $1,000. When you're talking about paying $200,000 to get the home of your dreams—what's another thousand clams?

Your gift doesn't have to be so glamorous—a box of chocolates can go a long way, or a vase of roses, gift certificate to a great restaurant, or a number of other freebies. In a buyers' market, you'll see these items on the other foot—but when you're trying to buy in a sellers' market—it doesn't hurt to throw in a little bit of friendly bribery!

Buyer Strategies in a Sellers' Market

Besides the common problems with a sellers' market—not enough inventory and too many buyers—there's also the problem that a house can actually sell for too much. This can happen when a contract price exceeds an appraisal from the bank. When this occurs the buyer must come up with the difference or the seller must reduce the sales price down to the appraisal.

Apart from taking the above-noted actions, buyers can beef up contracts without going over the appraised value of a property and having to renegotiate the contract or resulting in a failed contract altogether. Strategies for doing so include using monetary and non-monetary offers in the contract. I recently attended a panel discussion on multiple contract offers and how agents and brokers can compete in such an environment. The record so far was thirty contracts on one house over a weekend. The brokers were from three states (Virginia, Maryland, and Washington, D.C.) and have seen just about everything that buyers can throw at a seller to become the new homeowner.

In one winning contract, it wasn't the sales price alone and the bottom line to the seller that brought the contract to the top—but the offer from the buyer for the seller to stay in the buyer's Florida condo for a week after settlement. Quite clever. Kudos to this buyer who used a time-honored strategy for a sellers' market. Most times, it had been the sellers who offered unusual attachments to the contract instead of the buyer, but the tables had turned in this marketplace and the creative-minded buyer won.

Another addendum that can be used is to offer the seller a bonus instead of a larger sales price. (Keep in mind, the loan program may not allow this, but check with your mortgage provider first.) Simply, if you know the house will appraise for only $225,000—then it's a waste of time to offer $235,000. If you have the extra $10,000, then offer it in the contract as a bonus to the seller, rather than making it a part of the sales price. The bonus works well because it's outside the commission structure and is hard cold cash to the seller, not split with the agent.

One buyer won her bid by writing a strong contract and then having flowers that matched the dining room decor delivered right at the time her agent was conducting the contract presentation. This was the homey touch that took the contract over the edge. The sellers felt the contract was competitive and the buyer truly cared about their home.

When it comes time to write the contract, have your agent call the listing agent and find out what the sellers want. It sounds obvious, but too many agents write from a left-brain, analytical perspective. If you find out when the sellers are moving, why they are moving, where they are moving, and could they use some money for a vacation or a rental car—these can be the issues that win the contract.

There's a difference between selling to someone who plops down a bunch of money and a buyer who takes an interest in where you're going and what you're doing after the sale is complete.

The bottom line—financially—is not always the bottom line. Make the effort to find out what the seller really wants and go for it.

Selling the Deal as Important as Selling the House

Sellers' markets creep up on you. They don't just suddenly happen from one month to the next. As a local economy strengthens, jobs are created, bringing in workers, which creates a demand for more homes. As one builder told me, "Homes are where the jobs go at night."

Buyers' markets on the other hand, can materialize suddenly, like a really bad cold in the morning or the obnoxious brother-in-law at your front door. All it can take is a couple of stories in the local media about some sort of slow down or a possible factory closing and suddenly, buyers don't want to buy anymore. As the economy slows, people lose jobs and start moving elsewhere. With no one moving into town, those houses can sit on the market a long time.

This economic climate creates a glut of homes, which means you've moved into a buyers' market. Buyers are in control and get prices lowered, lots of seller subsidies, and even some extra perks and cash. The hardest part about a buyers' market is the education of the seller.

Sellers are slow to move from one market to the other, unwilling to drop the price by $5,000, $10,000, or even $25,000 to bring the price in line with what the market demands.

They can only remember what it was like when they bought the house a few years earlier—it was a sellers' market, they had to bid up by 5 or 10 percent, had to put down a lot of money, give away their first born, and make a blood pact with the loan officer. They just can't fathom that now the buyers will get to come in, bid 5 to 10 percent below their asking price, and ask for the seller's second born and one of the seller's cars.

Here are some strategies that are not as severe, but will work in a market that is becoming competitive from the seller's perspective. First—drop your price. That's it. Pretty simple, but it works. The buyer doesn't care how much you paid for the house eight years ago, how much work you put into the place, and that you put a three-tiered deck on the back. If you're overpriced, they'll buy someone else's house. So, if your home isn't moving, check the price first.

If you are bent on keeping the price, then sell the deal instead of the house. Take the initiative to place an offer on the table before any buyers even come into the house. Ask your agent to advertise this deal in the MLS or in the advertising: "Move in and make no payments for three months."

Here's how it works. If you're trying to sell for $195,000 and your agent is after you to drop the price, instead of dropping the price $5,000, figure out how many payments $5,000 will make and offer this as an incentive instead. In this case, if the buyer puts down 10 percent, the $5,000 would make four principal and interest payments on a $175,500 mortgage (30-year fixed with a 7 percent mortgage). Plenty of buyers would love to move into your house and live "free" for four months. The catch is—your offer is good only on a full-price contract.

Instead of just dropping the price, sellers can offer other incentives, such as vacations, home warranties, vehicles, even boats.

Some loan programs allow the seller to pay off a buyer's bills. The biggest key in all of this is to not wait for a buyer to show up and then offer it. Make the offer early and often to attract the buyers.

In essence, you're not selling the house as much as you're selling the deal. In a buyers' market, the question is not if the buyer can find a house, but which house offers the best value for the money.

Rent Backs Can Backfire on Buyers

Another contract clause I've seen used many times for sellers who can't move right away or for buyers who need to delay settlement is the rent-back clause.

In a perfect world, the seller asks for a certain price, the buyer agrees to it, and they head toward settlement. Rarely will you come across such a transaction. Instead, negotiations produce various diversions on the straightforward contract. Creative clauses, such as owner financing, seller subsidies, paying off a buyer's debts, and 100 percent financing, can help get a buyer into a house, a buyer who otherwise might not be able to buy.

In a fast market, sometimes a home shopper will find a seller who wants to sell the house quickly and take his time moving out or purchasing his next property. The seller will usually do what is called a "rent back" from the buyer. The transaction will settle and the title exchanges hands. The seller now becomes a renter with the new ownership at a prenegotiated rent. Then the buyer waits for the seller to move into his new house. Be careful with this strategy, as it can come back to bite you later.

A rent back can be negotiated several ways. The lease can be for a set time period or open ended. However, some mortgage programs won't allow a rent back to last more than sixty days. If the mortgage program was meant only for an owner occupant (meaning the person getting a loan for a particular property must actually live in the property), the underwriters will consider a home where the rent back exceeds sixty days to be a rental or investment purchase instead—which may require a higher interest rate or a higher down payment.

If the lease is open-ended, the seller-turned-renter has plenty of time to find a new home and move. Here's where the problems can begin and why it's always best to negotiate such a contract as if the worst will happen. The worst may include:

- The sellers-renters leave the house with lots of damage that was not present when the buyer first bought the house.

- The delayed move date gives the seller time to remove some pieces of the real property that should have been included in the property, such as chandeliers, special door hardware, or shelves and mirrors. The buyer-owner won't find these things missing till move-in day, which now is not immediately after settlement.

- The seller-renters end up losing their house on the other end of the deal or are not able to find a house to buy and want their old house back. This is probably the most prevalent hiccup in a rent-back situation—and the most distasteful. Some seller-renters can get downright nasty when they can't get the house back and commence to damage it before moving out. At this point, the only option for the buyer is to sue, but the damage has already been done and the expense of fixing it will most usually be picked up by the buyer until the suit is settled.

If you do negotiate a rent back, be sure to cover your bases on insurance coverage. Any damage to the house is now your responsibility. If the hot water heater goes out it's your water heater, now, not the former owner's. Be sure to cover all of these issues in the lease and add addenda if necessary for items not covered in it. As added protection, if the seller wants a rent back, then negotiate a home warranty to protect you from such breakdowns. Check the deductible on these warranties, as some will require as much as a couple hundred dollars per incident before they kick in.

A typical lease makes the landlord (in this case the buyer-owner) responsible for repairs and upkeep of the property. Because of the unique situation of the rent back, the buyer may want to negotiate that the seller is responsible for all damage until the buyer moves in. Don't leave anything up to assumption or to speculation. Cover all the bases for damage to the property.

The investor who knows contracts and what can be done with them is an investor well-educated. Work diligently with your team of professionals to write contracts with the contingencies that will protect you and the strategies that will get the deal done.

Note

1 American Society of Home Inspectors, www.ashi.com, 2004.

CHAPTER 7

Deciding on Your Investment of Choice

The simplest concept in real estate investing is buy low, rent high. Everyone generally understands that as a real estate investor, the idea is to let someone else's rent pay for your mortgage and to hopefully come out with a positive cash flow at the end of the month. However, holding onto bricks and mortar is not the only way to invest in real estate. There are many other approaches to take, and this chapter gives short descriptions of some of them. At the end of each description is a list of pros and cons for that approach. Later chapters will cover some of these methods in greater detail.

Fixer-Uppers

This is a property an investor buys knowing it will need repairs. In some markets, these repairs may entail a major overhaul; in others a little painting and woodworking is all that is needed. Most times, however, it's not a property that just needs paint and carpet, but one that has rot, flooring, roofing, basement, and other major problems. But that's what makes it so enticing.

Pros: For investors with their repair teams in line, this can be a real moneymaker. The key here is to hammer on the seller early in the negotiating process. Get the house for as low as possible and know what your bottom line really is. A fixer-upper held for long-term renting can provide returns in the 500 percent range.

Cons: For those wanting to flip the property, if you don't project $30,000 to $50,000 in profit, then you may want to pass. Why? An unseen defect can run into the tens of thousands of dollars real fast.

Retail Investment

Keep your eyes open for underpriced properties in an area where rentals are brisk. This should be a house that really does need just paint and new carpet. After making a few simple repairs, you will then rent it out. Be sure you know what the rents are before going into the property. You want a positive cash flow before you even walk into the property.

The bottom line is whether rental payments will cover an investor's monthly expenses. You have to be concerned about break-downs eating up any of your positive cash flow in the short term. There's nothing like buying a rental with a $200 positive cash flow and then the furnace goes out—$2,500! Wow, it would take more than a year to break even.

Pros: A house that is in good shape can rent for years without any major expenses if it was taken care of early on.

Cons: Good rental properties (say, in a college town or near a military base) don't come on the market often, so you may be waiting a while before you find one. (Experienced investors usually scoop these up before the novices even know they're on the market.)

Foreclosures

These properties are purchased at a courthouse auction—hopefully for less than they're worth. Depending on the state of the market, there may be several bidders for each property. In a hot real estate market, where appreciation is in the double digits, you'll find investors competing with individuals who just want to get into their first home. Consumers seeking a shelter over their heads find themselves writing contracts above the asking price. They'll even include "Acceleration Clauses" in the contract, giving their buyer-broker permission to outbid any competitive bids by a set dollar amount, just so they can win the bidding war. Investors know when to stop, but someone who is used to bidding over value for a retail market will have no concern about bidding up a foreclosure—to their detriment, I might add. Foreclosures usually need a lot of work to prep for market. The buyer accustomed to bidding up properties in the "retail" market will now have to dump even more money getting a foreclosure into move-in condition.

To effectively bid for a foreclosure, you must have your financing set up beforehand and be prepared to rehabilitate the property to put it on the rental or flip market. Pretty much, you're looking to fix it up, sell it, or rent it out.

Pros: This is a commonsense approach to getting started in real estate investing. If you can get the property for a wholesale price and then rent it out for less than your mortgage, you're on your way to building wealth one month at a time.

Cons: You get into the property and find out it has major problems costing a lot more than you'll ever recover. Ever heard of concrete being flushed down the drain (usually by a spiteful former owner)? It means having to remove all the sewage drains. Hidden defects can run costs up and give you a red ink bath before it's done. Since the bank or note holder is selling the property as is, there's not much recourse.

Condominiums

I've put condos in a separate category only because I want to point out the nuances of this type of property over single-family and townhouse dwellings. I like condos! Depending on the market, they can provide as much gain as single-family and townhouse markets, but frankly I like them as rentals for the following reasons:

- They are self-contained.

- There are no leaky roof and basement problems (and if you do get a roof leak, the whole condo association (COA) has to pay for it).

- The landscaping and exterior care is maintained by the COA, not the individual owners.

- Insurance is cheaper.

- If a major system goes down, it is more than likely that other units are having the same problem and you can bid it out for a lower price.

If you want to buy multiple properties and want to concentrate them in one area, condos are the way to go.

Pros: Self-contained units that rent easily because of the customary low price. Maintenance is easier than for single-family units.

Cons: They drop in value faster than any other type of real estate during a real estate downturn. Your neighbor's problem can become your problem real quick; that is, a leaky dishwasher upstairs can come running through your ceiling (but that's what a good insurance policy is for!).

Real Estate Notes

If you would like to get monthly payments from real estate, but don't want to be a landlord, maybe you should consider real estate notes. For these, you invest in the mortgages of real estate, instead of the real estate itself. Most notes held by private investors are second trusts taken at the table to help the buyer get into the property. If you buy a property at a good discount and can sell it for a higher price, you can sell the property with owner financing by wrapping a mortgage around your original mortgage, thus creating a note that pays you a higher dividend than what you're paying on. Here's how it works:

Let's say you bought a foreclosed or preforeclosed house for $150,000, but its fair market value is $180,000. If you bought it with a 10 percent down payment, on a thirty-year mortgage at 6 percent, your monthly principal and interest will run about $810 per month. If you turn around and sell the house for $180,000 with a zero-down payment, you can wrap a loan around your loan at a higher interest rate, let's say 8 percent (since you're taking a higher risk with a zero-down payment) and receive a P&I payment of $1,321. After making your mortgage payment of $810, you've created a positive cash flow of more than $500 per month.

The benefit of holding a note instead of being the landlord is that you don't have to take care of the property. Remember, you don't own the house, you own the note. If your buyer misses payments, your loan is always secured by the property, and you will be able to foreclose to sell the house a second time if necessary.

Buying and selling notes can be a very lucrative business. Some investors buy notes at a discount from other investors or from sellers who took back a second trust on a property they wanted to sell. Here's how it works:

A seller wants to sell a property for $200,000. He has $50,000 in equity in the house, so he stands to walk away with a large amount of money. Let's say, however, the buyer qualifies for only $180,000 through traditional financing. The seller can take back a $20,000 note to help the buyer get in the property. The seller then takes the proceeds from the sale—$30,000 cash from the buyer's first mortgage—and a promissory note for the final $20,000 at 12 percent, amortized over 10 years. This seller's note will provide the seller, now investor, with a monthly income of $286.

For some investors, a small cash flow from a note is just fine. Others may have preferred the $20,000 cash up front—enter the discount buyer. The discount note buyer will provide the seller-investor with a large amount of cash for the note—but at a discount. If the two investors can agree on, say $15,000, then the first investor now has $15,000 in his pocket and the new note owner has a note that's providing him with a return of 19 percent instead of 12 percent.

Pros: For those who have cash, this one can give major returns on your money. The interest rate is not going to fluctuate like the stock market, certificates of deposit, and bonds are sure to do.

Cons: It takes money to make money—without cash, you can't do this investment. Also, your mortgagee (the borrower) might skip town, leaving you to foreclose—right behind the first-trust note holder, who usually gets paid first in a foreclosure.

Another con, for some investors, is that notes are generally short-term investments (three, five, seven years, and so on), whereas if you own a property, it brings in money as long as you have the house.

Tax Liens

When homeowners fail to pay their property taxes, a tax lien is placed on the property and then sold to investors at auction. The local jurisdiction sells these liens so they can raise money they had budgeted to fund their day-to-day operations. The auctions occur once or twice each year and are open to the public. The taxes and penalties levied on these delinquent tax amounts can be substantial (upwards of an annualized 50 percent return!)—and the investor gets a portion of it during the time he holds the certificate.

If the homeowner doesn't pay the taxes she can lose her house to the tax lien purchaser. Many investors purchase tax liens, hoping that's exactly what happens. Actually, most liens are paid, the tax lien investor makes the interest on his money, and the homeowner stays in the property. Thus, if the jurisdiction is paying 18 percent, the investor will make $1,800 per year on a $10,000 tax lien investment.

I'm very excited to have a tax lien expert contributing the how-to's on this form of investment in chapter 14.

Pros: A high-yield investment with a secured note based on real property and enforceable by a local government.

Cons: Although state law requires the liens be paid off by property owners within one to three years, you can purchase a lien where the property owner goes bankrupt. You can then take possession of the property and get your money back that way; however, your lien may be secondary to a first-trust or IRS lien on the property. Other pitfalls apply. Read chapter 14 for details.

REITs

A real estate investment trust, or REIT (pronounced "reet"), is a company that owns and operates income-producing real estate such as apartments, shopping centers, offices, hotels, and warehouses. Some REITs finance real estate as well. As an investor, you will purchase shares of REITs, which are traded on major stock exchanges, such as the New York Stock Exchange and the American Stock Exchange. I actually own shares in several REITs through my IRA in a real estate mutual fund.

Created in 1960 by the federal government, REITs are permitted to deduct dividends paid to their shareholders from their corporate taxable income. Thus, most REITs pay out 100 percent of their taxable income to shareholders, reducing their taxable income to zero. The shareholders, in essence, are the ones who end up paying the taxes on the dividends and any capital gains. Most states honor this federal treatment and also do not require REITs to pay state income tax. This high percentage of annual revenue distribution (minimum 90 percent required) is a requirement by the federal government for a company to qualify as a REIT. However, like other businesses, but unlike partnerships, a REIT cannot pass any tax losses through to its investors.

Pros: If you're looking for a very low-risk approach to investing in real estate, then a REIT is for you. They appear to be safe harbors for long-term investments. For more details, visit www.NAREIT .com, the official site of the National Association of Real Estate Investment Trusts. Here, you'll find links to articles on REITs, REITs by state, and investments.

Cons: You are now at the mercy of the management team of a REIT, and you're not going to deal in as much cash flow as you would with a passive investment such as a rental property, tax lien, or note.

Real Estate Investing Offers Multiple Opportunities

As you can see, there are plenty of ways to invest and build wealth in real estate. The key for you is to:

1. Find a mentor who has blazed the trail before you.

2. Educate yourself on the details of a particular type of investment.

3. Take a deep breath and dive in!

Forget Location, Timing Is the Key to Real Estate Investing

Regardless of what type of investment you look into, just as the three key components to real estate are location, location, location, the three key components to profit are timing, timing, timing.

I remember in the spring of 1998 sitting at an awards ceremony for Weichert Realtors, one of the nation's largest independent real estate companies, when James Weichert, the president and founder of the company, predicted: "Anything with a door on it will sell in the next twelve months."

He was dead-on. What began that year was one of the largest real estate value surges in the markets where his company sold real estate. History has proven him right, as well, with average appreciation growing in many regions in double digits every year since his prediction. He had been watching the signs of economics that affect real estate trends.

If you're buying a house to live in, the three key aspects of real estate are: location, location, location. If you're looking to buy real estate as an investment, however, the three key aspects are: timing, timing, timing.

Robert M. Campbell notes this principle very well in his book *Timing the Real Estate Market* (www.realestatetiming.com). Every once in a while, a book comes out that you want to read thoroughly, thumb through regularly, and file as a reference work in your personal library. *Timing the Real Estate Market* is one of these books.

Many times, I'll read a real estate publication and it's timely—so timely, that it's no good to me, because the material is dated. In six months the principles it touts are obsolete because the nature of the economy upon which it's based has changed. The beauty of Campbell's *Timing* is that it offers the real estate investor proven methods of reading a regional economy, so she will know just when to buy and when to sell to maximize her returns.

The meat of the book can be found in chapter 4, "The Five Vital Signs Indicators: Your Window into the Future." If you're so busy you can't read all one hundred pages, then memorize these ten pages. Here are the five vital sign indicators in brief:

1. Existing Home Sales. This is the leading indicator of real estate price trends. As sales increase, the inventory of homes drops, thus pushing up prices. When the opposite happens, prices drop.

2. New Home Building Permits. This indicator is important for two reasons, Campbell writes: 1) Real estate construction is the largest single industry in the U.S. (making up roughly 15 to 20 percent of the total U.S. economy). The overall U.S. economy floats up and down on the new homes industry. 2) New homebuilders are keenly aware of the demand for housing. Watching them is like watching the future economy.

3. Mortgage Loan Defaults. This indicator is the first sign that the fourth indicator is about to rise. Mortgage loan defaults mean the local populace is undergoing financial stress—usually because of job loss. When you hear of layoffs coming to your region, mortgage loan defaults will follow, which brings us to the next indicator.

4. Foreclosure Sales. These sales can be watched in the classified ads section of your local newspaper—homes being sold by foreclosure will be located in the "Trustee Sale" heading. Watching these sales gives you an indication of how your local economy is doing. As they increase, the economy is softening, and investors should take note for opportunities.

5. Interest Rates. This is the only indicator not driven by the local economy. This indicator should also be judged in conjunction with the previous four. Interest rates will not necessarily provide an indicator of when to buy or sell, but they can and will accelerate or slow the upward or downward trends on pricing and availability of investment real estate. Interest rates headed up can have both effects on the market—speed it up or slow it down—depending on what the other four signs are doing. Higher rates hurt rising home prices, and they speed up declines in home prices when they're headed downward.

"The Vital Sign Indicators are market barometers for trend forecasting in real estate," according to Campbell. "They measure supply and demand changes that will lead to changes in market conditions."[1] Real estate investing can be very rewarding if the investor times entrances into, and exits out of, the market. Campbell's method of timing these moves is a great tool to do just that.

How to Foresee Real Estate Market Trends

At the beginning of each year I get the age-old question thrown at me by millionaire wannabes: "What's going to happen with the market?" Everyone knows real estate pays off in the long haul, but a lot of people are afraid to jump in when prices are escalating at a more-than-healthy clip.

Is there really a way to monitor interest rates and prices to eliminate your risks? First let's start with real estate prices.

Like any other product, real estate prices are driven by supply and demand. Frankly, this is one of the basic principles that helped sustain many real estate markets across the country through this latest recession. While metropolitan areas such as Northern California and the Washington, D.C., region were growing their job bases through the 1990s, local jurisdictions were afraid of losing open space to houses—so they passed laws to limit development.

Don't forget a key component of economics and how it affects real estate: "Homes are where the jobs go at night."

If economic development is bringing industry to a region, along with the jobs and prosperity that come with it, then the local jurisdiction must allow for the development of property that will supply housing for the new employees. When they don't—prices start going up.

Thus, in a region where jobs have been lost, puffing up unemployment numbers, how can sales outpace the year before and prices still inflate? Where there are not enough houses going up to meet the demand, prices will continue to increase.

So—indicator No. 1—where is your local economy headed? Listen to the local bean counters and prognosticators. If they are talking about the economy slowing down, then you have to watch for falling housing prices—IF—and this is principle No. 2—there is an ample supply or an overabundance of houses on the market.

In the Washington, D.C., region, for instance, we were hit with job losses just like many other regions this past recession; however, we had not supplied those with new jobs with enough housing. So when the recession hit, many were put out of work, but those who had jobs still needed to buy houses—thus, the prices kept increasing and sales remained brisk.

I'm watching the inventory numbers here in the Washington, D.C., market. At the end of the last recession, inventory began increasing by a rate of up to 50 percent compared to the same period a year before. Did that mean the market was headed toward a buyers' market? Not necessarily, but time will tell. And time is on the side of sellers; since there had been such a scant supply of houses to start with, the market may be leveling out to where it needed to be in the first place.

Lesson No. 1: Supply and demand in real estate controls home prices on a local level.

Lesson No. 2: The national economy affects interest rates. Remember when the latest hot real estate market was heating up? It was during the Clinton years and interest rates were pushed up to around 8 or 9 percent—but people kept buying. That's because the economy was so hot.

The Federal Reserve alters the prime lending rate to manipulate the supply of money in the market. If the economy is slow, it lowers rates so more companies will borrow money, hopefully, to invest in their businesses, thus increasing the need for jobs. When the economy starts heating up (determined by the Gross Domestic Product, manufacturing output, and other economic indicators), rates start edging up to rein in the growth so inflation doesn't run out of control. The idea being that if the economy is hot, more employees are needed, and the good ones demand more money and benefits, which eventually hits the employers' payroll. Increases in payroll and expenses for manufacturers mean higher prices at the store.

To make all that investment money harder to acquire keeps companies from building up inflationary policies. Make sense? Now, here's the funny part—the prime rate doesn't have all that much to do with what the interest rate will be on your home loan. However, it does affect the bond market where your interest rates are determined. It doesn't affect the bond rate directly; it's actually more of an emotion-based reaction to the market. If stockholders fear the economy has peaked and start selling, they'll put their money in something more stable—bonds. If bonds become more desirable, the rates increase—and so do the interest rates on home mortgages.

Timing and the effects of the overall economy on real estate investing are very important to understand as you launch your investment plan. As you begin to select your choice of investment, watch the market. Pay attention to the signs and then obey them! These are rules that if violated can cost you a lot of money. Don't get caught buying at the height of the real estate market when all the economic indicators are pointing to a slow down. Now, let's take a look at one of the most popular investments—fixer-uppers.

Note

1 Robert M. Campbell, *Timing the Real Estate Market* (San Diego, Calif.: The Campbell Method, 2002).

CHAPTER 8

Distressed Properties–
Fixer-Uppers

Buying a fixer-upper, repairing it, and then renting it out is the traditional way many investors get involved in real estate. These type of properties are easily found in a buyers' and even-level market (where it's neither a buyers' nor sellers' market). When real estate heats up to a sellers' market, you'll find fixer-uppers selling for more than their value. This means you will end up paying too much for a house, have to spend thousands more fixing it up, and then hope that the rent you receive covers your mortgage payment. The key word on fixer-uppers is: bottom line. If you can't retain a bottom line expense that can be covered by either the monthly rental or the final sales price, then walk away, walk very far away.

The term "fixer-upper" is a relative term. One person's fixer-upper can be another buyer's move-in condition. Meanwhile, another person's fixer-upper can be another person's condemnation project. Let's put a line of demarcation for this discussion: a fixer-upper is a property that needs more than just paint, caulking, and new carpet.

A Realtor friend of mine told me about a couple who wanted a fixer-upper. She searched the MLS for all the fixer-uppers on the market in their price range and then hit the road with these scavenger hunters in tow. House after house obviously needed some fixing up, but the buyers were not satisfied. In fact, they questioned the Realtor about her interpretation of a fixer-upper.

Finally, as they arrived at the last property, the couple got very excited. It was an older home that had been sitting vacant for quite a while. The yard was more than grown over, it looked like a cow pasture with all the thorns and small trees that had popped up. When the husband got out of the car, he approached the ivy-grown chimney (the brick couldn't even be seen underneath the growth). As he ripped at the ivy and nearly brought the whole chimney down, he dodged to keep from getting hit by the falling brick and exclaimed: "This is what I'm talking about!"

When you say you want a fixer-upper, tell your agent specifically what you mean by it. Are you talking about bringing in contractors to do the work or are you a Handy Dan or Dana who can do all the work yourself? Do you expect to rehab the place or remodel it? AND, how much are you willing to part with up front to find it? (Some investors won't touch a fixer-upper unless their margin is at least $50,000, while others will go in to make $10,000 on the backside.)

Before you consider fixer-uppers, you need to visit your lender and have a heart-to-heart talk about your financial situation, how much more money you can afford to borrow for an investment property, and whether he or she has loan programs that can finance the rehabilitation work, as well. These are the first questions you need answered before you can even think about shopping. Fixer-uppers on their face ring of money-making ventures . . . but like the old adage goes, "It takes money to make money." This is even more true with fixer-uppers.

The whole premise of this book is that these are commonsense approaches to building wealth. The first property you need to purchase is your personal residence. A fixer-upper can be the next logical step for many homeowners wanting to launch their real estate investment portfolio. Unlike foreclosures, you can get into these properties to see the damage before writing a contract. As you pursue fixer-uppers, it means you're going to need some cash for down payment, and then either cash or credit for the rehab work. We'll talk about financing all of this in a bit, but you need to have these moneys secured before starting your trek around town looking for the gold mine fixer-upper.

If your first residence has experienced a healthy appreciation over the past several years, it may be the source of money you need for a fixer-upper. The expenses you will need to cover investing in fixer-uppers include:

- **Acquisition Fee**. This includes the down payment, the origination fees for the mortgage, and the closing costs.

- **Inspection Fee**. Most of us don't know how much it would cost to replace a bad roof, fix the gutters, and replace all the windows. So we have to hire a professional home inspector to look over the property and help us find out what other tradespeople we will need to contact to fix everything. The home inspection should run a couple hundred dollars.

- **Costs of Fixing It Up**. This can cost a few hundred dollars if you were lucky enough to grab a property that needed just paint. Most likely, it's going to cost a few thousand dollars. How will you pay for this? Some folks have pulled out Visa, MasterCard, or Discover, while others already had a nest egg set aside to use. Still others, as mentioned above, have used the equity in their homes in the form of a home equity loan, a home equity line of credit (which operates much like a credit card), or a reverse mortgage. During my days as an agent, we would use the commission money we received from the transaction to pay for any rehab work we had to have done.

A fixer-upper may have arrived in its current condition in several ways: an investor let the property deteriorate, owners found themselves unable to keep it up because of financial difficulties, a house was simply abandoned, or heirs inherited a piece of property they had no financial means to prepare for renting and thus, allowed it to deteriorate even further.

Finding the Fixer-Upper

The search for fixer-uppers on the open market has gotten tougher in markets where appreciation is healthy. From the 1990s until today, the process of buying and selling property has gotten easier, and the secrets of acquiring properties are not so secret any longer.

The first people to ask are in your investment team, particularly your Realtor. Tell your Realtor you want to consider every fixer-upper that comes on the market (these may be also advertised as "handyman specials"). The Realtor can set up a search in a computerized MLS that will query the database for this keyword. As the properties come up, the Realtor will then notify you of them.

Secondly, you want to keep your eyes open for this type of property coming on the market through "for sale by owner" (FSBO) houses. Owners of property in need of repair often think they don't have enough equity to pay an agent a commission. Thus they want to skip the commission, sell the house themselves, and try to retain as much of the equity as possible. Ironically, the National Association of Realtors (NAR) "Buyer Profile for 2003" showed that the average home sale for FSBOs is $145,000, while Realtors' average sale price is $175,000.

In addition, targeting FSBOs will provide more opportunities without competition from other buyers. On average only about 20 percent of FSBOs use the Internet to market their homes, according to NAR, and that means more buyers won't even know the property is on the market. To find FSBOs, simply seek out your local newspaper and look under "Homes for Sale." The FSBO ads will be the ones that don't have a company or real estate agent name listed (which is required of real estate companies). Some will highlight that they are for sale by owner. More than 70 percent of buyers use the Internet to begin their home search and 44 percent find it through a real estate agent, according to the NAR study. Therefore, you may be able to target a good deal with FSBOs before other buyers even find out about them.

Sometimes a fixer-upper isn't advertised as such but may target investors instead. This is a targeted ad, because most buyers of property don't have the necessary resources and money it takes to fix up a property; the seller knows investors are not afraid of such a challenge.

The ad may start out: "Investor Special," or "Great Investor Opportunity." Keep in mind that sellers are trying to get as much out of the property as they can without putting any money into it. Therefore, they will try to make it sound enticing as a moneymaker for the buyer, hoping the buyer sees value and is willing to pay a premium for it. You really have to be ready to see the diamond in the rough. What you'll not see advertised is something like this:

"Fixer-Upper available to novice investor who wants an easy transaction. I'll turn over the property to you with no money out of your pocket, and you can put about $10,000 into it and make a lot of money in a flip! Come on down—I'll hold it for you so no one else knows it's available!"

You're also going to run into some home sellers who don't know their property is a fixer-upper—or worse, they know that since it's in such awful condition and you have the possibility of making a lot of money, they think they should get some sort of added benefit by selling it to you for more than it's worth because they are handing over this opportunity to you. Sheesh! It happens! But I digress . . . .

The final way of finding fixer-uppers is to cordon off an area of a community and drive through looking for properties in disrepair, or better yet, abandoned properties. You'll want a table that looks something like table 8-1.

Take down as much information as possible. You may even want to visit the neighbors to find out more about the house, owner, contact information, and so on. You'll be amazed at how much the neighbors will talk. They'll usually end up saying something like: "I wish someone would buy that house and fix it up."

Table 8-1. Finding fixer-uppers.

Photo #	Street Address	Condition	Notes
001	123 ABC St.	Broken front windows Steps rotted Cracked/sunken sidewalk	Owner: Mr. Wayne Thompson

Most houses in disrepair are rental properties; thus, the neighbor will be a good source of information. This is just your initial investigation. The neighbor may have old information, but at least you have somewhere to start. Gather as much information as possible—remember, you're in a business and need as much information as possible before you approach the owner, who, more than likely, is going to try to get as much from you as possible. You need to build a case that the house is in such disrepair that they'll be lucky to have you take it off their hands for such a low price.

The best place to look for these types of properties is in the older parts of the city or county. After driving block by block and jotting down the above information, head to your computer and log on to the Internet. Visit the county or city Web site and look for tax records under the Department of Taxation or Department of Revenue. If your county has tax records online, you'll be able to find the owner's name and mailing address to make a first contact. If it's not online via the Internet, then more than likely your Realtor teammate should be able to find that information via the tax records section of the local MLS.

Finally, if those two methods don't work, you'll have to visit the local courthouse and look up the property records. The clerk is there to help you, so ask him or her for a quick tutorial on how to search the records.

Once you have this spreadsheet full of names, you can start to contact each homeowner to see if any are interested in selling the property. I suggest you have several names ready because most of them are going to say "No."

When someone says, "Yes," get your team to work. The first item on the agenda is an inspection of the property to determine estimates for repairs, which will then affect your offer. While your Realtor or lawyer is putting together the contract, get the ball rolling on all the other aspects of the purchase:

- Line up an inspection by your work crew to find out all the defects of the property, including the following areas:

  Structural System
  Exterior
  Roof System
  Plumbing System
  Electrical System
  Heating System
  Air-Conditioning System
  Interior
  Insulation and Ventilation
  Fireplaces and Solid Fuel Burning Appliances

- Get estimates on repairing and renovating all of the affected systems and fold those into your offer price. You'll want these contractor estimates that your lender will use in determining the hard costs of renovation, which will determine the complete loan amount.

- Contact your lender and let him know you have a fixer-upper property you're going to purchase and you need to line up a renovation loan for the property.

  It's difficult to describe the financing available on this type of property because the lenders keep changing the programs (all their programs, for that matter). Here is some general information. You'll need to contact a loan officer to find out specifics.

Fix-It Financing

Suffice it to say, lenders have programs for investors to use in refurbishing and then selling or renting a property. For instance, here's a program that, at this writing, is being offered by Wells Fargo Home Mortgage, called Investor Renovation Mortgage. The product particulars include:

- Rolls purchase price plus all improvements into your loan.

- Finances up to three payments into your new loan.

- As low as 10 percent down on one- and two-unit properties.

- No prepayment penalties.

- Has 15-, 20-, and 30-year terms available.

- The Renovation Mortgage allows borrowers to utilize 50 percent of the "as completed" value of the property for renovations.

- There are no required improvements or restrictions to the type of repairs, nor is there a minimum amount of repairs required. The purpose of this loan is to allow for greater amount of funds available for remodeling than most conventional products.

- This is a full document loan. Income and asset verification are required. To qualify, applicants must have good credit and good cash reserves.

Another type of financing that isn't exactly for investors, but at the same time can be used for those who want to buy a single-family home and convert it to a two- to four-unit dwelling (living in one, renting out the others), comes from a U.S. Housing and Urban Development program called Section 203(k) loan, which is used for the purchase and refurbishing of a house. You must live in the unit to use this loan; however, as mentioned earlier, you can convert a property into a multiunit property and still use the program. The minimum loan amount is $5,000.

HUD explains online that "the extent of the rehabilitation covered by Section 203(k) insurance may range from relatively minor (though exceeding $5000 in cost) to virtual reconstruction: A home that has been demolished or will be razed as part of rehabilitation is eligible, for example, provided that the existing foundation system remains in place. Section 203(k)–insured loans can finance the rehabilitation of the residential portion of a property that also has nonresidential uses; they can also cover the conversion of a property of any size to a one- to four-unit structure. The types of improvements that borrowers may make using Section 203(k) financing include:

- Structural alterations and reconstruction

- Modernization and improvements to the home's function

- Elimination of health and safety hazards

- Changes that improve appearance and eliminate obsolescence

- Reconditioning or replacing plumbing; installing a well and/or septic system

- Adding or replacing roofing, gutters, and downspouts

- Adding or replacing floors and/or floor treatments

- Major landscape work and site improvements

- Enhancing accessibility for a disabled person

- Making energy conservation improvements

"HUD requires that properties financed under this program meet certain basic energy efficiency and structural standards. However, luxury items and improvements that do not become a permanent part of the property are not eligible uses of a 203(k) loan."[1]

To read more on this loan program, visit www.HUD.gov and click on the "Home Improvements" link.

Steps to Success!

One of the greatest roadblocks for all real estate investors is to be frozen by inaction and thinking you don't have enough knowledge to be successful in this endeavor. Let me encourage you to simply take one step at a time. Assuming you've already spoken to a loan officer and know your investor buying power, then walk through these steps.

1. Get your agent in search of fixer-uppers.

2. Drive around town as described above.

3. Find out the owners' names by searching your local tax records (usually readily available through the local MLS).

4. Follow up with the owners and ask if they are interested in selling their home in as-is condition.

These first four steps will be repeated time and time again until you find the property that meets your investment requirements; once you do, continue:

5. If the owner says "Yes," request an inspection of the property.

6. Conduct the inspection.

7. Get estimates for repairs and rehab projects.

8. Run the numbers for your return on investment (ROI).

9. Make an offer.

Once you've carried out these steps, you're at the final part of the process. If after the negotiations and counteroffers the contract falls through, then you're done and need to go back to step one.

If the owner accepts your offer, then the real work begins. Put together a construction schedule, prioritizing the fix-up projects, with carpeting or flooring coming last (you don't want to scar up your new flooring with work boots, nails, drips of paint, and construction dust).

It may work something like this:

Interior

☐ Fix leaky faucet in kitchen.

☐ Fix holes in drywall throughout house (bedroom 1, behind entrance door).

☐ Put new screen in sliding glass back door.

☐ Replace broken window in bedroom 2.

☐ Replace broken dishwasher.

☐ Fix ice maker in fridge.

☐ Add insulation in attic.

☐ Paint all rooms.

☐ Replace carpet throughout.

Exterior

☐ Service furnace.

☐ Cut back overgrown bushes.

❏ Mulch flower beds.

❏ Plant seasonal flowers.

❏ Caulk around all storm windows.

❏ Scrape wood around house.

❏ Paint all trim.

❏ Replace rotted panels at bottom of bay window.

❏ Prime and paint bay window.

❏ Replace gutters and downspouts.

As you move into the budgeting phase, keep in mind that this is a commodity that you are fixing up to sell or rent—it is not your personal residence. Forget the upgrades (but use quality-grade materials) on all your projects. The bottom line here is the bottom line—how much cash can you get from this transaction once you've rented it out or sold it.

Many first-time investors think about fixing up such a property and turning around and selling it for a killing . . . which can be done, but planning for the long haul is always better, though not as glamorous.

If you turn the property around and sell it, you have a short-term gain, which will earn less money than waiting for appreciation and the renter's money to build your wealth. I had a reader write me about a property she inherited asking whether she should hang on to it or sell it and take the gain from the last few years' appreciation.

Inherited Property Is the Perfect Investment

Question: I am the single owner of a house I inherited in 1995. I have never lived in this house and have rented it two separate times. Tenants have recently moved out and I would like to know whether I should continue renting or sell it now that the market value is high. What about capital gains, and so on? I realize that renting at this time would make more profit than selling and putting the money in the bank at such low interest rates. However, I think selling now, rather than waiting and having the value of the house go down in a few years, is a better choice. What's your advice?

Answer: What you do with the property now should be directed by your long-term financial goals. Frankly, right now, if I inherited a property—meaning I have NO money out of my pocket to get into it whatsoever—I would hang on to it until I retired or died. This is the ultimate cash machine if you're willing to look at the cash flow it's generating rather than how much it's worth at this point in time.

Real estate investors, while looking for a good time to cash in, rely on the long-term growth more than the short-term value to create wealth. You've had the property only eight years—how much money will it make for you over the next ten or twenty years with an average increase in rent at the rate of inflation (let's say 2 to 3 percent)?

If you're receiving $1,000 per month in rent now, moving forward at 3 percent per year over the next ten years would result in a cumulative cash flow of $137,520— AND you still have the equity in the property to use later if you so desire. Why would you get rid of that? This type of return is not available in the stock market (unless you know exactly what to invest in), CDs, or any other current investment.

Another difference between real estate and cash investments is how much cash it generates per month. Let's say the house is worth $150,000 and that it's currently bringing in $1,000 per month ($12,000 per year)—that's an 8 percent return on the value of the house. Now for you, since you inherited the property—it's an infinite percent return on the money you didn't even have to put into it.

If you do sell, capital gains are going to eat you up—at the minimum it's 5 percent of your gain—for every $100,000 in value that you're going to get in the sale, you're going to pay Uncle Sam $5,000. However, since this was an investment property, hopefully you have been depreciating the value of the property against your income. One of the tax rates that wasn't lowered through the recent Bush tax cuts was the tax imposed on depreciation taken on the sale of investment real estate—the rate is still at 25 percent.

You do get to reduce your gain by the amount of the value of the house when you inherited it (called your basis), plus the cost of selling the house (commissions, advertising, points, and so on). To tell you in this space how much you'll pay in taxes is impossible. Talk with your accountant to be sure. Unlike your personal residence, you do not get to exempt $250,000 of gain from the tax man.

Selling now at $150,000 would create a gross gain of that same amount. Now let's start the reductions—6 percent to sell ($9,000); a point to the buyer ($1,500); closing costs of roughly 3 percent ($4,500)—you're down $15,000. Now your gain is at $135,000. If the house was worth $100,000 when you inherited it, that's how much you get to reduce from the gain as well for tax purposes. That puts the gain around $35,000, on which you'll have to pay taxes.

Now, the cash you're walking away with (subtracting the cost of sale and maximum taxes) may roughly be $126,250. In the bank, that's going to return about 2 to 3 percent annual return ($2,525 to $3,788). Using the above examples, you've cut your cash flow by as much as $7,000 per year.

With these ROUGH numbers, which do you think is the better investment? Unless you have an amazingly good deal sitting on the side waiting for your money (like a gold mine that no one else knows about), I'd keep it in the property. If you need cash, then talk with a loan officer about pulling out some of your equity. Right now, you have in your possession what everyone who writes me is looking to get—a positive cash flow property that's building you wealth one month at a time.

Tables 8-2 and 8-3 below compare the numbers for selling a property immediately with renting it out and selling it down the road.

As you can see by looking over the two charts, the long-term hold will result in exponential growth on the $25,803 of your initial investment. While the return on your initial investment to fix up and sell a property immediately is quite high, at more than 85 percent on your money in just a few weeks, holding the property and renting it out, then selling after the value of the house has appreciated, returns a whopping 520 percent in ten years.

Now, you may have noticed, I didn't place capital gains taxes in the second table; that's because the equation assumes the investor will take those gains and roll them over into another investment property. When you do this (called a 1031 Exchange or Starker

Table 8-2. Fixer-upper: Fix up and sell immediately.

Home Price	$150,000
Down Payment of 10 Percent	– $15,000
Loan Amount	$135,000
Closing Costs	$4,500
Total Purchase Cost	**$19,500**
Repairs	$6,303
Subtotal	**$25,803**
Listing Price	$200,000
Sales Cost (Commission, Closing Costs, Etc.)	– $15,000
Subtotal Above	– $25,803
Net	$159,197
Less Mortgage Note	– $135,000
Gain	$24,197
Capital GainsTaxes @ 5–15%	$1,209–$3,629
Net Gain	**$22,988–$20,568**

Exchange) the capital gains are not taxed at this time. Until you finally cash out of real estate investments you don't owe taxes. Thank you Uncle Sam! (See chapter 13 for more information on 1031 Exchanges.)

Fixer-uppers—whether you rent them out or sell them—are a great way to get into real estate investing. Because of their condition, you know you're getting them at a discount. There are plenty of mortgage products made specifically for buying and refurbishing the fixer-upper, and they are more palatable for the first-time investor not wanting to deal with the legal and untested waters of foreclosures or other distressed investments. In addition, for the real estate investor who masters this style of investing, they can create a

Table 8-3. Fixer-upper: Rent and sell after ten years.

Home Price	$150,000
Down Payment of 10 Percent	− $15,000
Loan Amount	$135,000
Closing Costs	$4,500
Total Purchase Cost	**$19,500**
Repairs	$6,303
Subtotal	**$25,803**
Rental Income @ $1,100 per month (inflated @ 2% per year) × 10 years	$144,480
PITI @ $959 × 10 years	$115,080
Gross Rental Profit	**$29,400**
Year 10 Value of Home @ 2% per year appreciation	$243,799
Note Balance @ Year 10	− $112,976
Subtotal Gross Profit	**$130,823**
Rental Profit	$29,400
Total Gross Profit	**$160,223**
Less Purchase Cost/Repairs	$25,803
Net Gain	**$134,420**

fantastic portfolio that will withstand the test of time and economic storms.

Note

1 U.S. Department of Housing and Urban Development, Rehabilitation Mortgage Loan Insurance, www.hud.gov, 2004.

CHAPTER 9

Foreclosures–The King of Real Estate Investing

The king of all real estate investing! Here's where you start buying at wholesale and selling at retail. This chapter covers how to locate, purchase, finance, rehab, and sell or rent out foreclosures.

Periodically, I hear from readers who want to make millions in real estate working on foreclosures. They are right in that these properties can be a good place to invest for exponential growth (or loss).

Keep in mind, that once you get a foreclosure, you have to do something with it—fix it up and rent it out, fix it up and sell it, or fix it up and move into it. Many folks I talk with kind of forget that part. They want to pick up a property with a $5,000 down payment, fix it up with the remaining $5,000 they have for this endeavor, then make $50,000 in return. Nuh-uh—ain't gonna happen—at least not for most investors.

Foreclosures are properties of owners who have fallen on hard financial times. Most likely the house is in disrepair. The owners who can't keep up with a $1,000 mortgage payment more than likely don't have the $200 to $500 per month needed to keep up the property either, which means a lot of items have gone for months without being maintained by the time the property makes it to the auction block. You'll need money for paint and new flooring to be sure. But then there are the hidden expenses—dry rot, blocked plumbing (sometimes done intentionally as a means of revenge for being foreclosed upon), busted windows, drywall damage, roof and basement issues, just to name a few.

Whatever amount of money you think you'll need to get a property in shape—double it, so that you realize exponential gains, not suffer exponential losses.

Timeline of a Foreclosure

Here's a brief description of what's happening at the time a house goes to foreclosure.

When a borrower has defaulted on a mortgage, as a general rule, lenders begin foreclosure proceedings after three missed payments. By the time it's advertised in the newspaper, the borrower is in deep yogurt and won't be able to stop the proceedings without a reinstatement. (A reinstatement is where all the missed payments are brought current and all penalties and fees are paid.) The lender turns the mortgage over to a "trustee," which is a company or person who is legally empowered to handle the foreclosure process.

For our example, let's say the trustee of the note has foreclosed on the property and taken possession of the house. At an appointed time, the house is offered up for sale at the county courthouse (or at the trustee's office). Usually the highest bidder gets the property.

Keep in mind, the trustee is trying to get as much for the house as possible. He wants to recover the money for the lender, so he's not as likely to let it go for less than what the lender is owed. If he does, the borrower who just got foreclosed upon may end up owing money to the lender after the house is sold. For instance, if a foreclosure property has a note for $100,000 but the highest bid is only $75,000, the lender may decide to let it sell for $75,000 and then go after the former property owner for the remaining $25,000 note balance. This situation is called a deficiency judgment—some lenders exercise this option, others don't.

A bank may take title of the property rather than let it sell for less than its note amount. If this is the case, then the bank will most likely fix up the property, list it with an agent, and try to sell it for a retail price and walk away with as much profit as possible.

The best situation for a homeowner whose property has gone into foreclosure is for the house to sell for more than the note amount, before the bank takes over title on the property. After the note is paid as well as all additional expenses incurred, the remaining funds must be given to the borrower. Expenses lenders may recoup include:

■ Accrued interest

■ Legal fees

■ Court costs

■ Late penalties

■ Filing fees

■ Title work

The winning bidder on a foreclosure must have a deposit check ready to pay to the trustee to reserve the house until settlement or escrow. The deposit is usually 10 percent of the note amount. The details of the transaction are posted in the foreclosure notice. Keep in mind that there may be other liens on the property in addition to the one note. Homeowners association dues, taxes, and various other liens can be placed on the property as a means of getting past due money from the owners.

Finding Foreclosed Houses

Look for foreclosures in the "Trustee Sale" section of the local newspaper. If your area has a lot of newspapers, look through them regularly. Trustee sale notices often do not follow a particular schedule like other parts of the paper. They appear when the attorney handling the foreclosure gets it ready for auction. Usually there's no one publication that runs all ads, so you'll need to be vigilant in your detective work.

Also, the ad must appear several times before the foreclosure occurs. When you see a new trustee sale advertisement, you have several days to get ready for the auction. Auctions usually take place at a courthouse. (Later in this chapter we'll talk about HUD and VA foreclosures—the local courthouse is not where you will bid for these government properties.)

If you go to the courthouse steps, be ready for a lot of no-shows before you actually find a property that goes to auction. Many properties get advertised, but either the owner reinstates the loan or he files for bankruptcy, which stops the trustee sale (at least temporarily). You will find that often the same trustee name comes up again and again. Get to know these folks. They may not want to become your personal foreclosure trainers, but they can serve as a great resource of information about the local foreclosure process.

Here's how to prepare for the auction:

- Search for foreclosure sale listings in the local paper.

- Make a list of target properties.

- Hit the road! Drive by the properties for a physical inspection. (You won't be able to tour inside, but at least get a feel for the community and external condition.)

- Research values in the community:
  - Are they headed up, down, flat?
  - What were the last three sales?
  - What's the pricing/rental trend over the last six months?
  - What are list prices in the community now? (A Realtor, whom you've made part of your investment team, will help you with this part of the process.)

- Know the top dollar price that you'll bid (AND STICK TO IT!).

■ Call the trustee's office the day before to confirm the auction's date and time.

■ Go to the auction.

Be sure to bring to the auction the required deposit money advertised in the trustee sale notice in the required type of funding (cashier's check, bank check, or another type). You'll be using the trustee's contract, but you'll want to have your attorney look it over.

There are several things you need to do before making a bid:

1. **Financing.** This is a given (refer to chapter 3). The trustee is generally going to require a 10 percent deposit at the time of the auction.

2. **Insurance.** Discuss with your insurance agent all the policies you'll need once you take possession of the property: a homeowners policy, title insurance, mortgage insurance, a home warranty policy if desired.

3. **Inspection.** Contact a home inspector to complete a follow-up inspection to ensure you haven't missed a glaring defect. (This of course happens after the auction is complete.)

4. **Repair Crew.** Whether it's a person you hired or some of your family and friends, you'll need someone to take care of the obvious cosmetic issues and then the defects discovered by the home inspection. For those hiring out the repairs, you'll need an idea of the cost of hiring crews to work on the property before you get into it, so that you'll be able to determine if this foreclosure is as good a deal as it appears on paper. Unfortunately, most courthouse foreclosures sell the property as is, thus you can't find out the condition until after you've bought it. However, VA and HUD foreclosures are open inside and out for inspection with a real estate

agent. An investor can walk through these properties with a contractor to figure the cost of fix up.

5. **Realtor.** Line up a Realtor to list the property for sale or for rent.

Once you win your first bid, you'll want to line up a preparation calendar to get the property in shape as soon as possible to lessen your financial liabilities.

Three Paths to Wealth

As an investor, you have several options on how to make money in a foreclosure transaction. There are three basic scenarios to buying foreclosures:

1. Visit the courthouse steps during an auction, purchase a property, fix it up, and then rent it out, creating a positive monthly cash flow. At this point, the investor also becomes a landlord, having to be available for repairs or to hire someone to do them.

2. Buy the foreclosure, invest more money to fix it up, and then sell the house, taking the profit once the house is sold.

3. Purchase a foreclosure that is underpriced by say 30 percent or so and "flip" the house immediately by selling it to a second buyer and wrapping another loan around the property. This is just like buying and flipping a property discussed earlier; however, this time, the investor holds onto the second mortgage and makes money on a monthly basis.

Fix Up and Rent

Most foreclosures are going to need some type of repair work. If you intend to hold a property, you must include in your acquisition budget moneys for refurbishing or repairing the property. In addition, you must consider who is going to complete the repair work.

If completing the work yourself, you'll need a budget for all the materials. Talk to people who fix up and rent out foreclosures, and they will ALL tell you to budget for 25 to 30 percent more than you initially estimate. Once you start repairing walls, floors, and carpeting, you may uncover defects that were missed during your initial inspection. I've been fortunate to buy two condos that needed only surface painting and carpet cleaning—however, they are exceptions to the norm.

Once the house is repaired, you will then advertise for renters. You can try to rent it out yourself, but I suggest dipping into the experience and pool of renters from the Realtor member of your investment team. She can list the rental in the local MLS, and most important, she can process the applications of potential tenants and run background, employment, and financial checks to find the one who is truly appropriate for your property.

The key to converting a foreclosure into a rental is to purchase it at such a good price that your monthly payment is covered by the rent. Be sure to analyze the rents in the area as well to make sure you can get enough rent to cover your payment. If you can't, then remove that property from your target list.

Buy, Fix, Sell

Refurbishing property can be very rewarding. The biggest battle first-time investors face when working on refurbishing properties is psychological. It's a battle of the mind: What if we pay too much going in? What if we can't get our money's worth? What if we find more problems later that make it impossible to turn a profit?

Most investors have a story about a property that made them take a financial bath. Nevertheless, I know of more investors who have made good money on their investments than those who have not.

Keep in mind, this is a product. Don't approach the refurbishing as if you're going to live in the home for the next thirty years. While you may not want to go with the cheapest household accessories throughout the house, remember that most new homebuyers end up remodeling once they walk in the door. Off-white paint throughout, base carpet-flooring, low-end appliances will all work just fine. More than likely, you'll be working on an entry-level property that targets the first-time buyer—who has been renting. The low-end items are going to look great to them because this is their first house or their move-up house.

If you are going to modernize or fix up a few rooms, the highest return for your investment will be in the kitchen and the bathrooms. For the kitchen, replace dated appliances (turquoise colored, for example) and replace dated kitchen flooring and countertops. A clean coat of paint on the cabinets can do wonders and save you money.

The bathroom is the next place to look over. A clean sweep is always in order here. Start with the mildew—professional-level cleaning, new caulking, replace flooring if water damaged. New faucet fixtures don't cost a lot and are easy to replace. Check for rust around the medicine cabinet and replace if necessary—the same for the light fixture around the vanity. New towel racks and shower curtains can do wonders for the look. They don't cost a lot, but turn the renter's reaction from "Yuck," to "Wow!"

Flipping with Wraparounds

A third way to make money on foreclosures is to sell them immediately for a higher price than what you paid and create a note on the property that continues to pay you for an extended period of time. This way you have the benefits of selling and renting wrapped into one.

For example, let's say a house worth $100,000 on the open market is sold at a foreclosure auction to an investor for $50,000. The investor may put down 10 percent and assume or create a new mortgage for $45,000. The investor then advertises the property as-is and at a discount, say for $80,000, offering 100 percent seller financing (remember, it's worth $100,000). He hopes to create a sense of urgency by underpricing the house and pulling in buyer calls because of the low price and the 100 percent financing.

If he's successful, the investor takes a promissory note from the new purchaser for $80,000. He has now created a cash margin of $35,000 for himself. The buyer makes payments to the investor for an $80,000 loan and the investor makes payments on the original loan for $45,000. In real numbers, here's what it will look like.

If the original loan is for $45,000 at 7 percent over 30 years, the principal and interest is $299.39. When the second buyer takes a note for $80,000, the investor may charge a bit higher interest since he's offering 100 percent financing (which is normal in the mortgage world). Let's say he offers an $80,000 loan, 9.5 percent over 30 years. The monthly payment is $672.68, creating a positive cash flow of about $373.29 per month.

If the borrower stays in the house for 30 years, the investor will make $99,387 in interest and $30,000 in capital gains after he's paid his own interest on the first note for a total return of $129,387. Your gross percentage return is more than 2,400 percent on the $5,000 down payment! (That's not a typo—it's really 2,400 percent.)

For most transactions, the owners are either going to refinance or sell in five years. So let's see what the return on investment will be if this occurs.

Over five years, the investor will have received roughly $37,584 in interest and when the homeowner sells and pays off the loan, he gets his $35,000 from the spread created on the wraparound loan. Thus, he has grossed $72,584—less his $5,000, he has cleared $67,584. That's a return of 1,250 percent! That's still pretty good over five years!

Keep in mind that a lot of mortgages may call for a mortgage to be paid in full if the house is sold—this is called a due-on-sale clause, meaning if the property is sold, the first trust must be paid off immediately. However, if the payments are being made, most lenders will continue with the mortgage as it is. The loan is still secured by the property and can be foreclosed if any payments are missed in the future.

VA and FHA Foreclosures

Government-owned foreclosures offer the most controlled environment in which to bid on foreclosed properties, since the bidding process is operated by the federal government and requires the involvement of trained professional real estate agents.

For a list of HUD properties, visit the agency's Web site at www.hud.gov. VA hires out its property management to Orlando-based Ocwen Federal Bank. The Web site for listings is www.ocwen .com. To bid, however, you'll need to talk with a real estate licensee who has gone through the training for these government agencies. Unlike other foreclosures, you can even tour these properties with the agent before making a bid.

VA and HUD properties are held by the government because the purchaser of the original property used either an FHA- or VA-insured loan to buy the property. Although the money for the loan was provided by a private lender, the federal agency insured the loan so that if the borrower defaulted the federal government would take back the property, pay off the balance of the mortgage to the private lender, and then sell the property at auction.

As a general rule, a higher percentage of FHA and VA homes will go into foreclosure than nongovernment-insured mortgages, because the FHA and VA programs allow higher risk borrowers to get mortgages. On the other hand, in most markets, the FHA and VA programs make up a very small portion of the mortgages that are placed. If you live near a large military facility, you will obviously have a higher number of VA foreclosures available in your market.

One thing to know in this process is that it's all about money—VA and HUD are interested only in which deal gets them the best bottom line. If your bid comes under the highest bidder by $50—you just lost the house. It's a very black-and-white transaction for these sellers.

With this in mind—you may want to negotiate with your agent about the commission. If you have the money, pay the commission yourself instead of having the proceeds come from the transaction.

The government allows agents to charge 6 percent on the transaction (this is a commission not split with a listing agent as with most sales). You especially want to negotiate with your agent if you are bidding in a sellers' market. In addition, you'll also find yourself up against agent-buyers, who can get into the deal with no commission at all. I've seen some investors get their real estate licenses just so they can wheel and deal in foreclosures without worrying about how much commission to pay their agent—they are their agent!

Because of the controlled nature of VA and HUD foreclosures, there's not a lot to say about them except to locate the agents in your area who are certified to work with them. Otherwise, it works almost like a regular nonforeclosure sale—visit the property, write a contract, wait and see if your bid wins. The controlled process also makes them more popular than traditional foreclosures, since bidders are working with licensed professionals, thus, they may sell quicker and for higher prices than traditional properties.

Five Warnings About Foreclosure Investing

Before you go out, checkbook in hand, ready to bid away, take some advice first.

If you're deciding to invest in foreclosure properties as a husband and wife team, be sure that both of you are sold on this venue of investing. You are about to enter a world of high finance, property management, calls in the night from tenants (maybe even police!), and other risks that a regular homeowner will never experience. However, if you have the willingness to break away from the normal investment route and seek out real estate investment as part of your portfolio, it can also be very rewarding.

Next, get educated. Reading this one chapter does not constitute preparing the first-time investor to start bidding on properties. There are plenty of real estate agents and auctioneers who do this on a daily basis and will be happy to educate you in the world of foreclosure properties.

Don't worry, all the foreclosure properties are not about to disappear. Unfortunately, bankruptcies have been hitting record levels the last several years, and in a world of easy credit followed by even easier bankruptcy, those foreclosures are not going away very soon.

There's opportunity now for investors to step in and benefit from these properties that are about to hit the market. However, despite all the hyperbole, investors can lose money in real estate—a lot of money. If you have some cash itching a hole in your bank account and you're looking for positive cash flow and possible high returns on investment, be sure to avoid these five pitfalls in the foreclosure investor field.

1. Paying too much for a foreclosure. Many VA and HUD foreclosure buyers have found themselves getting caught up in the excitement of bidding on properties and watch, without even knowing it, their supposed cash cow die right in front of them. If you must have a 20 or 25 percent spread to make money on the purchase, then stop bidding when the price gets below that spread amount.

    In simple terms, if you're bidding on a property with a $150,000 value and you intend to sell it for a 20 percent gain, then stop bidding when the price gets above $120,000. In a hot market, even foreclosures sell at market price, but then the new owner moves in and will most likely have to fix up a dilapidated property that was neglected by the former owners. Usually, when an owner is headed toward foreclosure, fixing the leaky roof or basement is the last thing on his mind, leaving it up to the "bank" to fix instead.

2. Getting a house without clear title. Make sure you can get clear title to a property before you put your $10,000 earnest money deposit into the deal. Ask questions of the auctioneer-trustee who is conducting the auction. Is she conducting the title search, or must you have an attorney do a title search to

find out if you're going to have any problems taking title to the property. If you can't get title, you can't sell the property.

3. Having negative or unprofitable cash flows. The whole idea behind buying a foreclosure is to buy low enough so that rent checks will cover the investor's mortgage payment, taxes, insurance, and fees each month and then leave the investor some profit at the end of the month. Unless the property is in pristine condition and all the systems will last for years repair free, you're setting yourself up for financial hardship if an air conditioner breaks or the refrigerator has a compressor attack.

   The monthly cash flow should include enough to finance any breakdowns or repairs while a tenant lives in the dwelling. Negative cash flows are not deductible expenses.

4. Not taking care of little problems before they become big problems. Don't take the cheap way out on being a landlord. A house starts deteriorating from the day the builder completes its construction. Your new investment property is creating cash flow—take care of it. Paint it regularly, clean the carpets and floors between tenants, fix the broken windows, repair leaks promptly, replace rotted wood, and so on. If you let the property deteriorate until you can't rent it out any longer, you've waited too long to fix these problems. In addition, fixing defects quickly will save you money due if you wait and then the bill doubles or even triples.

5. Failing to educate yourself on tax benefits of owning investment properties. If you're going to invest in rental property, talk with professionals in the field who know how to maximize your financial benefits from this new form of investment. Accountants, attorneys, and real estate practitioners are all worth their fees, as they help you avoid pitfalls, increase your gain, and keep you out of trouble.

It may appear that buying foreclosure properties can be a daunting task. It requires a lot more work than just showing up at the courthouse steps with a checkbook in hand. For the real estate investor, however, it's a part of your portfolio that can escalate your net worth because of the potential equity obtained by purchasing properties for dimes on the dollar. Read this chapter again. Digest the nuances of finding foreclosures, developing financing schemes, and working your to-do list, all of which are required to be a successful foreclosure investor. Then take that final step—put this information into practice and make your first bid!

Distressed Sellers–Working Foreclosures Before They Hit the Auction Block

How would you like to reduce your competition at the foreclosure sale? Get rid of the tire kickers? And, how would you like to look at a property before it goes to foreclosure? I'm talking about preforeclosures. These are properties held by a distressed homeowner who has missed several payments and is facing foreclosure. He or she has already received notices from the lender that they're late and a foreclosure is pending. This category is a bit trickier and it takes a little more work, but the return is worth the extra effort.

Up till now, we've spent most of the time explaining about how to buy foreclosures after the lender has taken possession and the owner is no longer in the dwelling. You will have found these properties by showing up at the courthouse steps, by searching trustee sale classifieds, and by looking online through VA and FHA property listings. In these scenarios, you will be dealing with the trustee of the property rather than the former owner who defaulted on the loans. If you would like to work with a seller who is about to lose his house to foreclosure, then you're going to have to do some advertising and marketing to make the phone ring.

You've probably seen signs with messages such as: "AVOID

177

FORECLOSURE" and "WE BUY HOMES FOR CASH," stapled to traffic signs at a local intersection or printed in the real estate classified section of your local newspaper. These signs are from investors looking for two types of property owners: 1) those suffering financial stress, which selling can relieve, and 2) those who have already missed several payments on a mortgage. What's even more exciting is that many of these "investors" don't have the money to purchase properties—they're going to find another buyer who does—and will make thousands of dollars on this referred transaction. (I'll tell you more about this later in the chapter.)

If you choose this mode of investing, you'll need to work up a marketing budget, which may include printing, advertising, postcards, and postage, just to name a few. I have three sample marketing pieces to mail in this chapter. You'll also need to visit the local courthouse to pull some records. You can make your phone ring by marketing to preforeclosure property owners in one of several ways.

Advertising

Simply, you're looking for owners of distressed properties to call you with their problems. Newspaper ads, posters, and signs touting "Avoid Foreclosure," "We Buy Homes As-Is," and "Cash For Your House" are targeting homeowners who need to get out from underneath a burgeoning mortgage and are willing to let go of their properties at a discount.

Farming

As you drive around your area, make note of properties that are in disrepair. Most preforeclosure properties need fixing up. It stands to reason that if a homeowner cannot make the mortgage payment, then he also has no money to take care of the place. Put these properties on your mailing list.

Mailing

This involves creating a database of names of targeted properties. It will more than likely be a short-term list as the recipients of your marketing piece will either call and avoid foreclosure, or they won't and they'll lose their house. You'll need to send a letter to these folks about three times, then delete them from your list.

You can create a database of names in several programs, such as Microsoft Excel, Microsoft Access, WordPerfect, Outlook, and various other software applications. Regardless of what you use, the optimum program will allow you to record notes on your marketing progress, such as dates mailed, responses, and so on.

How to Find Homes in Preforeclosure

So where do you get these names? They are readily available at the land records department at your local courthouse. As borrowers become delinquent on their mortgage, they will eventually receive a "Notice of Default" from the lender. These notices must also be recorded at the courthouse and that's where you'll go to start building your list.

I can't say if this process will be easy or difficult because each locality has different processes. Some of the records are in land record books, others are computerized. Some jurisdictions may require fees to be paid for access while others may just hand them over. You'll have to find out once you go to the courthouse. If you're as fortunate as we are in Fairfax County, Virginia, your local government will have set up a searchable online database available to the public for a nominal monthly fee.

There's an online service that collects listings of "Notice of Default" properties across the country. Visit www.DataQuick.com and you'll find plenty of real estate data and services to get you going in your real estate investing career. This group also provides a valuation service whereby you can receive sales comparables (values of similar properties in the same geographic area) for any target property you are considering. For a monthly fee, you gain access to all their services, as well as 250 searches per month. They can also be contacted toll free at (888) 604-3282.

Homeowners who have received the "Notice of Default" are in trouble. Hopefully, they realize it, but some are in total denial. They are about to lose their home through foreclosure. Some of them file for bankruptcy to stop the foreclosure but soon find out that the note holder can petition the court to turn over the house to the foreclosure process. The court will agree and the owner now has not only a bankruptcy, but also a foreclosure blight on his credit report. A bankruptcy can delay consumers from getting a loan for a house for a couple of years—a foreclosure takes up to ten years to be removed from a credit report.

Now that you have your database, start putting together your letters or postcards to mail. In addition, look up the phone numbers of the people in your database, as you are going to call them once you mail your marketing letter or postcard.

Preforeclosure Marketing Letter #1
Dear [HOMEOWNER'S NAME]:
   YOU ARE ABOUT TO LOSE YOUR HOME TO A FORECLOSURE SALE, according to county courthouse records, but this DOESN'T HAVE TO HAPPEN!

In a few weeks, YOUR HOME WILL BE AUCTIONED AT THE COURTHOUSE STEPS in a Trustee Sale and you'll no longer own your house. You'll have to **move into temporary housing, try to find an apartment, or ask friends and family to let you live with them**.

In addition, you'll LOSE ALL THE EQUITY in your home. Even if your mortgage company sells the house for more than your loan amount, they can charge fees, penalties, and interest that will come out of your equity.

A foreclosure or bankruptcy will **RUIN YOUR CREDIT**—you won't be able to buy another home for ten years! You'll be renting for a long time with no tax benefits, no appreciation, no way to build wealth through your home. **I know you don't want this to happen**. The mortgage company just wants their money and, frankly, they don't care if you get any money.

I DO CARE!

[Homeowner's Name Here], **I know this is a tough time for you**. It's stressful and is causing trouble with your family. It's simply embarrassing. **BUT YOU CAN TAKE CONTROL OF YOUR SITUATION, SAVE YOUR CREDIT, AND PUT SOME CASH IN YOUR POCKET!**

Don't wait until it's too late, like most homeowners facing foreclosure.

If you want to STOP the foreclosure—save your future—get some needed cash in your pocket—then call me now!! **Here's my direct line: (555) 555-1234.** There's no obligation. I have a few questions to ask you about your property and then we can schedule an appointment for me to see your house and make an offer!

YOUR CALL IS STRICTLY CONFIDENTIAL!

Sincerely,
[YOUR NAME]

Preforeclosure Marketing Letter #2
Dear [HOMEOWNER'S NAME]:

I STILL HAVEN'T HEARD FROM YOU! I wanted to write you and let you know what you can expect to happen in the next few weeks if you don't **STOP THE FORECLO-SURE PROCEEDINGS NOW!**

First, you may get another notice from the Sheriff's Department posted on your door that you are about to lose your house. Then **Sheriff's Deputies will eventually show up to evict you from YOUR OWN HOME!** DON'T KEEP

WAITING, HOPING SOMETHING WILL HAPPEN TO SAVE YOU!

If **YOU** don't stop the foreclosure process, then **who will?** Your next step at this point is to find an apartment or a family member or friend to move in with in the next few days. You must understand that TIME IS OF THE ESSENCE! **Your home is being advertised now in the local newspaper to be sold at auction to the highest bidder.** This is a VERY SERIOUS MATTER!

If you recall from my last letter—**I CAN HELP YOU!** Don't be embarrassed to ask a professional investor like myself to:

- **Save the equity in your home,**
- **Save your credit, and**
- **Put cash in your pocket so you can pay off bills or move into another property that you can afford.**

By letting your home sell at auction you won't get a dime from the sale. **AND if your home sells for less than the mortgage amount,** the lender will still come after you to get the balance—the foreclosure won't necessarily get you off the hook!

WHAT WILL YOU DO?? Wait for the Sheriff to evict you and your family? Or call me to buy your home, stop the foreclosure, save your credit, and put LOTS OF MONEY IN YOUR POCKET.

In A COUPLE OF WEEKS I can purchase your house with cash and you'll have enough money to get on with your life! Doesn't that sound better than a foreclosure sale? I'm as close as the phone. Call me today so we can get started immediately. My phone number (555) 555-1234.

Again, our conversation is strictly confidential.

Sincerely,
[YOUR NAME]

Figure 10-1 shows a sample postcard that can be used.

Figure 10-1. Foreclosure postcard.

YOU ARE ABOUT TO LOSE YOUR HOME TO

<u>FORECLOSURE!</u>

STOP IT by calling me now at the number below:
(555) 555-1234

[Local jurisdiction] Courthouse records show that your lender has filed a Notice of Default on your house. If your home goes to foreclosure, you won't be able to buy another house for 10 years. DON'T LET THIS HAPPEN!

LET ME PUT CASH IN YOUR POCKET!

Stop Foreclosure? Protect Your Credit? Call NOW!

Assigns: Turning Your Contract Over to Someone Else

You're probably wondering by now—"Great! How can I buy this house in two weeks when I don't have that kind of cash?" Well, that's where the phrase: ". . . and assigns" comes in handy.

When you write the contract to purchase a property, you will have in the purchaser's line, [Your Name and/or Assigns].

This simply means that you can either buy the property or you can assign the contract to someone else. This "someone else" is the investor you will find who has the cash to buy the house. You will receive a finder's fee from the proceeds of the house. You can also be part owner of the house or arrange several other scenarios, but for our purposes, we'll assume you're going to assign it or it doesn't go to settlement.

Another phrase you need in the contract to make this happen is an addendum that states: "Seller also agrees and understands that this contract is contingent on the approval by the purchaser's partner." Who's your partner? The investor buyer you have lined up to front the cash for the purchase.

The investor, who is more than likely the mentor we talked about earlier, is going to look over the contract and the homework you've done to see if the deal will make enough money for him, less your fee. If it will, he agrees, and you move forward with the deal.

The process works like this:

- Find property.

- Contact owner.

- Inspect property.

- Conduct comparative market analysis of the house (use your team members if necessary).

- Determine potential profit.

- Make offer.

- If accepted, have investor/partner review contract.

- If accepted, go to settlement.

- Go to bank with check.

This mode of investing obviously requires a partner or investor who has money ready to purchase property. Your mentor may not be that person—but she should know some contacts in the investor circles around your market who are. If not, visit real estate clubs in your area to find other investors who are willing to take assigned contracts. Creative Real Estate Online offers a great resource at its Web site (www.creonline.com), where you can search by state for clubs in your area.

Ambulance Chasing?

When you see how much money you can make by buying preforeclosure properties, some may argue this is a type of real estate am-
bulance chasing, but the hard-core facts are these:

- The investors are looking to pick up the house for what I call
  a wholesale price. For instance, if a property owner receives
  notice that his foreclosure date has been set and the bank or
  note holder has told him to vacate the premises in two weeks,
  he doesn't have time to pursue a traditional sale process. A
  call to one of these investors may be his only option.

- Investors have plenty of cash and want to get the house at a
  deep discount.

- The owner is in default—most likely several months if he has
  received a foreclosure notice.

- The owner doesn't have the cash to bring the payments current—presumably he's sitting on several thousand dollars
  worth of missed payments.

- More than likely the house needs repairs. If the owner lacks
  the funds to keep the mortgage current, then he definitely
  hasn't been spending money to keep the property in good
  shape. If he has kept the property in good shape in exchange
  for the house payments, then he lacks good judgment.

- Since the mortgage is in arrears, probably so are the taxes,
  homeowner association dues, homeowners insurance, and a
  plethora of other bills connected with the property.

- There may even be liens on the house the owner doesn't
  know about. If he has missed home payments, he has probably missed other creditors' payments. There's a good chance
  the title to the house is cloudy, meaning there are liens and
  judgments attached to it from the creditors and tax collec-
  tors.

- The investor is willing to solve all of the above problems with cash if the owner will provide the title to her at a discount.

- With the sale of the house, the investor pays off all the loans and gets the owner on his way, usually with cash in his pocket, at least enough cash to move out and get set up in an apartment somewhere. In addition, by avoiding foreclosure, the owner's credit has been rescued from years of detrimental reports.

Now, is the investor a pariah? I think not. She has assumed all the risks to take the property; pay off all the debts, liens, taxes, and so on; finance the fix-up costs for a sale—and then will walk away with the profit.

Working with distressed sellers to save them from foreclosure is a good way to get ahead of your competition. It takes a lot more work than buying regular foreclosures or traditional investment properties, but it can be a gold mine for the investor willing to deal with property owners who are financially stressed and may be emotionally stressed as well. Following the approaches outlined in this chapter, you'll find that you can help homeowners facing foreclosure actually get back on their feet and protect their credit, and make yourself a nice profit.

CHAPTER 11

Prepping for the Rental

Once you've purchased your first investment property (which may actually be your first primary residence that you're going to convert to a rental in a few years), you have to look at preparing this puppy for the rental market.

The preparation process includes several steps: maintaining the physical property, analyzing the market, listing the unit, reviewing applications, and, finally, choosing an appropriate tenant. I'll deal with each step and also provide you some tips on avoiding pitfalls along the way in the area of tenant selection and property management.

Improve Before You Move

The first step in preparing a house for rental is to conduct an inventory of the property to see what you'll have to do to prepare the house for its next resident. After all, you and your last tenants may not have noticed the worn spot on the carpet in the den, but what about the next couple you show the apartment to? They may point it out and decide to pass on your unit.

Prevention and regular maintenance are the best ways to get a property ready for renting. If you're regularly dropping by for a physical inspection of the house or condo, then you won't be surprised by a large problem when your current tenant gives notice.

If you wait until you've received a notice from your current tenant to do maintenance and basic upkeep, the amount of work will be overwhelming and you may need to call in professionals (read—write checks) to get it done. Eventually, if you have more than one or two investment properties, you will want to have a team of professionals doing all the fix-up. Remember, you've set up a real estate investment business, not a property management company.

When you're getting the property ready to rent out the first time, you may want to add some upgrades to the house so it rents quickly and your new amenities last longer than the first year. Fix-ups and upgrades don't have to be expensive.

You will want to look at several items.

Cleanliness

In the big scheme of things, many properties can best be prepared with just a really good cleaning. I've seen many private landlords make a huge mistake by not paying to have a unit professionally cleaned and not giving the cleaning process its due attention.

This is more than just a Saturday morning cleaning. We're talking deep cleaning. Since the last tenant has moved out, this is one of the easiest deep cleanings that can be done. Some of this may be review, but it's best to have a checklist when getting this done:

Whole Unit

❑ Vacuum.

❑ Dust.

❑ Shampoo carpet.

❑ Mop all hard-surface floors and use appropriate postwaxing applicant (wax, flax seed oil, and so on).

❑ Wipe down all walls.

❏ Patch all picture holes.

❏ Paint when and where necessary.

❏ Clean light fixtures (you can put light globes and covers in the dishwasher).

❏ Clean windows.

❏ Replace torn screens.

❏ Check windows for ease of opening and closing.

❏ Check all smoke and CO2 detectors.

❏ Open all doors and listen for squeaking hinges—oil.

Kitchen

❏ Thoroughly clean kitchen appliances.

❏ Check garbage disposal seals.

❏ Vacuum bottom of refrigerator and around compressor.

❏ Check ice maker (if applicable).

❏ Replace exhaust fan filters.

❏ Thoroughly clean inside cabinets, consider new contact paper.

❏ Clean ovens and drip pans on stove.

❏ Replace any broken appliance light bulbs.

Bathrooms

❏ Clean and disinfect with strong detergents (bleach-based preferred)! This is probably the room that gets the dirtiest. I don't want to get into too much graphic detail, you can imagine, I am sure.

❏ Remove all soap scum from mirrors, glass, tile walls, tub, shower, and so on.

❏ Replace shower curtain.

❏ Remove all mildew at all costs—and this doesn't mean cover it up. If you have a mildew problem, take care of it!

❏ Vacuum exhaust fan.

❏ Replace exhaust fan if broken.

❏ Clean out medicine cabinet.

❏ Check under vanity for leakage.

❏ Check inside toilet tank mechanism to ensure proper flushing.

❏ Tighten towel rack brackets.

Washer/Dryer

❏ Run empty load through washer with bleach.

❏ Wipe out thoroughly.

❏ Check fixtures, check pipes for rust, replacing hoses, and so on.

❏ Clean external surfaces.

❏ Clean lint net.

❏ Remove exhaust hose and inspect; clean and reattach.

❏ Run cycle on both to ensure they work properly.

Decor

After cleaning up, take a look at the decor. What's out of date? What's cracked and needs replacing?

If you want to know how important this is, then visit some of your competition to see what their units look like. Specifically, look over apartments that are in your rental price range and see how they've prepared their units that are on the market. You'll see that professionally managed units look great when they are in between tenants.

Some simple and relatively inexpensive changes when preparing to rent your unit the first time include:

- New medicine cabinet and lighting in the bathroom

- New kitchen appliances

- New flooring in the kitchen

- New paint throughout

- Upgraded curtain rods and blinds

Home Inspection

By the time you get to the major systems, you may want to hire a professional, certified, or licensed home inspector. Not all states require certification and licensing. For a professional in your area, refer to the American Society of Home Inspectors (ASHI) at www .ashi.org.

A home inspector can check all aspects of the house and at least let you get familiar with the property before you start renting it out.

ASHI's home inspector "Standards of Practice" include the inspection of the following areas of the house:

Structural system

Exterior

Roof system

Plumbing system

Electrical system

Heating system

Air-conditioning system

Interior

Insulation and ventilation

Fireplaces and solid fuel burning appliances

Painting

Applying a new coat of paint to the interior can do wonders to the look and feel of your house. Painting is one of the most inexpensive improvements, yet one of the most effective. A couple of cans of good paint run about $50. Additional equipment (brushes, rollers, drop-cloths, and so on) will run between $30 and $50 and in a day, you've given one of your rooms a completely new look.

Painting the exterior on a regular basis is something for which every homeowner should budget time and money. Painting your investment every two to three years keeps the exterior in good condition and provides you with the opportunity to inspect more closely the parts of the house you normally would not get access to on a regular basis, such as the eaves and overhangs.

While it is difficult to paint the whole house for under $200, try attacking the trim first. With a couple of cans of paint, you can probably take care of the shutters and door. A fresh coat of paint on these items does wonders for the look of the rest of your house.

Keeping up with the above items provides you with an investment property that will last for years. In addition, it gives you the opportunity to inspect your property while the tenants live there, AND it makes for happy tenants who will want to stay in the house year after year after year!

Mold Is Not the Only Environmental Concern for Homeowners

As a landlord, you are responsible for providing a safe, healthy environment to your tenants in exchange for the rent they've promised to pay you to live in your investment property. Part of that preparation is making sure the house is free of threats to your renters' healthy well-being.

Mold, while providing really big payoffs to infected consumers right now (as well as lining some aggressive attorneys' pockets), is not the only environmental attack you may be facing in your home. Long before mold became the buzzword in real estate circles, there have been environmental concerns for homeowners.

Real estate professionals have begun to attend training sessions in droves to find out what they need to know about in-home mold. In a nutshell, the mold problem is really a moisture problem. Without moisture, there is no mold. You can find plenty of information on the Web about mold and ways to take care of it. Amazingly, however, there are other health hazards in properties that have been passed over in the hyperbolic reaction to the mold issue. Below I've listed other hazards that have always been with us, but I fear may get less attention because they haven't created big headlines about really large monetary awards from lawsuits. Nevertheless, many of them can cause as much health risk—even death.

■ **Radon.** The U.S. Environmental Protection Agency blames this invisible gas for thousands of deaths each year due to lung cancer. The gas radiates from concentrations of uranium in the soil. The average indoor radon level is 1.3 picocuries per liter (pcl) in the United States. A house has a radon problem if the measurement reaches above 4 pcl.

■ **Lead.** Houses built before 1978 most likely had lead-based paint in them, and this is now a required disclosure whether you're renting out a unit or selling a house to someone. The current supply of paint used in houses is lead-free. In some states, there are other requirements besides the federally mandated disclosure, such as required participation in insurance programs to cover possible lead poisoning.

Your Realtor should have a copy of the government-required disclosure form in his listing package as you put the house on the market, but it is the owner's responsibility to make sure her tenants or buyers have been informed of the presence of lead-based paint in the house. Federal regulators treat this part of the code very seriously. A Maryland landlord made national headlines when he faced criminal charges for not disclosing and was fined tens of thousands of dollars as a result.

If your house was built before 1978, then disclose to your tenants and let them decide whether or not they are willing to live in your house. By the way, painting over the lead-based paint doesn't take away your liability. For the federally mandated brochure warning about lead, visit www.hud.gov.

■ **Asbestos.** Again, homes built before 1978 may have asbestos present in various forms. The American Lung Association says the mineral fiber can be positively identified only with a special type of microscope. The fiber was added to a variety of products years ago to strengthen them and to provide heat insulation and fire resistance. Visit the following site for guidelines on what to do if asbestos is present in your home: http://www.lungusa.org/air/air00_aesbestos.html.

■ **Water Quality.** The one area that carries a lot of pollutants that most homeowners don't think much about is our drinking water. The Environmental Protection Agency has a great site about water at http://www.epa.gov/OGWDW. Though the United States has the safest water supply in the world, there are still plenty of ways it can become polluted—industrial and agricultural run off, natural occurring pollutants, and even by-products from chemicals used to disinfect water.

■ **Carbon Monoxide.** Carbon monoxide (CO) is a colorless, odorless, and poisonous gas that results from the incomplete combustion of fuels such as natural or liquefied petroleum (LP) gas, oil, wood, coal, and other fuels. If you use natural gas as a heating source or to operate appliances, it would be wise to have CO detectors in your home. The U.S. Consumer Product Safety Commission has plenty of information about this device. See the Web site at www.cpsc.gov for more information.

A good home inspector is the first place to start for testing for many of the hazards above. If he doesn't conduct some of the tests for these environmental hazards, he may have referrals of environmental testing organizations in your area.

Are Landlords Always the Bad Guys?

As you enter the world of real estate investing, you have to come to grips with the fact that you are in a business and you are going to make money on the backs of your tenants. Like any other business, you are going to have expenses and more than likely they will grow—not shrink.

Depending on the type of property you decide to invest in, your expenses will increase in the area of taxes, utilities, homeowner association dues, and various other categories. So what are you going to do?

Just when I thought I had answered this question for the last time and pointed renters to a good "How to Buy a Home" Web site, I received this letter from a disgruntled high-rise tenant in Arlington, Virginia, a suburb of Washington, D.C.

"I have been a loyal renter for over five years at the same apartment building in the Crystal City area. I have seen annual rental increases go from 2 percent to 3 percent to 5 percent to 8 percent to now 11 percent. Isn't there some kind of limit to this ridiculousness? This just is not fair. Do rules vary from jurisdiction to jurisdiction?"

In the world of low- and moderate-income rental property,

there are rules. The government steps in with its calculations on what the property owner can charge. The formula includes such factors as the net operating income for the multifamily complex and the median household income of renters to determine fair market values. And in many areas, though not as many as in the past, there are local rent control regulations, which often limit yearly rent increases.

With private-sector housing, all that matters is the NOI (net operating income). The NOI represents gross rent less uncollected rent, taxes, government fees, insurance, maintenance, and repairs. As time passes, landlords face rising taxes, utility bills, repair costs, and other expenses, increases that must be covered by pushing up the rent.

Coupled with the NOI is supply and demand. If you live in an area where the supply of rental properties (as well as homes for sale) is dwindling, then it's likely you'll see higher rents than in areas with a surplus of housing units.

A good Web site to research your area's rent statutes is Rental Housing Online (http://www.rhol.org/), where you can find information for landlords, tenants, investors, and more. The U.S. Department of Housing and Urban Development (www.HUD.gov) also has some good resources for renters, and that means you as a landlord should look it over.

Numbers Are Just as Important for the Rental Market

Whether you're buying or renting a house, it always comes down to the numbers. Many renters don't think they can buy a home, when in reality, it costs almost as much money to move into a rental and takes nearly as much financial scrutiny to determine a renter's qualification. Some rentals require a security deposit, first month's rent, pet deposit, move-in deposit, and other fees before you can even open the moving truck doors. For an apartment rental of $1,200, that can quickly add up to nearly $3,000 just to rent a pad the first month. With the right loan program, a renter could turn that deposit money into a down payment and purchase his or her own piece of the American dream. But let's stick with rentals for now.

As an investor, it's good for you to understand that it's a misnomer to think that because the home sales market is hot, that means rentals will always be available. A hot sales market can be a landlord's best friend. When sales pick up, causing inventory to shrink, the inventory for rentals may narrow as well. Since there are not as many houses for sale in the community, the would-be buyers stay put and the rentals also become scarce—this is when you can increase your rent. Keep in mind, a hot market is indicative of a thriving economy, which means more people are working and jobs are growing. If more people are moving in than the number of homes being built, both rental and sale prices will increase. In a more level sales market, rentals may be soft because it may be cheaper to buy than to rent. In preparing your new investment to rent out, I advise hiring a professional Realtor who has worked rentals in the past and has the connections to check backgrounds on all the applicants. When looking over applications, keep in mind you are looking for reasons to eliminate, not to rent out.

When you find an applicant who has nothing on his application that would eliminate him from the tenant pile, then you have found the tenant for you.

The Realtor will help with this process by running rent to debt ratios and using a reputable background-check company to look over each applicant. This company will check out the validity of the applicant's information.

Does he really make $30,000 per year? How did he leave the last property? What's his credit rating? Any judgments, bankruptcies, or history of late payments? In a tight market and with a heightened sense of fair housing law, property managers have begun to systematize the way they screen rental applicants. Online screening services are growing. Property managers can now log on to find out if applicants paid their rent on time.

Property Owners' Exchange (www.poeknows.com) in Baltimore operates a consumer-reporting agency. By putting applicant-rejecting criteria on a form (or by letting a third-party conduct the screening), property managers can reduce their liability and receive a cleaner profile of the potential renter. POE president Howard Levin said in *Realtor* magazine (the National Association of Realtors' monthly publication), "If you're not thorough, you'll wind up dealing with residents everyone else rejected."

The questioning and investigation of potential renters is getting as intensive as the process for buyers. RentGrow, a third-party screening company based in Waltham, Massachusetts, operates a pretty sophisticated screening Web site (www.rentgrow.com) to help multifamily property owners create an online screening process. Despite the system you use, there are some basic issues that MUST be dealt with.

- Check the credit history, obviously.

- Look at employment and income. On the income, you want to consider whether it's hourly or salary and how much of it is based on overtime or bonuses versus the base salary.

- Examine housing history, including payment history.

- Check up on the potential tenant's rental background by calling past landlords.

- Do a criminal record search. Need I say more?

- Search eviction records. This checks for judgments filed at the courthouse and any evictions from the past.

- Do a co-applicant check. You may have a second or third applicant on your rental application. Treat all of them equally in making your final decision. With roommates, one or two could pull out in just a few weeks or months—leaving the primary renter to pay all the expenses on her own.

By taking care of your investment properties and the people who rent them, you'll find that you have happy tenants who take care of your property for years to come.

Tenant Rights Backfire on Seller

Some tenant laws can be so obtuse as to be funny and make for sitcom fodder. In fact, the rush around to seize rental units from recently deceased tenants has humorously been played out on popular comedy shows such as *Seinfeld*, *Friends*, and *Frasier*.

These scripts are based on the sadly true ways properties can change hands in localities that have very stringent rental regulations. In New York City, increasing rent is a cumbersome ordeal; thus, stories abound of children and grandchildren scurrying to move into grandma's apartment when she kicks the bucket, but they hide her death from the landlord.

Under most landlord-tenant laws, the property can be sold at any time, usually subject to the lease, meaning that the new owner must abide by the lease until it is fulfilled and that the former owner is no longer liable for anything required in the lease. In the case where the property is being converted into condos or converted from a rental to a private residence, such as a town house or single-family home, some tenant protections require the landlord to at least offer the sale of the property to the current tenant before offering the property on the open market. This is usually called a Right of First Refusal.

An example of how these laws can bite real estate investors was played out in Washington, D.C., which has such a law. In many instances, this decree has helped many properties change hands effortlessly, as well as maintain affordable housing for some tenants.

On the other hand, some unscrupulous folks will take advantage of any loophole to make a quick buck. To sew up these loopholes, it is important for investors who want to become landlords to read up on the law, have a real estate professional review contracts, and get legal advice on what is required of you as a landlord.

A letter was forwarded to me from a buyer in our nation's capital who states that her transaction had been hijacked by the tenants living in the house she and her husband were trying to purchase. As I talked with the buyer and reviewed the D.C. tenant laws (though I'm not an attorney), I saw that the seller overlooked some protections for herself, and it may cost her some money.

In a nutshell, the single-family house was rented by four people—and here's the first mistake—without a lease. Since the landlord wanted to sell the property as a single-family home again, she must first give notice to the tenants and allow them Right of First Refusal.

The story is quite fascinating. The buyers (an attorney and an editor with their first child on the way) wrote in an e-mail that they were amazed to watch this tenant law played out before them:

> In accordance with D.C. law, the tenants were given ample notice that the owner was interested in selling the house. However, after reviewing our ratified contract, they decided to exercise their right of first refusal. (This is after they demanded that the seller pay them to leave. She offered them one month's free rent, their security deposits, and $500 each, which they flat-out refused.)
>
> Their intent, as we have been informed, is to sell their right to another buyer/developer and make a fast buck. In the meantime, because of such liberal tenant laws in the district, we all are forced to wait them out. The tenants' attorney told us today that most of these cases are 'resolved' when the parties get so frustrated they pay the tenants to leave. In our case, these three guys want $20,000.

At this point, the parties involved are playing a game of legal chicken, a stare down to see who blinks first, as it were.

Basically, the tenants are operating within the law and their rights.

Unfortunately, the buyers are facing a delayed settlement, which could cost them more money. The seller should have taken more precaution, planned the sale accordingly, and these headaches would not have happened. Without a lease, she had no closure capability in place to make sure the tenants had a firm date when they must leave.

If you're considering the real estate investment track, read up. Cornell Law School's Legal Information Institute has plenty of links to state landlord and tenant Web sites. Get ready for some slow, deliberate reading when you visit http://www.law.cornell.edu/topics/landlord_tenant.html, as you will find it has a lot of headings, subheadings, and tedious legalese. But if you crawl through these statutes, you can learn a lot about what you can and cannot do as both a landlord and a tenant.

Need Renters? Uncle Sam Can Help

As you place your property on the market, unless it's in a high-rent district, you want to be sure you've covered all your bases as far as marketing your property to the widest audience. The quickest way to lose money in real estate investing is for your cash flow machine to sit empty with no rent dollars coming in each month.

There are government programs that pack a powerful punch for low-income home renters, and they can mean consistent rental payments to you as a landlord, as well.

Households with 50 to 60 percent of the median income in a particular area can get assistance from a local or state housing authority that uses funds from a U.S. Housing and Urban Development program called Section 8. This program was the successor to public housing as we know it in this country. Instead of the government taking on the task of building and maintaining housing projects, like it did in great numbers during the 1960s and 1970s, now it provides financial assistance to home dwellers who need a helping hand.

Basically, Section 8 funds pay the landlord rent money. The

renter applies for a voucher (and there are several types to choose from—check out HUD's renting section at its Web site: www.hud .gov). The housing choice voucher program places the choice of housing in the hands of the individual family, according to HUD. "A very low-income family selected by the public housing authority (PHA) to participate is encouraged to consider several housing choices to secure the best housing for the family needs . . . The housing unit selected by the family must meet an acceptable level of health and safety before the PHA can approve the unit. When the voucher holder finds a unit that it wishes to occupy and reaches an agreement with the landlord over the lease terms, the PHA must inspect the dwelling and determine that the rent requested is reasonable," according to HUD's Web site on voucher programs.[1]

Other stipulations of which a landlord should be aware regarding the voucher program include:

- The PHA determines a payment standard that is the amount generally needed to rent a moderately priced dwelling unit in the local housing market and that is used to calculate the amount of housing assistance a family will receive.

- Payment standard does not limit and does not affect the amount of rent a landlord may charge or the family may pay. A family who receives a housing voucher can select a unit with a rent that is below or above the payment standard.

- The housing voucher family must pay 30 percent of its monthly adjusted gross income for rent and utilities, and if the unit rent is greater than the payment standard the family is required to pay the additional amount.

- By law, whenever a family moves to a new unit where the rent exceeds the payment standard, the family may not pay more than 40 percent of its adjusted monthly income for rent.

The final decision on the housing assistance is determined by the local PHA. The calculation for this figure is generally determined by taking the lesser of:

1. The payment standard minus 30 percent of the family's monthly adjusted income or

2. The gross rent for the unit minus 30 percent of monthly adjusted income.

Most landlords will be concerned with only the following vouchers:

Family Unification Vouchers

Tenant-based Vouchers

Vouchers for People with Disabilities

Welfare-to-Work Vouchers

The value of the voucher varies. The public housing authority pays the owner the difference between 30 percent of adjusted family income and a PHA-determined payment standard or the gross rent for the unit, whichever is lower. The family may choose a unit with a higher rent than the payment standard and pay the owner the difference. It's a busy formula to figure, but your local PHA staff can help determine your voucher level.

This voucher is what the renter then uses to rent a unit. I use the word unit, because it can be an apartment, condo, town house, or single-family home. In some states, property owners can decide whether or not to use Section 8 vouchers, while other states require investors to use them if they're going to offer rental properties in the state.

Section 8 housing has helped a lot of people when they need it most, giving them a leg up on the tough job of saving up money for a down payment. By using the Section 8 program, the renter can now save more of his or her own money in preparation for buying a house in the future.

Many low-income renters know about Section 8. What they may not know about is Section 42—the government program that can give Section 8 voucher holders extra punch for their dollar.

Section 42 administers the Low-Income Housing Tax Credit, introduced in 1986. LIHTC is a tax credit program developers use to construct or refurbish multifamily housing with the understanding that only residents who make 50 or 60 percent of the local median income can rent the units. With that limitation, the developer can save hundreds of thousands, if not millions, of dollars in tax payments because they are helping fill the need for low-income housing. With these savings, they can then offer apartments under the market-rate rent.

"Although there is considerable variation among properties, tax-credit properties tend to be small, newly constructed, and managed by their owners. Most are situated in central cities. The properties are intended to serve families, elderly persons, and disabled persons," according to www.huduser.org, an online information source for housing and community development researchers and policymakers.[2]

Because of the quality of some of these units, potential renters in high-rent markets have been caught lying to get into these properties. Basically, the application process is the reverse of most housing processes—the landlord tries to eliminate you because you make too much money, rather than the other way around.

The vouchers are administered by the state, but the properties that accept Section 8 are privately owned and maintained—and that's where you find the disconnect.

Interested renters can find their state public housing authority Web site by visiting the National Council of State Housing Agencies Web site (http://www.ncsha.org/). There's no national or state-by-state database available for voucher holders to find private homes that accept Section 8 vouchers. Hopefully, HUD and the state-level PHAs can rectify this problem to make the process less painful.

If you decide to use the Section 8 voucher program as part of your marketing efforts, be sure to conduct due diligence research on your responsibilities as the landlord. In some areas, a landlord can place a property into the program and remove it at will, while other jurisdictions have a "once you're in, you stay in" approach. Below is HUD's description of the roles of the tenant, the landlord, the housing agency, and HUD in the use of the voucher program:

Tenant's Obligations

When a family selects a housing unit, and the PHA approves the unit and lease, the family signs a lease with the landlord for at least one year. The tenant may be required to pay a security deposit to the landlord. After the first year the landlord may initiate a new lease or allow the family to remain in the unit on a month-to-month lease.

When the family is settled in a new home, the family is expected to comply with the lease and the program requirements, pay its share of rent on time, maintain the unit in good condition, and notify the PHA of any changes in income or family composition.

Landlord's Obligations

The role of the landlord in the voucher program is to provide decent, safe, and sanitary housing to a tenant at a reasonable rent. The dwelling unit must pass the program's housing quality standards and be maintained up to those standards as long as the owner receives housing-assistance payments. In addition, the landlord is expected to provide the services agreed to as part of the lease signed with the tenant and the contract signed with the PHA.

Housing Authority's Obligations

The PHA administers the voucher program locally. The PHA provides a family with the housing assistance that enables the family to seek out suitable housing, and the PHA enters into a contract with the landlord to provide housing-assistance payments on behalf of the family. If the landlord fails to meet the owner's obligations under the lease, the PHA has the right to terminate assistance payments. The PHA must reexamine the family's income and composition at least annually and must inspect each unit at least annually to ensure that it meets minimum housing quality standards.

HUD's Role

To cover the cost of the program, HUD provides funds to allow PHAs to make housing-assistance payments on behalf of the families. HUD also pays the PHA a fee for the costs of administering the program. When additional funds become available to assist new families, HUD invites PHAs to submit applications for funds for additional housing vouchers. Applications are then reviewed and funds awarded to the selected PHAs on a competitive basis. HUD monitors PHA administration of the program to ensure program rules are properly followed.

The Rental Game: What Are the Rules?

Let's take a look at what to do when the dishwasher has spewed soapy water across the kitchen floor and leaked down on your neighbor below. In other words, who is responsible when things go wrong at your rental property—and be sure you understand, things will indubitably go wrong! Across the country, tenant law differs as much as the geography. Nevertheless, some principles remain the same regardless of the local nuances of tenant and landlord rights.

Besides the rules and principles of finance, return on investment, and passive cash flow, there are also laws and regulations that even the fledgling landlord must master. Unlike the land holders of centuries ago, who were "lords" of the land, and therefore could rule as either a benevolent or despotic dictator, the landlord in twenty-first-century America will find him or herself girded with a plethora of local, state, and federal rules that govern the practice of dealing in real estate.

One of the first places to visit is the landlord/tenant area posted

online by Cornell University's Law School (http://www.law.cornell
.edu/topics/landlord_tenant.html).

Commonly speaking (because the biggest problem I find with
legal Web sites is they don't speak in such basic terms), there are
certain rights reserved for the landlord and certain rights reserved
for the tenant. Visit your state's Web site to search for the tenant
laws for your state. You'll find that some of the laws are triggered
by how many properties an investor owns. For instance, in Virginia,
many of the regulations and laws from the Landlord–Tenant Act
do not kick in until the investor has a fourth property. If you are
going to rent out property to tenants, you need to get real personal
with your state's document. Once you've read it, contact the housing agency in your county or city, and see if it has even more requirements.

A tenant–landlord act regulates the actions between a landlord
and his or her tenants. It lays out the guidelines for what tenants
and landlords will and won't be held responsible. For instance,
while you may be able to sell a house "as is," this is not the case
with a rental. All appliances and systems (at least in most tenant–
landlord acts I've seen) require them to be in working order. This
is what you might call an anti-slumlord provision.

The contents of a tenant–landlord act will differ state to state.
Some will go on for volumes, while others may not even have a
dozen pages to peruse. Nevertheless, this is the real estate investor's
Bible of sorts and something that should be studied. It may not be
the most exciting reading, but you'll enjoy even less reading a sum-
mons for your appearance in court.

Real estate investment is one of the most invigorating ways to
build personal wealth and participate in the American Dream, but
it should be pursued with much respect and due diligence.

Now, I bring Cornell's Web site to the forefront, as it is an
official sounding, and most of all, a reputable, place for all of us to
seek out what the law says. However, a site based in Cleveland puts
the responsibilities of landlords and tenants into simple language.

NeighborhoodLink (http://little.nhlink.net/nhlink) is a product of Levin College of Urban Affairs, a part of Cleveland State University. An easily navigable site with plenty of information on rental laws in Cleveland, the site also includes form letters for tenants who must deal with unresponsive landlords. (This is a very cool part of the site—check it out— http://little.nhlink.net/nhlink/housing/cto/letters/letrs.htm.) Now the reason you should check it out is to understand that tenants have a slew of legal resources at their disposal to get your attention as a landlord. You MUST be familiar with the law of your land and ready to respond when you get a letter from one of the local housing groups or an attorney.

Nevertheless, the lists of landlord and tenant duties found here give a simple approach to who is responsible for what in a lease agreement, and these duties are generally relevant across the country. Most lease agreements will include the fact that the landlord has several items to maintain at the property, including:

- Keep the unit fit and habitable—at the least.

- Comply with local and state codes regulating the building, housing, health, and safety.

- Keep all systems in good working order—plumbing, electric, heating, and so on.

- Maintain all required appliances and equipment. This may be negotiable if the unit doesn't come with appliances or if the tenant insists on using his or her own appliances.

- Give notice before entering the property. You may own the property, but you do not have free reign over the dwelling. You must give adequate notice, at least twenty-four hours in some jurisdictions, before entering a tenant's unit—except in emergencies.

And what about tenants? Again, look over your lease agreement to see what the tenant will be obliged to maintain. Usually, it will include:

- Keep the premises clean and safe.

- Comply with housing, health, and safety codes that apply to tenants.

- Refrain from damaging the premises and keep guests from causing damage.

- Maintain landlord-supplied appliances.

- Allow entry by the landlord if the request is reasonable and proper notice is given.

- Comply with state or municipal drug laws in connection with the premises and require household members and guests to do likewise.

Oh—who is responsible for that leaky dishwasher? Most likely, the tenant has an obligation to limit the damage by shutting off the machine and drying the floor. The landlord who supplied the appliance should have it repaired or replaced as soon as possible.

Keep in mind, tenant laws differ by jurisdiction. For details regarding your area, speak with local realty brokers, attorneys, and housing offices.

The regulations real estate landlords face include fair housing (local, state, and federal), disclosures on lead-based paint (federal), and state-level tenant–landlord acts that regulate the responsibilities and privileges of both the renter and the landlord.

Who Pays for Rent-Back Damage?

In the event that you're buying a property where the owners are moving out, but need to rent back from you for a few weeks or months, you'll find that there are particular circumstances in this instance about property damage. The Realtor involved in the transaction may have you and the seller-turned-renter sign a "standard" Post Settlement Occupancy Agreement.

Many of these types of agreements state that "all electrical, heating, air-conditioning, plumbing, and any other mechanical systems and related equipment, appliances, and smoke detectors included in this contract, shall be in working condition." The review of these items becomes very important once the old owners move out. Who knows, but that since the date of settlement, the garage door opener breaks and the hot water heater develops a slow water leak.

Depending on the contract language, the tenant may be responsible for these types of breakdowns. When it comes to interpreting contracts and legal agreements, please consult with an attorney. However, when it comes to real estate agreements, the contract says what the contract says—or in this case, the Post Settlement Occupancy Agreement says what it says.

Before you sign anything, read it. I know that sounds pretty basic, but read it and then go over it with your Realtor or attorney. When the form says, "all electrical, heating, air-conditioning, plumbing, and any other mechanical systems," are to be in working order the day you walk in as the new owner, you should expect all these items to be so.

With most contracts and forms, you don't have to really ask the question, as our former President Clinton asked, "What is, 'is'?" It means what it says, and, rest assured, the buyer or his attorney or Realtor will enforce it to the nth degree of the law.

When you look at signing this type of agreement, walk through it with your home inspection report at your side. What are the inspector's notes on plumbing, electrical, heating/air, and all other parts of the dwelling?

If these items are working now, what about appliances on their last leg? If any of the appliances seem to have age on them, the renter may consider writing exclusions for those items and insist on an "as is" phrase in the occupancy agreement. Not many buyers will go for that unless you have gotten a really good deal on this property and the appliances are going to be replaced anyway.

Even though the renter is no longer the owner of your property, the intent of letting him stay there is not for an investment, such as a landlord-tenant situation. In such a case, the investor-owner would expect to absorb the costs of the new water heater and garage door opener. However, the new owner is doing a rent back to help the renter with the timing of his move. Thus, you obviously want a home that is in relative move-in condition for your future renters.

To avoid many of these headaches, especially if you're purchasing older properties, you may want to consider a home warranty. Most homeowners are under the assumption that home warranties are only for those in the midst of buying or selling a home. Actually, most home warranties can be purchased at any time you own the property. The basic requirement is that your house is in good shape and that all the items covered by the warranty are in working order.

Warranties carry a deductible for each incident, and the policies require you to call the warranty company first before making arrangements to have the system or appliance fixed. Usually, the policy underwriter has a list of vendors to use. For more information on home warranties, click by any of the sites listed below:

2-10 Home Buyers Warranty http://www.2-10.com

American Home Shield http://www.ahswarranty.com

Best Home Warranty Company http://www.bhwc.com

Fidelity National Home Warranty http://www.homewarranty.com

HMS Warranty http://www.hmsnet.com

Home Warranty of America http://www.hwahomewarranty.com

Government Has Property Rights—To Your House

You may have heard of the police confiscating real estate in the pursuit of drug dealers. Hopefully, you aren't considering real estate as a means to launder dirty money, but be aware that drug use in your properties by your tenants can cause you much pain and sorrow.

In the United States of America your property can be seized, condemned, and turned over to another owner if the government finds a good enough reason to do so. In addition, if you are suspected of being involved in the drug market, your house can be confiscated and sold by local authorities—before you've even been tried or convicted of a crime.

"No criminal arrest or conviction is necessary to subject property to forfeiture," according to the American Civil Liberties Union's Web site (www.aclu.org). "Indeed, nearly 80 percent of the victims of forfeiture have never been indicted of a crime. All the police have to do is satisfy a requirement of probable cause that the property was used in an illicit activity or was purchased with funds from illicit activity."

The concept of taking your property is not a theory, but a hard, cold reality. In the area of law enforcement, many crime-ridden communities have been cleaned up using this particular practice, but many innocent citizens have also been victimized by this mode of law enforcement.

An online piece by FindLaw.com in 2000, "If the Government Wants Your Property," states, "If you've been convicted of a crime, the federal government can seize any property used in the crime, including your house. The property may then be sold and the proceeds used to further the government's crime-fighting efforts. So if you own a crack house, your arrest and conviction may lead not only to jail time but to permanent loss of the house and your equity in it."

The above-mentioned legal action can also be taken against a property owned by an investor who has a tenant suspected or convicted of illicit drug activity. Fortunately, Congress amended these laws a few years ago to protect innocent homeowners from aggressive civil forfeitures. FindLaw.com reported: "The new law prohibits the government from confiscating property unless it can show 'by a preponderance of the evidence' that the property is substantially connected to the crime. This is a much higher standard of proof than 'probable cause'. . . . If a property owner successfully challenges the seizure in court, the government has to pay legal fees. And if the confiscation causes substantial hardship to the owner, the government just may release the property."

If you find yourself in this type of land-forfeiture situation, by all means, contact an attorney. Please don't waste your time e-mailing me or any other real estate writers, for that matter. Call an attorney. Period.

Unfortunately, even people who stay away from the crime scene can have property condemned and forcibly sold to the government if a local jurisdiction decides there's a better use for the house. Such is the case of one elderly lady in Illinois.

"In Des Plaines, Illinois, Irene Angell still lives in the house where she was born more than eighty years ago," reports Castle Coalition. "The city is currently threatening to condemn her home for a Walgreens drugstore. Ironically, Ms. Angell worked for Walgreens many years ago and met her husband there."

This process of property seizure is called "eminent domain." The Internet is full of sites operated by a lot of irate people who have had their homes and property taken through the process of eminent domain. There are also many sites for eminent domain professionals—the people who use eminent domain as a means of acquiring property for transportation and commercial development. One such site is EminentDomainOnline.com.

LawInfo.com contains a clear explanation of how eminent domain works:

"Eminent domain is the right of the government to take ownership of privately-held real estate regardless of the owner's wishes. Land for schools, freeways, parks, public housing, and other social and public interests are obtained in this manner, and the structures on the existing land may be condemned and destroyed. Quasi-public organizations, such as utility companies and railroads, are also permitted to obtain land needed for utility lines, pipes, and tracks. The property owner must be paid the fair market value of the property taken from him or her."

To be fair, eminent domain is not entered into lightly. Most eminent domain actions are for the greater good of the larger community; however, if you find yourself at the "taking" side of the eminent domain stick, contact a lawyer first to find out your rights under the law, then get a good Realtor to help you get the best price on your property.

Below are several resources for homeowners facing this government action:

- Home of the Eminent Domain Abuse Survival Guide (http://www.castlecoalition.com/)

- Property Owner's Guide to Eminent Domain (www.EminentDomainLaw.net)

- Public site for consumers and professionals regarding eminent domain (www.RightOfWay.com)

- Official site of Owners Counsel of America to help homeowners with eminent domain issues (www.ownerscounsel.com)

- Institute for Justice (www.ij.org), which defended an Atlantic City homeowner from condemnation of her home to construct a parking garage for a casino

•••

Fair Housing Important Part of Rental Process

Before you start eliminating applicants from your pool of tenants, make sure you are eliminating for all the right—and legal—reasons. Below is an excerpt from the Fair Housing section of the U.S. Housing and Urban Development's Web site. For a full version of this section, visit www.hud.gov and click on the "Fair Housing" link.

Keep in mind that this information is in regard to the federal laws. Your local and state laws may include other fair housing requirements, such as sexual orientation, age, matriculation, political affiliation, and appearance. Research your local fair housing laws before accepting your first application.

Basic Facts About the Fair Housing Act

What Housing Is Covered? The Fair Housing Act covers most housing. In some circumstances, the act exempts owner-occupied buildings with no more than four units, single-family housing sold or rented without the use of a broker, and housing operated by organizations and private clubs that limit occupancy to members.

What Is Prohibited in the Sale and Rental of Housing? No one may take any of the following actions based on race, color, national origin, religion, sex, familial status, or handicap:

- Refuse to rent or sell housing

- Refuse to negotiate for housing

- Make housing unavailable

- Deny a dwelling

- Set different terms, conditions, or privileges for sale or rental of a dwelling

- Provide different housing services or facilities

- Falsely deny that housing is available for inspection, sale, or rental

- For profit, persuade owners to sell or rent (blockbusting)

- Deny anyone access to or membership in a facility or service (such as a multiple listing service) related to the sale or rental of housing

What Is Prohibited in Mortgage Lending? No one may take any of the following actions based on race, color, national origin, religion, sex, familial status, or handicap (disability):

■ Refuse to make a mortgage loan

■ Refuse to provide information regarding loans

■ Impose different terms or conditions on a loan, such as different interest rates, points, or fees

■ Discriminate in appraising property

■ Refuse to purchase a loan

■ Set different terms or conditions for purchasing a loan.

It is also Illegal for anyone to:

■ Threaten, coerce, intimidate, or interfere with anyone exercising a fair housing right or assisting others who exercise that right.

■ Advertise or make any statement that indicates a limitation or preference based on race, color, national origin, religion, sex, familial status, or handicap. This prohibition against discriminatory advertising applies to single-family and owner-occupied housing that is otherwise exempt from the Fair Housing Act.

Additional Protection if You Have a Disability

If you or someone associated with you:

■ Has a physical or mental disability (including hearing, mobility, and visual impairments, chronic alcoholism, chronic mental illness, AIDS, AIDS-related complex, and mental retardation) that substantially limits one or more major life activities

■ Has a record of such a disability

■ Is regarded as having such a disability

Your landlord **may not:**

■ Refuse to let you make reasonable modifications to your dwelling or common use areas, at your expense, if necessary for the disabled person to use the housing. (Where reasonable, the landlord may permit changes only if you agree to restore the property to its original condition when you move.)

■ Refuse to make reasonable accommodations in rules, policies, practices, or services if necessary for the disabled person to use the housing.

> • **Example:** A building with a ''no pets'' policy must allow a visually impaired tenant to keep a guide dog.

> • **Example:** An apartment complex that offers tenants ample, unassigned parking must honor a request from a mobility-impaired tenant for a reserved space near her apartment if necessary to assure that she can have access to her apartment.

However, housing need not be made available to a person who is a direct threat to the health or safety of others or who currently uses illegal drugs.

Housing Opportunities for Families

Unless a building or community qualifies as housing for older persons, it may not discriminate based on familial status. That is, it may not discriminate against families in which one or more children under eighteen live with:

- A parent

- A person who has legal custody of the child or children

- The designee of the parent or legal custodian, with the parent or custodian's written permission

Familial status protection also applies to pregnant women and anyone securing legal custody of a child under 18. (Source: U.S. Department of Fair Housing, www.HUD.gov.)

As you can see from this chapter—once you have purchased and refurbished a rental property, the real work begins as you actively rent out the property and start servicing your customer—the tenant. This is a very important part of your real estate business. Ignorance is not bliss and, in fact, can come back to haunt you if you do not know the law and the regulations governing the renting of residential real estate. My best advice regarding the preparation of your property to rent is to simply avoid stupidity and ignorance at all cost. Collect all the referenced materials you'll need to be a good landlord and study them thoroughly.

Notes

1 U.S. Department of Housing and Urban Development, www.hud .gov, 2004.

2 U.S. Department of Housing and Urban Development, www.hud user.org, 2004.

CHAPTER 12

Happy Paper Trails

When it comes time to finish the paperwork for your first piece of real estate (investment or otherwise) you're going to find out that a lot of trees have lost their lives because of the paper shuffled back and forth to buy, sell, rent, insure, list, survey, and record the transaction.

There's a lot of paperwork required in real estate. You eventually need to understand what all these papers mean: deeds, liens, notes, insurance papers, and other forms. I'll go through many of them in this chapter, but suffice it to say a whole book could be written on this subject. The descriptions are abbreviated, but provide a brief explanation of what the papers are and what they mean to you. So let's get started.

Deeds

There are several ways you can hold title to a property. Just like the title on a car, you must also have a title to the land and home that you have purchased. To take title, you must declare the form of ownership in one of several ways. Each state governs how property can be held within its boundaries, so there may be other ways to hold title than just the three covered here. Discuss the best way of holding title with your team attorney.

- Joint tenancy

- Tenancy in common

- Tenancy by the entirety

Which is best? Well, they each offer various advantages and disadvantages, depending on your particular circumstances and how you want the property to pass if you die, sell it, or get a divorce (for married owners). After the transaction is completed, the settlement attorney records this transfer of the deed at the courthouse to prove to all around that you are the property's rightful owner. The American Land Title Association defines these titles thusly:

- **Joint Tenants**. "Two or more persons who hold title to real estate jointly, with equal rights to share in its enjoyment during their respective lives with the provision that upon the death of a joint tenant, his share in the property passes to the surviving tenants, and so on, until the full title is vested in the last survivor. A joint tenant cannot legally sell or encumber his interest without the consent or joinder of all of the other joint tenants."

In simple terms, joint tenancy is similar to tenants by the entirety (described below) but the co-owners are not married. If you partner with two other people to purchase a house, this may be one method of title. If one dies, title remains in the surviving joint tenant without required further action. This means if you die, you cannot leave your share to your heirs. Joint tenants are not married, thus are not treated as one legal entity. If an owner wants out of the title, he or she may petition the court to divide the property or order its sale. The property can also be divided if a judgment creditor petitions the court to collect the judgment from one of the owner's shares.

- **Tenants in Common**. "Two or more persons in whom title to a single piece of real estate is vested in such a manner that they have a common or equal right to possession and enjoyment of the property, but each holds a separate individual interest or estate in the property. Each owner may sell or encumber his respective interest or dispose of it by will, and if he dies without leaving a will, his heirs inherit his undivided."

Some state laws presume *tenants in common* unless the deed specifies otherwise. In this case, if one owner dies that share does pass to his or her heirs, not necessarily the surviving owner. Unmarried property owners usually use tenants in common. A tenant in common may sell his interest without approval of the other owner and, unless specified otherwise, the law assumes you meant to have equal ownership.

■ **Estate by Entireties**. "An estate or interest in real estate predicated upon the legal fiction that a husband and wife are one person. A conveyance or devise to them (unless contrary intent is expressed) vests title in them as one person. Upon the death of either husband or wife, full title passes to the survivor."[1]

Tenancy by the entirety is possible only when the joint owners are husband and wife. This type of title provides for a common law right of survivorship, which means property goes automatically to the surviving spouse. No will, probate, or other legal action is necessary; thus, one spouse can not use a will to leave an interest to someone else.

This form of title follows the ancient legal theory that a married couple is one entity. Conveyance of the property must be done together and the property cannot be divided without the other. If a divorce occurs, tenancy by the entirety automatically converts to tenants in common.

Liens

Most home purchasers must buy a property with a mortgage, or note. This is in the form of a lien, and is also recorded at the courthouse as part of the land record file. When a buyer takes possession of the house after settlement, he or she truly owns the house. Some buyers believe they don't own the house until the mortgage is paid off—in reality, you own the deed to the house and land, but the lender has a lien on the house for a mortgage. Once the mortgage is paid in full, the lien is removed—you hope.

Liens are used by creditors to ensure payment from someone who owes them money. As I said, the most well-known lien is the mortgage. This is considered a voluntary lien, but there are other types of liens, as well.

A judgment lien is usually placed on your house from a creditor who claims you owe them money. This judgment can damage your credit report and seriously impair your ability to borrow money in the future.

There's also a mechanics lien, which is a lien to force payment for subcontractors who provide labor and material during the construction of a home or development. Property owners more susceptible to this type of lien are those who purchase a new construction home. If the builder doesn't pay the service provider, such as electricians, plumbers, or the lumberyard, the house can't be sold without the debt being paid off and the lien being removed.

Then there's the tax lien–ouch. This can hurt, because you're dealing with the Internal Revenue Service, state revenuers, or even the local tax board. If you're behind on your taxes, these agencies have the right to place a lien on your house in their efforts to collect back taxes.

Liens have been known to remain on a property even though the debt has been paid off. The lender may have simply failed to have the lien removed. That doesn't pose too much of a problem if you can get in touch with the lender and have it removed. Problems arise when the old creditor is nowhere to be found.

The way most people find out about liens is during a home sale or refinance. If you find an old lien on your property, talk with an attorney to have it removed (assuming it's not because you really do owe someone money and haven't paid it off). Nevertheless, you've really got a problem when you know you've paid off the mortgage or debt, and the lien remains attached to your property. That's when a good lawyer comes in handy.

Closing Forms

I had twenty-eight forms in my last refinance and thirteen of them were what I call "I told you so," forms. These forms serve no other purpose than for the settlement/escrow service provider to be able to say, "I told you that you have the right to hire your own attorney to represent you in this transaction and here's the form you signed acknowledging that it says you agree that I gave you notice to hire your own attorney if you wanted to." Or something like that.

Is all this paperwork really necessary? Unfortunately, it is. I talked it over with the attorney conducting my latest settlement and it all came down to this—people aren't honest these days. If they were, a handshake would seal the deal. So when you look at that mound of paper on the settlement or escrow table, here's some insight as to what it is you're about to dive into. It may differ from state to state and locale to locale.

■ **Settlement Statement Notice.** The first notice I had to sign was that the settlement company had actually given me the HUD-1 Settlement Statement. The HUD-1 is a document published by the U.S. Department of Housing and Urban Development. It tabulates the funds flowing through the transaction, whether it's the sale of house or a refinance. (By the way, more than 21 percent of my $6,295.60 of closing costs were taxes.) You want to hang on to this form come tax time for deductions of points paid.

■ **Payoff Acknowledgment.** This form lets me know that my bank has given the title and escrow company a "verbal and/or written confirmation of payoff figures." This form also notifies the seller/note holder that if the payoff amount given to them was inaccurate—meaning it was less than the actual amount—that the note holder (in this case, me) would pay the difference.

■ **Privacy Policy**. Now here's a "told you so" form that's worth keeping. This was a form I had not seen in a settlement before, or at least I didn't remember this from earlier purchases and refinances. I received two of these: one from the title company, the second from my new mortgage provider. They both told me from where they collected nonpublic personal information and what they intended to do with it.

■ **Initial Escrow Account Disclosure Statement**. Here's a pretty important form. This way you're not surprised about all the extras that are coming out of your pocket for taxes and insurance each month. It is out of the Escrow Account that the lender pays your local taxes and hazard insurance premiums.

■ **Truth in Lending Disclosure Statement**. This is from the lender and lays out before you the annual percentage rate (mine was 5.75 percent), the finance charges, the amount financed, and the total payments you're gong to make over the term of the loan. Quickly go through this one or you may get buyers' remorse once you see that you may be paying as much in interest as you are for the value of the house.

■ **FAQs to Truth in Lending Act**. This has six questions and their answers about the above statement. Here's one of those forms that the government required lenders to put out there so you know what it is you just signed.

■ **Notice of No Oral Agreements**. With this form, any oral agreements between the borrower and the lender are null and void.

■ **Notice of Right to Receive a Copy of the Appraisal Report**. It's what it sounds like—I have a right to the appraisal and the title company has told me so.

■ **Servicing of Disclosure Statement**. Have you ever gotten a loan through Acme Lending, then by your second payment you get a statement saying your loan has been sold to Triple Z Mortgage? This statement tells you this may happen. When you get this form, don't get too cozy with the lender, because he's about to be replaced.

■ **Notice of Right to Cancel.** Ahhh, the buyers remorse form, at least that's what I call it. You have a right to cancel your loan "within three (3) business days" from whichever of the following events occurs last: 1) the date of the transaction, 2) the date you received your Truth in Lending Disclosures, or 3) the date you received this Notice of Right to Cancel.

These are but a few of the forms you may find in your mortgage file, and they may differ according to your state and local laws. If you end up using a government-insured loan (FHA, VA, and so on), your file full of various disclosure and statement forms will be even thicker. Happy reading and signing.

Insurance

There are several types of insurance policies that must be activated when purchasing a property. The three main policies are homeowners, title insurance, and private mortgage insurance. There are other types of policies as well, such as an umbrella liability policy and mortgage payment insurance.

Homeowners Insurance

The homeowners policy is to protect the rebuilding of your house in case of fire, flood, or other disaster. Depending on the riders you purchase, it also protects the homeowner's possessions. If you want to know what the replacement cost of your house would be, there's a handy tool for all homeowners on the Countrywide Insurance Web site (www.cwinsurance.com)—their insurance calculator. Plug in your city, zip, and the square footage of your house, and it will calculate the replacement coverage you should be carrying.

Here's the coverage amounts required for a 2,400-square-foot home in the following Springfield cities:

Springfield, Va.	$299,000 @ $124.58/sq. ft.
Springfield, Ill.	$282,000 @ $117.50/sq. ft.
Springfield, Calif.	$277,000 @ $115.41/sq. ft.
Springfield, Ohio	$268,000 @ $111.66/sq. ft.
Springfield, Ark.	$217,000 @ $90.41/sq. ft.
Springfield, N.C.	$215,000 @ $89.58/sq.ft.
Springfield, Mass.	$215,000 @ $89.50/sq. ft.
Springfield, Tenn.	$208,000 @ $86.66/sq. ft.
Springfield, Mo.	$188,000 @ $78.33/sq. ft.
Springfield, Tx.	$167,000 @ $69.58/sq. ft.

As an investor, you definitely want to know what the policy does and doesn't cover since your property will be at the mercy of someone other than yourself. That point became very clear to me when I read a "stupid criminal" story, in which a man got caught in a chimney in a San Diego suburb trying to enter a building through the opening usually reserved for Santa Claus.

Apparently, nineteen-year-old Josh Marteen found himself stuck in a chimney for five hours and was later arrested once firefighters used chainsaws to cut through the siding of the building, then cut through the masonry to release the man.

Mr. Marteen told officials he was stargazing, which leaves me wondering what his two friends were doing inside the building where police found them. Nevertheless, the firefighter crews really did a number on the house. During an emergency, homeowners can't take precautions like they would during regular construction and remodeling. Thus, the sawing into the side of the house and eventually into the chimney left more than just damage to the walls.

All in all, the chimney had to be reconstructed; the walls repaired, spackled, and painted; the carpet replaced or at least thoroughly cleaned. The damage obviously cost a few thousand dollars, at least. So who's going to pay for it?

Well, according to the Insurance Information Institute (www .iii.org) there are several perils most insurance policies will cover. These include:

- Fire or lightning

- Windstorm or hail

- Explosion

- Riot or civil commotion

- Damage caused by aircraft

- Damage caused by vehicles

- Smoke

- Vandalism or malicious mischief

- Theft

- Volcanic eruption

- Falling object

- Weight of ice, snow, or sleet

- Accidental discharge or overflow of water or steam from within a plumbing, heating, air-conditioning, or automatic fire-protective sprinkler system, or from a household appliance

- Sudden and accidental tearing apart, cracking, burning, or bulging of a steam or hot water heating system, an air-conditioning or automatic fire-protective system

- Freezing of a plumbing, heating, air-conditioning, or automatic, fire-protective sprinkler system, or of a household appliance

- Sudden and accidental damage from artificially generated electrical current (does not include loss to a tube, a transistor, or similar electronic components)

So in this instance, where the friendly neighborhood chimney burglar causes damage to your house, it could be considered vandalism and malicious mischief and your policy may pay for it. My first inclination would be to sue the criminal for damages. However, even if the criminal has homeowners or liability insurance, the perpetrator may not be covered for intentional criminal acts.

In another case (another stupid criminal case) two friends were drinking alcohol and smoking pot when one decided to aim a gun at his friend and pull the trigger. It didn't fire; then he pumped it and shot again—bingo—the friend got shot. The trigger friend was found guilty of a felony. His victim friend (formerly? we don't know) sued him for damages, but since the injurious shot was not INTENTIONAL the trigger friend wanted his insurance company to pay off the victim who was suing him for damages. The New York State Court of Appeals ruled that this insurance company does not have to pay damages for one of its policyholders' negligence conducted in an intentional criminal act.

This being the case, the chimney climber's insurance coverage could refuse to pay the victim's damages since the policyholder was criminally negligent (assuming he is convicted of the charges), thus excluding that damage from coverage. (The ruling can be read in full at Cornell University's Law School site, http://www.law.cornell.edu/ny/ctap/I02_0095.htm.)

In essence, the liability coverage under the traditional homeowners policy is specifically for true accidents—not for criminals to protect themselves for possible damage caused by their heinous acts.

Bottom line—if you're worried about insurance coverage from criminal acts, contact your insurer to make sure you have such coverage. If you're in the midst of such a claim and having problems getting paid by the insurance company, you may want to contact a good lawyer.

Title Insurance

Title insurance is a policy that protects the lender (lender's policy) or the buyer (owner's policy) against loss arising from disputes over ownership of a property.

Did you know that Abraham Lincoln lost his house twice because of a cloudy title? It's true. First American Corporation, which is one of the country's largest title insurance underwriters, reports about the losses on its Web site and in a promotional brochure about the dangers of not having a clear title to land. To read the whole story, you can visit this prolonged URL (http://www.firstam .com/faf/html/news/lawrept/lr960202.html) for the details. While you're there, you can look up the article "70 Something Ways To Lose Your Property."

Title insurance protects you from someone arriving at your house and asking you to leave because they are the rightful owners of the property. It protects your title to the property. If a rightful owner turns up at your door, then the policy is supposed to pay off the mortgages on the land and dwelling to protect both the lender and the buyer. It doesn't keep people from laying claim on the land, it just protects you from the losses you may occur in such a case.

Private Mortgage Insurance

This is a document that you'll find in your stack of papers when you are purchasing a home with less than a 20 percent down payment. Paid for by the buyer, the policy actually protects the lender in case the buyer defaults on the loan. This policy can run into thousands of dollars per year to provide—completely out of the pocket of the homeowner. Fortunately, an act of Congress a few years ago allowed homeowners who were required to purchase such a policy to remove the policy once the value of the property surpassed the 20 percent level.

For instance, if you bought a house for $150,000, using a 5 percent down payment, your mortgage would be $142,500. Included in the mortgage payment is a monthly private mortgage insurance (PMI) premium. In a few years, however, with mortgage payments and appreciation, you are now well vested beyond the 20 percent equity and you no longer need PMI to protect the lender. You must provide to the lender an appraisal of the property to have the PMI dropped. It's well worth the homework to save the hundreds of dollars you will need to continue the payment.

Mortgage Payment Insurance

Mortgage payment insurance is a policy offered through various companies, such as Mortgage Guardian, Inc. Like many insurance companies, its promotional materials point out all the horrible things that can happen to you if you lose your job and how this policy can protect you from not being able to make your mortgage payment. The agency's particular policy pays up to six months of mortgage payments for you, allowing your largest payment to be made while you concentrate on your smaller bills, like your car payment, household expenses, credit cards, and so on.

Mortgage payment insurance also gives you time to list and sell your house if you need to find a new job and it makes your lender real happy, which goes without saying.

Countrywide Insurance promotes two other types of mortgage payment policies: Mortgage Life Insurance and Mortgage Accidental Death and Disability policies. These two pay out more than just monthly payments—they pay off the whole mortgage in case of your death or disability, always depending on what type of policy you have in place. (I've always wondered about the value of this type of coverage, since most regular life insurance policies are created for this very task.)

Mortgage Life Insurance pays off most home loans, according to www.cwinsurance.com, the Web site for Countrywide Insurance. In the event of death, Mortgage Life Insurance will pay off your mortgage up to a specified amount. The policy requires no medical exam in most cases (unlike many life insurance policies). The policy is determined by three factors:

1. Amount of the home loan

2. Borrower's age

3. Tobacco use

There may be limitations to this type of insurance, according to Legal & General, an England-based group that sells mortgage payment insurance. If you receive some other type of insurance during your unemployment or disability, for instance, your benefit could be reduced. Be sure to ask about the limitations of any type of these policies to make sure you're not paying a monthly installment for protection you may already have through some other type of insurance provider. The mortgage payment insurance provider may offer a monthly payment, all right, but only after all other insurances pay out. Obviously, check the fine print and ask the agent tough questions.

In addition, check with your current disability insurance coverage (if you have it) and see how it pays out in case of long-term illness. Any benefit must first be approved by the underwriter before you receive a check. Does it pay within a few days, weeks, or months?

Good Fences Make Good Neighbors— What About a Bad Fence?

Homeownership is the American Dream. But did you know you can lose your land to squatters in this great country? (Now you see why in the old westerns, squatters were treated badly.) I've had readers write me regularly about this type of issue. You would think that in a modern culture this type of situation would not exist. As you'll see, you must be aggressive in protecting your own property rights—if you don't who else will? The letter usually goes something like this:

Question. My next-door neighbor's shed roof overhangs into my yard by nine inches, using the back wall of the shed as part of the fence. We have a straight line between the properties, but some of his posts are on our property. He refused to use a plumb line—instead he just eyed it. While nine inches is not the end of the world, the fence is right next to my house. The neighbor threatened us after I told him we would take legal action if he did not move his fence back to the property line. He tried to take sixty-five square feet of my front yard, contending that the mark on the sidewalk designates the property line. We are currently refinancing our house. Will the appraiser care?

I would have taken him to court months ago but I got laid off and he built the fence the day our son was born. We had more important things to do. The city will have nothing to do with this.

Answer. You are describing a brazen example of "encroachment," which is an unauthorized use and infringement on a neighboring piece of property. Let there be no mistake: This is a serious offense against your property rights.

You must take the following actions as soon as possible (meaning, within the next few days):

1. Dig out your survey from when you purchased the house. If you can't locate it, then pay for a new one. The survey removes all debate from the discussion with your neighbor as to what post, sidewalk line, old maple tree, or other supposed marker indicates where his property line begins and yours ends.

2. Schedule a meeting with your neighbor to go over the survey so he cannot claim that he didn't know where the real property line is located.

If this piece of information is enough to bring him to his senses, then that means the fence and the shed need to be moved. If the relationship with the neighbor is important to you (and I hope it is), you may even offer to help him with the moving of the additions. This will show him that you're willing to go the extra step to help him adhere to the survey. I know it seems like a lot of work on your part, even though you've been victimized here, but I also believe your relationship with this person—regardless of how strained—needs to be mended, as well as the fence. Living happily together with our neighbors is what makes a community.

3. Take the survey to the planning commission and see what it will do about it. If the commission says it's not its concern, then proceed to the next step.

4. Contact an attorney. You must understand that even though the neighbor has encroached on your property, if it goes uncontested for a particular length of time the property could revert to him through a process called "adverse possession."

Adverse possession is a means by which title may be acquired through a hostile occupancy of a piece of property—usually it's open land being used by an adjacent landowner without the actual property owner's knowledge.

5. One other possibility is for you and your neighbor to strike a deal. Have both lots resurveyed with his lot being expanded, yours reduced, and have the new surveys recorded at the courthouse. If you're in a cookie-cutter development that is ruled by homeowner association regulations, this may not be an option. Check with your HOA board of directors to see if you have any recourse through it, as well.

Otherwise, as you try to sell the house, title insurance companies may not be willing to insure against title issues when they see that the neighbor's fence and shed are on your property. It may affect your refinance as well—check with the loan officer.

6. Finally, dig out your title insurance policy. You may actually be covered for encroachment. I know of some policies that cover up to $5,000 to handle such a situation.

Real Estate Investing Means Paperwork

Paper is an important element of the real estate ownership process. If you desire to invest in multiple properties, then when it comes to these sheets of paper—get to know them well. As you can see, to start with you'll need to understand sales contracts, mortgage applications, deeds, liens, surveys, and a plethora of other legal documents that can make or break the deal. It can seem overwhelming when you look at just one file from a sale, but once you get familiar with these documents, you'll be able to identify them from ten paces out. Make note of the Web sites and companies I've referenced in this chapter, as they will be great resources for your real estate investing education.

Note

1 American Land Title Association, www.alta.org, Washington, D.C.

CHAPTER 13

Tax Benefits and Responsibilities of the Real Estate Investor

For crying out loud, don't make a bunch of money and then give it all to Uncle Sam! Here's a resource chapter on what you can expect to pay in taxes, but also how you can expect to benefit from the tax code for doing your part in repairing and maintaining the national housing pool as a real estate investor. Before going much further, let me provide you with one good tip. . . .

Get professional legal and financial advice. This chapter is not to be construed as being a substitute for professional legal, financial, tax, or any other kind of advice. Keep in mind that tax laws change all the time—at least annually. I implore you, my friends, seek out the professionals!

While you'll find plenty of tips and explanations of the law and real estate tax requirements, this one chapter does not provide all you can or need to know about your tax liabilities with regard to real estate investing. Everyone's situation is different. Your active and passive income will determine what's deductible and what's not. Your state and local governments will also govern what you can and cannot do with your business. The information in this chapter provides you with a good resource for where you need to go to ensure you abide by the letter of the tax law.

Deductions to Lower Your Tax Bill

There are a lot of deductions available to homeowners and investors alike. Some of them are going to cross over, so I'll deal with the homeowner deductions first. Keep in mind that the ownership of real estate is considered a business expense; thus, the cost of upkeep on the rental property (paint, maintenance, landscaping, and so on) and the cost of operations (property management, commissions, closing costs, and so on) are deductible. Some of these expenses may not be deductible for a private residence; however, some of them are deductible if you operate a business out of your home and have a home office.

While it may have appeared that the tax bill of 2001 wouldn't affect homeowners overall, you had to look at the fine print to realize the new rates and tables would actually knock some homeowners out of the mortgage interest deduction game. (For a look at current federal income tax rates, visit http://taxes.yahoo.com/rates.html.) At the same time, for taxpayers who earned more than $47,450 in 2002 you will notice a tremendous reduction in taxes, as you drop from a tax rate of 27 percent down to 15 percent.

If you were on the cusp of the two tax brackets, your mortgage interest deduction should now become a very important part of your tax strategy. If it brings you down to the lower bracket, you're going to save hundreds of dollars over your previous year's numbers. Keep in mind, I'm not an accountant, but just look at the tables at www.cch.com (the Web site for CCH Incorporated, a leading provider of tax and business law information and software) and you'll see what I'm talking about.

For those in the lower tax brackets, it may work best for you to look at taking the standard deduction instead of deducting your home mortgage interest. In the past, a taxpayer would weigh the difference by adding up all allowable deductions and comparing them to the standard deduction. For taxpayers filing jointly, the standard deduction jumps from $7,950 to $9,500 with the new tables.

Here's what I'm talking about: Let's say you're the owner of a condo or manufactured home in Florida with a mortgage that started out at $35,000, 6 percent, 30 years—your interest payments the first year will be only $2,983.28, according to the mortgage/amortization calculator I used at www.AccessNational.com.

This means you will have to come up with nearly $6,500 more deductions elsewhere to be able to use that home mortgage interest as a substantial itemized deduction on your Form 1040. With charitable donations and a kid or two, that might not be a problem. If not, I'm no rocket scientist, but go for the higher standard deduction—it looks like it would make sense (talk with your accountant).

Regardless of what your mortgage interest deduction ends up being, the new rates (all brackets above 15 percent) will most likely drop your tax bill. If you meet the itemized deduction limit, your mortgage interest deduction will lower your tax bill even more.

In addition, by expanding the 15 percent bracket by $9,350 for the "married filing jointly class"—the marriage penalty just got a lot less taxing (no pun intended). The mortgage interest deduction really takes a bite out of your tax bill if you were earning between $55,000 and $58,000 (married filing jointly), because now, you don't have to hunt around for that extra $9,350 in deductions to drop into a lower rate.

Finally, the marriage penalty is starting to look more like a marriage bonus. (If you've been holding off tying the knot, take the extra tax savings, make a down payment on a ring, and take your intended out to dinner.)

Another area of tax savings will be on capital gains. All the talk about cutting capital gains kept focusing on the rich and famous and how this benefits them in their sales of stocks and bonds. Well, I know a few middle-income old folks who have invested in real estate all their lives who are going to benefit immensely from this rate change.

The 20 percent tax on long-term capital gains will now drop to 15 percent. Long-term capital gains are gains acquired from assets held more than a year. (Keep this in mind when you're talking about fixing up and flipping properties. Those gains are short-term gains and will be taxed at the same rate as ordinary income, like wages and interest income, unless you have a capital loss that eliminates it.)

If your income is in the 10 or 15 percent brackets, your capital gains tax rate is cut in half to 5 percent and eventually will be dropped to zero by 2008. The tax bill can help a lot of people who have investments or equity in real estate. Get to know the law to find out how it will benefit you.

Upkeep Costs Deductible for Home-Based Business Owners

If you operate a business out of your home, you may have some substantial deductions coming your way. Let me direct your attention to IRS Publication 587 "Business Use of Your Home (Including Use By Day-Care Providers)." Now, simmer down—I know this sounds like excitin' readin', but trust me, you can substantially cut your tax bill by operating your real estate business (or any other business, for that matter) out of your home. To see if your home office qualifies, look at the chart in figure 13-1.

To claim expenses for business use of your home, you must meet the following tests:

1. Your use of the business part of your home must be:
   - Exclusive
   - Regular
   - For your business, AND

2. The business part of your home must be ONE of the following:

Figure 13-1. Is your home office deductible?

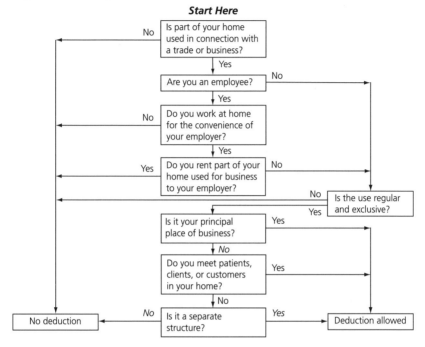

SOURCE: *www.IRS.gov:* "Is Your Home Office Deductible?"

- ▣ Your principal place of business
- ▣ A place where you meet or deal with patients, clients, or customers in the normal course of your business
- ▣ A separate structure (not attached to your home) you use in connection with your business

I'm not going to define "exclusive, regular, and for your business," here. You can do that with the online publications. However, let's run through an example of how a homeowner who uses her house in her business can deduct the expenses for her office.

The taxpayer must understand there are limits to this deduction. If the deductions are less than the gross income from the business use of your home, you can deduct all your business expenses related to the use of your home. If your gross income from the business use of your home is less than your total business expenses, your deduction for certain expenses is limited.

Expenses for a home office are reported on "Form 8829, Expenses for Business Use of Your Home." This form will walk you through several calculations for:

- Part of your home used for business

- Figure your allowable deduction

- Depreciation of your home

- Carryover of unallowed expenses to the next tax year

Let's talk about the fine print in IRS Publication 587. The fine print is where you get the tax savings. If you want the whole picture about how to qualify for all these deductions, then definitely get to this publication online at www.irs.gov. Type in "587" in the search line under "Forms & Publications" for the form. Search the site with "home office deduction" and you'll have plenty of great forms and publications at your fingertips.

What's really exciting is that when I had to fix my heat pump this winter, a portion of that bill will be deductible for me, since I operate a business out of my home. In fact, nearly all home-care expenses can be deductible as long as the office area is affected. The percentage calculation depends on the square footage of your house or the number of rooms in your house. If your office is 120 square feet and your house has 2,400 square feet, then your office makes up 5 percent of your house.

The rooms in my house are relatively the same size as those in most homes built in the mid-1970s, so I use the room formula. There are eight rooms in my house, so I deduct one-eighth of my qualified expenses from the income derived from my home-based business.

To find the nitty gritty of deductions, turn or scroll down to page 8 of Publication 587. You'll find clear instructions on what type of expenses are allowed.

IRS.gov says: "The part of a home operating expense you can use to figure your deduction depends on both of the following.

1. Whether the expense is direct, indirect, or unrelated.

2. The percentage of your home used for business."

Publication 587 even has a table, describing some sample expenses that are deductible and those that aren't.

Direct expenses are those that are only for the business part of your home. For example, if you painted and carpeted your office space, that expense is totally deductible (but be careful if you operate a day care—see instructions).

Indirect expenses include upkeep and operation of the entire home, such as insurance, utilities, and general repairs. Then the deduction is determined based on the percentage of your office space. If your utility bills for the year ran $5,000 and your home office makes up 5 percent of your house, you can deduct 5 percent of those utility bills, or $250. Other indirect expenses include mortgage interest, real estate taxes, insurance, repairs, and maintenance.

An unrelated expense is something like lawn maintenance or painting a room in your house that is not used for business. These expenses are not deductible as expenses on the home office.

Publication 587 lists the following expenses as items that can be used in your home office deduction:

■ Depreciation

■ Insurance

■ Rent

■ Repairs

■ Security system

■ Utilities and services

I was most intrigued by the home repair deductions. Just so there's no misunderstanding, I'll quote the IRS directly on this one:

The cost of repairs that relate to your business, including labor (other than your own labor), is a deductible expense. For example, a furnace repair benefits the entire home. If you use 10 percent of your home for business, you can deduct 10 percent of the cost of the furnace repair. Repairs keep your home in good working order over its useful life. Examples of common repairs are patching walls and floors, painting, wallpapering, repairing roofs and gutters, and mending leaks.

Here's an example for you to calculate the indirect deductions: If you bring in $25,000 in your business and your indirect expenses total $3,600, you'll get to deduct $360 (if your office makes up 10 percent of your square footage) from your $25,000 income. If you paid $300 to have the office painted, however, that is a direct expense and fully deductible.

The entries on your Form 8829 might look like this:

I. Part of your home used for business

Area of home office:	200
Area of whole house:	2,000
Percentage of home office:	10 percent

II. Allowable deduction for indirect expenses

Deductible mortgage interest:	$4,500
Real estate taxes:	$1,000
Insurance:	$400
Repairs & maintenance:	$1,400
Utilities:	$1,800
Total:	$9,100
Times percentage of home office:	10 percent
Subtotal Deduction:	$910
Direct Expenses	
Repairs & maintenance:	$300
Subtotal Deduction:	$300
Total Deduction	$1,210

III. Depreciation of your home
      Smaller of home's adjusted basis or fair

market value:	$130,000
Value of land included in above figure:	$20,000
Basis of building:	$110,000
Business basis of building ($\times$ 10 percent)	$11,000
Depreciation percentage	$\times$ 2.461%
Depreciation allowed:	$271

When you add up all the appropriate lines calculated above, you have a $1,481 deduction off the income from this home-based business. However, if after the depreciation you were at a loss instead of a positive income, your deduction is limited (of course, see instructions from www.irs.gov or Publication 587).

Record Keeping

One man's record keeping is another man's trash heap; however, the IRS has a few words to say about keeping records. While the agency doesn't require a particular record-keeping methodology, you do have to keep records that substantiate the business use of your home. Items such as canceled checks and receipts are always good ammunition in case of a tax audit. The IRS does provide guidelines on what information should be kept:

- The part of your home you use for business.

- That you use part of your home exclusively and regularly for business as either your principal place of business or as the place where you meet or deal with clients or customers in the normal course of your business.

- The depreciation and expenses for the business part. You must keep your records for as long as they are important for any tax law. This is usually the later of the following dates:
  1. Three years from the return due date or the date filed
  2. Two years after the tax was paid

If you're depreciating part of your home for tax purposes, then keep records that prove such depreciation—tax assessments, your acquisition papers (sales contract, HUD-1, and so on). Basis records are vital and include documentation of your original purchase price, any improvements to your home, and any depreciation you are allowed because you maintained an office in your home. Form 8829 or the Publication 587 worksheets are allowed as records of depreciation. For more information on record keeping, see IRS Publication 583.

If you decide to use these deductions in your business, keep in mind there's always a string attached. As you deduct and depreciate these expenses to reduce your tax bill, at the time you sell your house, that portion of your capital gain exclusion will be reduced by that area of your house. In other words, since you're not paying taxes on it now, you will later. Be sure to talk to a professional to determine if this deduction is worth your time and money.

And yet another warning—once you sell the house, all those deductions you took for the home office are then calculated to determine your recapture tax (currently at 25 percent). There's some really good news on the recapture tax front, however. In the last year, the IRS decided to no longer collect capital gains taxes on the proportion of your home that was used as an office.

While taxpayers will still pay taxes on the depreciation previously claimed on the home office, you'll no longer have to calculate what portion of the gain is commensurate with the amount of square footage deduction that was taken.

Here's an example: for $50,000 profit on a house with a home office that accounted for 10 percent of the home (one room out of ten finished rooms), you will have to pay gain on $5,000, which is the 10 percent of the $50,000 gain. At the current top tax rate of 15 percent on capital gains, that's a $750 bill you otherwise wouldn't have. Now you have to pay taxes on only the depreciation taken, but in the end it's still a reduction in your tax load.

Not All Mortgage Interest Is Deductible

The deduction for mortgage interest is one of the largest benefits of homeownership. Generally, it is 100 percent deductible. However, there are times when it's not—or portions of it are not. According to IRS Publication 936: "Home Mortgage Interest Deduction," there are limits on home mortgage interest deductions depending on several factors, of which income and the interest amount are two.

One limit on your mortgage interest deduction is based on your income. If your adjusted gross income (AGI) is more than $137,300 ($68,650 if you are married filing separately) as of tax year 2003, you will have limits; those are found in the instructions for Schedule A (Form 1040).

Secondly, you will have limits on mortgage interest deductions if the acquisition mortgages on your primary and secondary homes exceed $1 million ($500,000 if married filing separately) on homes purchased after October 13, 1987.

If you are a married filer, and meet the above criteria, then your equity loan interest deductions are allowed on a home equity mortgage of $100,000. (Your individual tax situation may be different than the above example; please check with your accountant.)

For more examples and scenarios, refer to IRS Publication 936.

How to Lessen Your Tax Liability

One of the exciting things about real estate investing is that the law lets you postpone paying capital gains taxes for as long as you own the property. In fact, when you sell an investment property, you still don't have to pay Uncle Sam right away IF you are going to buy yet another real estate property.

The Section 1031 Exchange (also known as the Starker Exchange) is a great tool for real estate investors to defer capital gains taxes and keep expanding their equity in real estate at the same time.

One of the good things about real estate investing is that you don't have to pay on your gain until you finally sell the property AND take the money. However, investors can delay that tax day by exchanging the property for another property that is the same value or higher.

Simply put, you have the opportunity to take the equity that has grown in your investment property and place it into a second replacement property that may have a higher level of appreciation, thus allowing your wealth to grow even faster or greater. It's kind of like a rollover for real estate investors.

A suitable exchange would be any property or properties that are of the same value. The like-kind requirement only means that it's the same type of property, that is, real estate for real estate, trucks for trucks. You can sell your duplex and buy four condos or one single-family home, if you so desire.

Keep in mind that you cannot take any of the proceeds from the sale or even have access to them in between the transactions, and the replacement property or properties must be identified within forty-five days.

Here are the steps necessary to carry out a legal real estate exchange:

First line up the necessary parties to the transaction: The investor/exchanger, the buyer, the seller, and a qualified intermediary. In the process of a 1031 Exchange, you are the exchanger or investor. The other two parties involved in the transaction are the buyer of your property and the seller(s) of your target replacement property. There is a fourth party required for the investor to complete a like-kind exchange, the qualified intermediary. The qualified intermediary acts as a proxy with whom the exchanger executes the exchange. Through the qualified intermediary, the investor obtains the "Safe Harbor" protections of the tax code because the exchange of cash proceeds pass through the qualified intermediary.

Next, you execute a contract to sell an investment property to a buyer. This sold property is called the relinquished property. The exchanger assigns his or her rights in the sales contract to the qualified intermediary.

At closing, the deed of the relinquished property passes from the exchanger to the buyer as in any normal sale, but the purchase money passes from the buyer to the qualified intermediary. This is so the investor/exchanger doesn't touch the proceeds and thus is absolved from paying capital gains taxes.

After closing, the investor/exchanger is now on a deadline. He or she has a maximum of 180 days from the closing on the relinquished property to acquire a replacement property. Within 45 days from the closing of the relinquished property, the investor sends a list of possible replacement properties to the qualified intermediary.

Now, the investor enters into a contract with a seller to purchase a replacement property and, again, assigns his or her rights in the purchase contract to the qualified intermediary.

At the closing of the replacement property, the seller receives payment from the qualified intermediary and transfers the deed directly to the investor.

There are some limitations on this intermediary, by the way. Since this person will help you move the funds from the first property to the second property, he CANNOT be any of the following people: "your agent at the time of the transaction, employee, attorney, accountant, investment banker or broker, or real estate agent or broker within the 2-year period before the transfer of property you give up," according to IRS Publication 544: "Sales and Other Dispositions of Assets." The person cannot be related to you, either.

You may, indeed, purchase your dream vacation home for your future primary residence and hold it as an investment property (recommended at least one year) before moving into it as your primary residence. My research shows that once you have moved into the property and lived there for two years, it then converts over to your primary residence and thus you may reduce your gain again by the basis of the property, expenses of selling the house, and then take your exclusion—$250,000 for single filers, $500,000 for married, joint filers. So far the IRS has not closed this loophole, but keep your legal eyes open in case it does so in the future.

As usual, the Internal Revenue Service also has plenty of information about Section 1031 Exchanges available at www.irs.gov.

Capital Gains: Determining Basis and Gain Easier Than You Think

For private homeowners, you'll need to calculate your gain each time you sell a house to determine if you owe capital gains taxes. Since the national median sales price of a home stands around $171,000, not many homeowners will ever have to pay gains taxes on their personal residence. Homeowners have an exclusion of $250,000 each on capital gains from a home sale ($250,000 for single filers, $500,000 for married filers).

When calculating your capital gains, you must first understand your basis. Basis is how much it cost you to acquire a property—or the amount the home was worth when you inherited it or took sole possession of it through a divorce. The basis is the figure you will use to determine your gain in the future once you finally sell the house.

Generally, the basis of your property is determined by the cost you incurred to take possession of it. When you bought your house, the price you paid is the beginning of your basis. However, there are expenses you may incur that add to the basis throughout the time you own the property. This additional basis can also reduce the amount of gain realized when the house is sold. For instance, the following items (this is not an all-inclusive list) can increase the basis of property:

Capital Improvements

- Putting an addition on your home

- Replacing an entire roof

- Paving your driveway

- Installing central air-conditioning

- Rewiring your home

Assessments for Local Improvements

■ Water connections

■ Sidewalks

■ Roads

Casualty Losses

■ Restoring damaged property

■ Zoning costs

Thus if you bought a house for $200,000, your basis starts at that price. If you add an extra wing to the house in a couple years at a cost of $30,000, the cost of construction is added to your basis (now it's $230,000).

If a twister comes through and wipes out the roof on the addition and you restore the damage at $15,000, the basis increases to $245,000.

Now, you cannot take a double dip on an expense. If you can deduct the expense from your current taxes, then you cannot add that cost to your basis.

Once you know your basis, then you can work on your gain. Gain is determined by subtracting the basis from the amount realized in the sale of your property. This is not as simple as taking your gross proceeds and subtracting the basis amount. Uncle Sam actually lets a seller deduct selling expenses from the gross proceeds to determine the amount realized.

Selling expenses include: commissions, advertising fees, legal fees, and loan charges paid by the seller, such as loan placement fees or "points."

Using the above house, if it now sells for $400,000, first you subtract your basis ($400,000 − $245,000). Your initial gain is $155,000. Immediately, we see that you will not owe any capital gains if the house was your personal residence and you had lived in it for two of the last five years, remembering that personal residence gain is not taxed until it tops $250,000 for single tax filers or $500,000 for married tax filers.

If it was an investment property, then this is your initial gain. Now we subtract the selling costs:

Commission fees @ 6 percent:	$24,000
1 point paid for buyer on loan of $360,000:	$ 3,600
Estimated legal fees:	$ 1,000
Total cost of selling:	$28,600

The formula for determining reportable gain looks like this:

Net Gain:	$155,000
Cost of selling:	$ 28,600
Net Capital Gains:	$126,400

Now you're ready to calculate your capital gains tax based on your income level.

Remember that determining gain on an inherited property is different from determining gain on a home purchase. If you inherit a property, the basis is calculated according to the fair market value of the property from the date you take title. If you received the property as a result of a divorce, through the death of spouse, in a trade, or through some other means, then grab a copy of "Publication 523: Selling Your Home" and use the worksheet that starts on page 8 to calculate your new basis.

IRS Publications for Homeowners and Investors

523 Selling Your Home

527 Residential Rental Property

530 Tax Information for First-Time Homeowners

535 Business Expenses

551 Basis of Assets

936 Home Mortgage Interest Deduction

Taxes Increase with Property Values and Assessments

Obviously, you want to see your investment grow by virtue of appreciation. Without appreciation, the exponential growth in real estate investments would not be as impressive. There is a downside, and that is your property taxes will inflate with the property values.

A hazard of increased market values is the shadowing jumps you'll see in assessed values as well. Assessed values are what the local and some state governments use to tax your castle. As assessed values increase, your monthly escrows will also rise once your mortgage company gets the message on increased assessment values.

It won't hurt you financially to look over your tax assessment very carefully when your tax bill comes in. Tax assessors are human, too, and could possibly add a bathroom or bedroom to your property description by accident, thus increasing your tax bill.

Once you receive your tax assessment, that's the time to look over the bill and get online if possible, to see where you stand. In most jurisdictions, there is a limited amount of time for you to challenge the assessment.

The odds of finding such information online have become increasingly good. While tax assessment values and market values often differ, tax assessments are important. They are the benchmark that is used to establish your property taxes, perhaps thousands of dollars each year.

Why do assessments and market values differ?

Market values—the price of homes for sale now—are instant

and immediate. Assessments reflect home evaluations made every two or three years in most jurisdictions. Moreover, assessments may be limited by such things as annual caps and special provisions for seniors, veterans, and others.

The Internet makes public records research a breeze. One of the best places to find property records is a site called Portico: Web Resources for Advancement Professionals, a site hosted by the University of Virginia in Charlottesville. This is not just a site for property owners in Virginia. Instead, it offers links to property records sites internationally. If you own property and pay taxes, this site can be very useful if your public data is digitized and available through your county or city's Web sites. The front page of Portico first offers a collection of Web sites containing publicly available information. At this writing, the public assessor's information is located under the "Personal Property" section located at the top and center of the front page. Once you click the link, you're taken to a long page (I suggest creating these pages in a columnar format for even easier navigation) with states listed and their locales linked. From there, you can check out whatever it is your tax assessor's office has deemed pertinent enough to place online, assuming, of course, that your hometown has made digitizing land records a priority.

In my own backyard—Fairfax County, Virginia—not only did I find my current assessed value, but also the last two transactions of my property, acreage of the lot, house description, comparable sales used to determine the assessed value of my house, a parcel map of my neighborhood, and an aerial view of the whole community with my property highlighted in yellow.

Amazing. Scary, but amazing. While I like having access to the Portico and its subsequent public records, so does anyone else in the world—not just my address, taxes, names, and so on, but now satellite photos of my roof line, albeit from thousands of miles away.

If you don't find your jurisdiction available at UVA's site, then click over to www.Appraisers.com, a commercial site that has 3,200 pages—including a page with local appraisers for every county in the United States.

This one is high on graphics and ease of navigation, mainly directing surfers to its paid-listing directory for appraisers. Click a state, click a region, click a county, and you are then presented with a directory of appraisers using the site.

Tax Resources: Getting Ready for Next Tax Season

If you've bought or sold a home in the past year, now is the time to go through your paperwork to find the forms, bills, and old checks you'll need in April—and beyond.

A few years ago, I sold three personal residences within a thirteen-month period. I learned quite a bit about what records the IRS requires to claim certain deductions, gains, losses, and so on, versus what records I actually could find. The silver lining in all the cloudiness about taxes and your home is that the IRS has a great Web site (www.irs.gov) filled with plenty of useful information. The site is easily navigable and searchable.

To get started, click over to the site and take a look at Publication 552, "Recordkeeping for Individuals." Here you can find several important issues to consider.

Under "Why Keep Records," the importance of the home as a strategic part of tax planning becomes evident when you notice the IRS advises that one of the reasons to keep records is to: "Keep track of the basis of property. You need to keep records that show the basis of your property. This includes the original cost or other basis of the property and any improvements you made."[1]

With that said, every homeowner should start tracking the basis of his or her home from the day of settlement. Within Publication 523 there is, naturally enough, a section devoted to determining the basis of your home.

On the paper side, put together a folder that includes the records you'll need in the future to determine the basis of your home. (Reminder: The "basis" of your home is the cost of acquiring it, whether you pay cash, use mortgage financing, or a little bit of both. For real estate, the "basis" can include other items, such as recording fees and certain closing costs. For details, review the IRS publications and confer with your tax adviser.)

If you purchased a fixer-upper, rehabilitation costs can be added to basis, with certain restrictions. Other additions to the property (such as a new deck) that add to its value may also be added to your basis.

To add these to the basis, however, you must keep good records on how much you spent for each improvement. If you're faced with a big bill for capital gains, these dollar amounts can be added to the basis, which can reduce your tax bill.

IRS Customer Service Failure Leads to More Online Self-Help

There are some jobs on this planet I would never want, regardless of how much money I was offered. Bungee cord tester, crime scene janitor, and IRS employee all rank right up there—especially working for the IRS. A Treasury Department report from three years ago revealed that the information provided to taxpayers at the agency's walk-in centers around the country was wrong 73 percent of the time.[2] While the number of erroneous answers was down from 81 percent in 2000, it's still a scary thought that the IRS could answer your question in one mailing, then call for an audit in the next.

Frankly, it's hard for me to criticize these folks. Living in the D.C. area provides a different face of the "bureaucrat." Some of these hard-working federal employees are my neighbors, and I'm not going to cast the first stone. Imagine having to process a bazillion tax forms every year, each with various deductions, credits, incomes, and so on, and having to tell the difference between the real tax cheats and the right-brain filers (like myself) who just aren't good with numbers.

Regardless of this most recent failing grade, I am one of the biggest proponents (and users) of the IRS's consumer-friendly Web site.

The best section of this site for researching tax information as it relates to your real estate investments can be found at the "Topical Index for Forms and Publications." As you seek out more information on tax benefits and responsibilities, it's worth your time to get to know the tax publications and forms that you'll need as you move into the field of real estate investing.

Click around the site and find out all the publications and forms you'll need to gain the most tax benefit out of your investments. Hopefully, this index will save you some time (and tax dollars).

Generally, this index simply lists the name of the publication and a small explanation of why the homeowner needs it for filing. Depending on your filing status, most of the forms will be needed for homeowners every tax year, but check back before each tax season for updates and revisions from the IRS. (The online index also provides downloads of the actual tax forms to be used during filing; the latest service is the auto-fill form section.) The index includes publications and forms for Harry Homeowner as well as for investors:

521. Moving Expenses. This publication explains the deduction of certain expenses of moving to a new home because you changed job locations or started a new job. It explains who can deduct moving expenses, what moving expenses are and are not deductible, and how to report your moving expenses.

523. Selling Your Home. If you sold your primary residence, this is the publication you want to look over. Generally, your main home is the one in which you live most of the time. The publication also has worksheets to help you figure the adjusted basis of the home you sold, the gain (or loss) on the sale, and the amount of the gain that you can exclude.

527. Residential Rental Property. Investors take note of this publication, which discusses rental income and expenses, including depreciation, and explains how to report them on your return. It also covers casualty losses on rental property and the passive activity and at-risk rules. Take note, this is for investment owners who just have a few properties. There's also information for those who sold a rental property. (For information on figuring gain or loss from the sale or other disposition of a rental property, see chapter 3 in Publication 544, "Sales and Other Dispositions of Assets.")

530. Tax Information for First-Time Homeowners. Your first home may be a mobile home, a single-family house, a town house, a condominium, or a cooperative apartment. This is a great booklet that covers the following topics:

- How you treat items such as settlement and closing costs, real estate taxes, home mortgage interest, and repairs

- What you can and cannot deduct on your tax return

- The tax credit you can claim if you received a mortgage credit certificate (usually provided via your state or city) when you bought your home

- Why you should keep track of adjustments to the basis of your home

- What records you should keep as proof of the basis and adjusted basis

547. Casualties, Disasters, and Thefts. This explains the tax treatment of casualties, thefts, and losses on deposits. A casualty occurs when your property is damaged from a disaster such as a hurricane, fire, or car accident. A loss on deposits occurs when your financial institution becomes insolvent or bankrupt. Here, you'll find definitions of a casualty, theft, and loss on deposits; how to figure the amount of your gain or loss; how to treat insurance and other reimbursements you receive; the deduction limits; when and how to report a casualty or theft; and the special rules for disaster area losses.

551. Basis of Assets. Once you sell your house and cash out, you'll need to determine the basis of your home. Basis is the amount of your investment in property for tax purposes. Basis is also necessary in the case of transferring property, such as in a divorce or estate settlement. Use the basis of property to figure depreciation, amortization, depletion, and casualty losses. Also use it to figure gain or loss on the sale or other disposition of property. You must keep accurate records of all items that affect the basis of property—like permanent improvements to the property. This is one of those publications you will hate to read, but love what it does for you.

555. Community Property. Community property laws affect how filers figure income on their federal income tax returns if they are married, live in a community property state or country, and file separate returns. Although your tax may be less by filing a joint return if you are married, sometimes separate returns can work more to your advantage. If you and your spouse file separate returns, you have to determine your community income and your separate income. Community property states include: Arizona, California, Idaho, Louisiana, Nevada, New Mexico, Texas, Washington, and Wisconsin. (Alaska does not use this method of community income calculation.)

556. Appeal Rights Primary Publication.
    Examination of Returns, Appeal Rights, and Claims for Refund-Related Publications
    Publication 1: "Your Rights as a Taxpayer"
    Publication 5: "Your Appeal Rights and How To Prepare a Protest If You Don't Agree"

While these really don't have a lot to do with the tax benefits of your house, it's good to know they exist in case you come out on the short end of the stick with the IRS.

561. Determining the Value of Donated Property. If you decide to donate real property instead of sell it, this booklet helps donors and appraisers determine the value of the property that is given to qualified organizations. It also explains what supporting documentation you'll need to claim the charitable contribution on your return.

587. Business Use of Your Home (including use by day-care providers). If you have a home office, this publication is a must. It includes guidelines on figuring and claiming the deduction for business use of your home—which includes a house, apartment, condominium, mobile home, or boat. This publication covers information on:

- The requirements for qualifying to deduct expenses for the business use of your home (including special rules for storing inventory or product samples)
- What types of expenses you can deduct
- How to figure the deduction (including depreciation of your home)
- Special rules for day-care providers
- Selling a home that was used partly for business
- Deducting expenses for furniture and equipment used in your business
- What records you should keep
- Where to deduct your expenses

936. Home Mortgage Interest Deduction. Here's the publication all homeowners should read and digest—rules for deducting home mortgage interest. Part I contains general information on home mortgage interest, including points. It also explains how to report deductible interest on your tax return, while part II explains any limits you may face on your interest deduction. There's also a worksheet to help figure the limit on your deduction.

In addition to publications, the IRS has a series of forms and instructions that can also be found online. For those with an interest in real estate, the most important forms are probably:

Schedule D (Form 1040): "Capital Gains and Losses"

Form 1040X: "Amended U.S. Individual Income Tax Return"

Form 8822: "Change of Address"

Form 8828: "Recapture of Federal Mortgage Subsidy"

As with any tax issues, forms can be helpful but it's always in your best interest to consult with a tax professional.

Tax Relief Available When Disaster Strikes

Another government-sanctioned way of reducing your tax liability is available if your property has been the victim of a disaster. If you get a call in the middle of the night that your duplex just burned to the ground, you will be able to deal with this misfortune a little more easily through the tax code, which provides for residential casualty losses. Publication 547, "Casualties, Disasters, and Thefts" gives all the guidelines a homeowner needs to claim losses from a catastrophe.

There is plenty of information from the IRS about the how-to's, whats, and wherewithalls regarding losses to personal property at http://www.irs.ustreas.gov. Here are the highlights of what it takes to claim losses and where to go for more information.

Substantiation

First of all, what can homeowners claim? You may be able to deduct losses from incidents including car accidents, earthquakes, fires, floods, government-ordered demolition or relocation of a home deemed unsafe because of a disaster, weather (such as hurricanes, storms, and tornadoes), mine cave-ins, shipwrecks, sonic booms, and vandalism, even volcanic eruptions.

Nevertheless, a bona fide casualty loss deduction requires you to show you actually sustained a casualty loss and support the amount you take as a deduction. It's not enough to say, "I lost my home in a tornado."

Believe it or not, before and after pictures aren't enough. You'll have to provide the date it happened and document that the loss was a direct result of the casualty and that you are either the owner of the property or, if you rent, that you're contractually responsible for damage to the property.

When to Deduct

If your losses were in a locale declared by the president as a "disaster area" you may be able to take advantage of the loss in your current tax year and not have to wait till next year's tax-filing time to claim it.

For instance, if you sustain losses in 2003 on your home, you are allowed to either take the loss when you file your return for the current (2004) year, or you can amend the prior year's return (2002). If you make the latter choice, the loss is treated as having occurred in the preceding year, which may result in a lower tax for that year, often producing or increasing a cash refund.

How Much Loss?

To figure your deduction from the loss, you must first determine the allowable loss. Here are the three steps you need to take:

1. Determine your adjusted basis in the property before the casualty. (This is how much the house cost you when you bought it.)

2. Determine the decrease in fair market value (FMV) of the property as a result of the casualty. (To determine fair market value, you may want to consider using a professional appraiser, the cost of which is not deductible.)

3. From the smaller of the amounts you determined in (1) and (2), subtract any insurance or other reimbursement you received or expect to receive.

What Is My Deduction?

And now, the envelope please. For personal-use property, such as a house that you own, the loss has two limitations called the "$100 Rule" and the "10 Percent Rule."

First, take the total loss and subtract $100. (Don't ask me why, ask your accountant—it's the federal government, remember.) Then you must subtract 10 percent of your adjusted gross income from the loss and that is your bottom line number to reduce on your income.

For example: In June, a fire destroyed your lakeside cottage, which cost $44,800 (including $4,500 for the land) several years ago. (Your land was not damaged.) This was your only casualty loss for the year. The fair market value (FMV) of the property immediately before the fire was $80,000 ($45,000 for the cottage and $35,000 for the land). The FMV immediately after the fire was $35,000 (value of the land). You collected $30,000 from the insurance company. Your adjusted gross income is $40,000. Your deduction for the casualty loss is $10,700, figured in the following manner.

Adjusted basis of the entire property (cost in this example):	$44,800
FMV of entire property before fire:	$80,000
FMV of entire property after fire:	$35,000
Decrease in FMV of entire property (line 2 − line 3):	$45,000
Amount of loss (smaller of line 1 or line 4):	$44,800
Subtract insurance:	$30,000
Loss after reimbursement:	$14,800
Subtract:	$100
Loss after $100 rule:	$14,700
Subtract 10 percent of $40,000 AGI:	$4,000
Casualty loss deduction:	$10,700

While loss or damage of a home is a frustrating and expensive event, at least there are ways to limit the losses through this section of the tax code.

Helpful Sites for Tax Season and Your House

When it comes to tax season, I hit the Internet big time, looking for sites that can help me squeeze every dollar of tax savings out of my house and mortgage. Here are a few I highly recommend as you prepare for the next tax season.

Daily Digital: http://www.irs.gov/

This site is operated by the Internal Revenue Service. It's been a favorite of mine for about a year now and they've just revamped the site with some handy new features.

Once you arrive at the above URL, there are several links on the front to drill into the site for information. I have found the best way to navigate this rich source of tax information, however, is to use the search engine. For instance, "Tax Trails" on this site is one of the best resources I've ever seen on a tax Web site—but you would never find it from the front page. The reason being, it's from an older version of the site and, thus, hidden from normal people who don't hang out here! Search "Tax Trails" and you'll find an interactive area where the user can answer yes and no questions for insights into deductions, limits, credits, and more; tax tables that can be found by simply typing in "[Year] Tax Table"; a tax calendar to help pinpoint individual, business, and excise dates for 2001; a W-4 calculator to help you figure your federal income tax withholding; and more.

"Tax Trails" really caught my attention. If you've had questions about how your house expenses are affected by taxes, now you can get some answers from the IRS. The "Tax Trails" section has several questions to click through on home-related deductions and tax issues.

The click through questions about homeownership include:

- Is my home mortgage interest deductible?
- Are my home mortgage points deductible?
- Can you deduct business use of the home expenses?
- Sale of residence.
- Capital gains and losses.
- Basis of real property.

By clicking the question or section, the site then presents the user with "yes/no" questions. For instance, on "Is my home interest fully deductible?" the question was: "Were your total mortgage balances $100,000 or less ($50,000 or less if married filing separately)?" If you clicked "Yes," then, yes, your interest is fully deductible. The answer comes complete with links to the IRS publications that deal with the mortgage interest deduction and the forms that should be filled out to report the information to the IRS—all linked in PDF files. (You must have Adobe Acrobat Reader to read the files. Acrobat Reader is a free software program—go to http://www.adobe.com/ for a free download.) The site also provides toll-free numbers to call if you would rather have the forms mailed to you.

In addition to the above services, the other sections include "Tax Stats," "Tax Info for Business," "Electronic Services," "Taxpayer Help & Ed," "Tax Regs in English," "IRS Newsstand," "Forms & Pubs," and "What's Hot" on the site.

HomeAdvisor.com: http://homeadvisor.msn.com/selling/guides/taxconsequences.asp

Yes, this is a long URL, but it's worth the tips you can get from Microsoft's home information Web site. You always want to know your tax consequences when you buy or sell a home and you always want to talk with a tax professional before making big-ticket item decisions. But HomeAdvisor.com has put together a pretty good resource guide here with some helpful links to capital gains taxes, lucrative long-term savings, capital improvements, and other related information.

Homestore.com: http://www.homestore.com

Type "taxes" in this site's "Find" box for a great list of articles about taxes and your home, whether you're buying, selling, investing, or renting. The tax area is populated with plenty of tips on such issues as moving and taxes, lowering your tax bill with smart remodeling, and what renters can deduct even though they don't own a home.

H&R Block: http://www.hrblock.com

H&R Block has a clean and easy to navigate site. By typing in "real estate" in the "Find" section at the top of the homepage, the user is presented with thirty-seven pages of answers to questions regarding real estate and taxes, such as the use of your home in your business, deductions for depreciation and other expenses, and deducting points from your income.

As you can see one of the largest benefits of owning real estate is the ability to grow wealth without interference from the Tax Man. If you're going to take on the task yourself of monitoring your tax liability, I suggest using one of many tax software programs available to help you keep tabs with the numbers and changes in tax law.

No other investment I know of allows your money to grow at an accelerated rate because of the leverage of the investment (that is, $10,000 controlling $100,000 in value). In addition, it allows you to depreciate, to count off expenses, to add on to value with certain upgrades, and to take cash from the investment on a regular basis through payments called rent, as well as to take deductions when disaster strikes.

I've planted plenty of information in this chapter—it's now up to you to pull down these resources and get to know them intimately.

Notes

1 "Why Keep Records," www.IRS.gov, 2003.

2 Fowler W. Martin, "Taxpayers Seeking Help Often Received Wrong Advice," *The Wall Street Journal*, May 15, 2001, p. B7L.

CHAPTER 14

Tax Liens

How would you like to make money paying someone else's real estate (property) taxes? There's a little known investment opportunity available in thirty-one states where investors can put up as little as a couple hundred dollars to as much as tens of thousands of dollars and earn interest on the money.

You may be thinking, "I pay enough taxes as it is, why would I want to pay someone else's taxes, too?" Well, how does a consistent, annual interest return of 10 to 15 percent (and at times up to 50 percent) sound?

These are available through tax lien certificates and tax deeds sold throughout the country by county tax collection offices. Tax liens are what the local government places on a property held by a taxpayer delinquent in real estate taxes. Instead of bearing the debt of delinquent taxpayers, the local government auctions off the liens to investors at different times of the year to collect these tax amounts. These are called "tax sales."

If Mr. Smith owes $2,000 in real estate taxes and hasn't paid it, the county will place a lien on his property and then auction that lien to an investor. The investor gets the lien for $2,000 and the county gets the money it needs right away to pay its ongoing expenses. Meanwhile the investor begins to earn interest on that money. This interest can be as high as 50 percent.

The place to find these nifty investments is at the local tax collector's office. There are also Web sites where the information has been compiled in either print or electronic format. You could end up paying as much as $39 per state for the information or, as one site reports, $199 for the whole country (encompassing 3,300 counties). You can contact your local tax collector's office for a lot of this information as well. If you don't know where that is, then just call the main information number for your county or city and ask for the tax collector's office—they can help you from there. Some are more cooperative than others.

Basically, these are short-term investment opportunities. After the lien has been auctioned off, the county lets the owners know that they may lose their property to the tax lien certificate holder if they don't pay the taxes—and now with even more interest and penalties. This gives the property owner another opportunity and possibly the inclination to redeem the tax bill and keep his or her property. If they don't, then the tax lien certificate holder can foreclose on the property.

Most of property owners (about 95 to 98 percent) actually pay the taxes. So most folks who invest in these certificates are doing so for the high interest paid on their money. Nevertheless, if you're not willing to accept the risk of having to foreclose on someone (and taking on the added expenses of that action) then this may not be an investment for you.

In some jurisdictions, you may "win" the property, but then you may be responsible for all past years of unpaid taxes on the property. You are not responsible for mortgages, though, only property taxes and possibly some city liens due to fines on a property that was not maintained—the mortgage company can either choose to pay you the taxes owed plus the interest you have earned or write off the property if it feels the investment is not worth it. Property tax liens are superior to all mortgages. Be aware of these risks and act accordingly. *Investors must carry out due diligence on the properties to limit risk.* This means researching the properties, which are usually publicized in a local newspaper or on the tax collector's Web site a few weeks before the sale.

I've asked tax liens expert Brian Lee of TaxLiens.com to take over from here. Brian has purchased and traded more than $20 million in tax liens and has twenty-two years of experience in the financial markets, Internet-related sales and marketing, and tax lien industries.

Tax Lien Basics
by Brian R. Lee, IronClad Realty Services, Palm Beach, Florida, (www.TaxLiens.com)

The Hype
The first thing we want to point out is that if you expect to get regular returns of 50 percent, 100 percent, and 1,000 percent as portrayed by infomercials and slick Web salesmen, you may as well not read any further. Tax lien investing should be looked at as a lower-risk investment that offers a modest return. Goals should be set between 10 percent and 15 percent as a net return each year. Sure, you may get a foreclosure and hit a home run once in a while, but after your overall costs and almost guaranteed mistakes or foreclosure difficulties, your return will probably match these numbers. If your return is any higher, you have been very thorough in your research, efficient in your due diligence, and very lucky in foreclosures. Foreclosures do not come easy or as often as portrayed in most "sales" literature and seminars.

The Market
Property tax liens are issued by municipal taxing authorities (counties) in return for the payment of delinquent property taxes. For municipalities with poor tax collection rates, the sale of liens not only generates revenue from nonperforming assets, but also spares governments the politically awkward chores of eviction and foreclosure. They earn interest as specified by state statutes (8 to 50 percent) and are secured by the underlying real property. The liens are issued when a property is delinquent on its property taxes. This includes industrial, residential, commercial, and specially zoned

property and land. These liens are then auctioned on the open marketplace to individuals, firms, large corporations, and whoever else shows up.

Tax liens are superior to all other liens, including IRS liens. However, it is recommended that you do not buy liens on properties that have IRS liens. They can be a headache. Tax deeds are the actual conveyance of the real property itself subsequent to foreclosure by the municipal taxing authority.

Each year, more than $7.6 billion in delinquent property taxes is created, with the total size of the market at any given time being in the $20 billion range. There are 566 municipalities that sell municipal liens in New Jersey alone. The industry is growing at a rate of 8 to 12 percent per year.

Making Money

There are two types of returns in tax lien investing:

1. Redemption. A lien redeems (pays off) during its redemption period and you make back your principal, fees, and a percentage return on your principal investment. Redemption periods vary state to state and range from a period of one to four years.

2. Foreclosure. This entails taking possession of the underlying property after the property owner has failed to redeem within the redemption period. Foreclosure laws vary from state to state and difficulty of foreclosure is just as varied from state to state.

There are various parts of the marketplace where you can make money in one of these two ways. However, almost all "product" begins at the auctions.

Depending on time of redemption, the bidding system, and state law, a tax buyer can earn anywhere from 12 percent to 24 percent interest the first year by purchasing certificates. Interest earned for the second year can range upwards from 24 percent to 50 percent. Each redemption rate of interest can be found in the code or statute of a given tax lien type state. This interest rate is set into law and can be changed only by an act of legislation.

In each case, the individual, estate, or other entity that owes the taxes has a period within which they have absolute right to pay off the lien (this is what is referred to as "redeeming" the lien). This process varies by state (Florida is two years, South Carolina, one year). The redemption pays your principal (what you paid for the lien at the auction), fees (filing, notices, and so on), and any penalties that may be issued according to state statute. If the property owner does not redeem the deed within this time period, the lien holder has the right to file for deed. The statutes and procedures vary by state, so refer to the state statutes for exact details and process. The tax collector's office is a good source for this information.

Causes of Delinquency

Understanding the underlying causes of delinquency is important because they reflect the taxpayer's ability to eventually make payment. There are reasons, other than the inability to pay, that taxes are delinquent. The main ones are listed below.

- Taxpayers may miss payments simply because a municipality lacks the resources or expertise to effectively service receivables. These taxpayers will typically pay after the introduction of more aggressive servicing techniques, such as the threat of foreclosure.

- Taxpayers may skip payments due to short-term financial distress or temporary lack of liquidity, but they are likely to redeem outstanding liens. When these taxpayers lack necessary funds or face more insistent creditors, municipal redemption periods of one or two years typically provide sufficient opportunity for them to become current. Because tax obligations are relatively small, these taxpayers generally make payments after their more pressing financial difficulties are resolved.

- Some commercial property owners and larger taxpayers do possess sufficient resources for payment, but use delinquency as a form of financing. If the jurisdiction's delinquency penalties are competitive with the rates charged by regular lenders, a tax lien, in essence, offers property owners a "no documentation" loan for the length of the redemption period. "No documentation loan" delinquencies will realize a high voluntary payment rate, but only as foreclosure becomes imminent.

- Voluntary redemptions (where payment is received without threatening foreclosure) are dramatically lower if the underlying property value is less than the sum of outstanding taxes and other claims on the property. Cash flows from this type of property are limited to liquidation proceeds. If foreclosure and liquidation expenses exceed the property's liquidation proceeds, these properties will not generate any cash flow.

Is Tax Lien Investing for Me?

There are several questions you must ask yourself first to help determine whether or not you should even be investing in tax liens and by what means.

1. Does this fit my investment goals and strategies?

2. Is an investment instrument that brings the return of 10 to 20 percent something that interests me?

3. Can I afford to have capital illiquid for a number of years if that's how long it will take to redeem or foreclose?

You should answer *yes* to all of these questions before investing in tax liens.

4. Can I handle the investment?

5. Do I have the time to go to auctions, to perform due diligence work, to find opportunities, and to assess data or afford to pay for these services?

6. If I end up with real estate, will I have the means to manage the foreclosure and the property realized through foreclosure? Remember, over 95 percent of all liens pay off, but you should be prepared for the tasks at hand if the property becomes yours.

You should answer *yes* to all of these questions before investing in tax liens.

7. Do I mind getting my hands dirty?

8. Do I mind competition (and sometimes stiff competition) at an auction?

9. Do I have the wherewithal to deal with the inconsistencies, and sometimes downright stubbornness, of the county?

10. Can I really take someone's property from them if that is what it comes down to?

You should answer *no* to the first two questions before investing in tax liens. You can always pass on taking someone's property, but you will also pass on profits.

Time & Costs

There are commitments of time and money involved in tax lien investing. You will need funds to purchase tax liens and to maintain those purchases. The amount of time and money you put in will vary depending on how involved you become with the project and the amount of research you do.

Due Diligence

A list of tax liens is typically available three to four weeks prior to an auction, published in the local newspaper or available from the local jurisdiction. The list will often have the property's parcel number, its owner's name and address, or a legal description, land use, and assessed value. Some counties have tens of thousands of parcel numbers (Broward County, Florida, had approximately 33,000 in 2002), meaning your time for doing research may be limited. Since these lists are all that investors typically have available to them, we will use them as examples. When they are available differs by jurisdiction.

The first tasks include the five listed below; the amount of time needed to complete them will depend on the size of the list.

1. Decide what kind of properties you will bid on.

2. Determine the amount of investment capital you have for the auction.

3. Decide what price range you will bid on.

4. Decide what areas you will bid on.

5. Mark those on the list.

Cost: $0.00, if you use the list that is published in the local paper prior to the sale. Those running the auction will also have a list available; sometimes they charge a few dollars for it. You may then decide that you want to look at these properties, like any smart person would do. How many properties can you drive by in three weeks and do you have the time to do it at all? Some people skip this altogether and take their chances by buying based on the list information. You can decide if the risk that comes with not knowing exactly what you are buying is acceptable based on your time constraints. However, if you are going to look at the properties, follow these steps:

1. Decide which properties you are going to look at.

2. Map these properties.

3. Drive by these properties.

Either make notes on the value of the property and the area or simply mark *yes* on properties that are up to your standards. You can also develop your own rating system.

Cost: The price of gas and film, if you are taking pictures and not using a digital camera. If there is a property without an address, you may choose to go to the tax collector's office to retrieve tax maps. Tax maps are either aerial or platt maps that identify the exact location of a property and its confines. In some municipalities the county address information is inconsistent; in such cases we recommend getting tax maps for every property you plan to purchase liens on. Nearly every municipality has a different system for pulling tax maps; for assistance go to the tax collector's or tax assessor's office. Some map systems are very hard to read, and each property may take five to ten minutes just to locate. So, if you have a list of more than twenty properties that need tax maps, plan on spending at least a full day retrieving them.

When retrieving maps, have your list of properties with parcel or property account numbers ready.

- Pull maps and locate each one.

- Have copies made.

- Map.

- Physically look at property.

Now you have your list of what you are bidding on.

Auctions

Some auctions charge a bidder fee, but other than that you just need to bring the money you are planning to invest. Some counties require you to pay at the end of the auction for everything and some will allow twenty-four hours for payment, but I would not count on that. Be prepared to pay at the end of the auction.

Cost: up to $150

Servicing

During the life of your portfolio you are going to have to maintain it if you want a better outcome, which includes filing notices and receiving redemption checks (which takes tracking and accounting). If you are a larger investor and your portfolio is $500,000 or more, it may make sense to hire a professional servicer to manage your portfolio. Typically this will cost you about 2 percent of the value of your portfolio each year.

Cost: Be prepared to pay filing fees (which vary), and depending on your level of investment you may have to pay subsequent or prior taxes if you want to proceed to foreclosure. These taxes, filing fees, and other minor charges from the county are "rolled" up into your initial investment and you will earn interest on that as well.

Rules of the Game

■ **Ground Rules**. These are handouts, mail outs, or information given to potential investors from county governments outlining the requirements for the sale. The information in these ground rules usually includes the time, place, and date of sale; the deposit requirements, if any; the interest rate; the redemption periods; the bidding system; the bidding increments; and the summarization of statutes. These ground rules do not necessarily teach you how to become a successful tax lien investor and will not include very specific information about all the other aspects of investing, filing deeds, filing notices, or foreclosure details.

To find out what the exact rules are on tax lien investing and foreclosure laws for your area, refer to your state statutes. Some counties or state Web sites have this information posted or the tax collector's office may provide it. (At www.TaxLiens.com, we post links to many Web sites that can help you with this investment strategy.)

■ **Registering for the Sale**. Procedures vary by county. You must have a social security or tax ID number and complete a W-9

Form (W-8 Form for foreign individuals or entities). In addition, the county may require its own registration form for general contact information. A bidder number, also known as a buyer number, is assigned by the tax collector at the time of registration, allowing you to bid under that number. In most counties your bidder number stays the same from year to year. You may have more than one bidder number if you want to have two separate portfolios. When you win a successful bid, that bid will be assigned to your number for that particular parcel.

■ **Bidding Systems.** Some states bid down an interest rate, meaning that bidding starts at a particular percentage (in Florida it is 18 percent) and participants bid in increments. The bidder willing to take the least amount of interest on the money owed wins the bid. If you bid 10 percent on a particular tax lien, you get that rate of return over the redemption period. If the lien is paid off in one year and the lien was $10,000, then you will make $1,000 plus filing fees and sometimes other penalties.

In other states bidding starts at the amount of taxes owed and goes up from there. Depending on the competition, bidding may continue up to the assessed value or more. The winning bidder will then have to pay the taxes owed and leave the amount of the overbid as a good faith deposit.

Some states, such as New Jersey, employ a mixture of both types of auctions. Bidding will start at a certain percentage rate, bid down to zero, and then bidding with a premium attached begins. States using these latter two bidding systems obviously require more investment capital and are not recommended for beginners.

■ **Competition.** There are basically five groups at the auctions:
1. Spectators (25–35 percent)
2. Moms & Pops (45–55 percent)
3. Local real estate experts (10 percent)
4. Midsize portfolio holders (5 percent)
5. Institutional and corporate investors (including banks) (1–2 percent)

The characteristics of auctions vary from place to place, but the examples above offer a good sense of what you will experience at many of them. Over the last several years, the institutional and corporate investors have created the most competition.

Developing an Investment Strategy

In general, choose the type of properties you want to purchase liens on and then do one of three things:

1. Buy liens that are more likely to foreclose.

2. Buy liens that are more likely to redeem.

3. If you are a bit more sophisticated in your strategy and want to try and realize foreclosure but also want a relatively steady cash flow in the interim—buy both.

Once you think you have a strategy down for buying liens that are more likely to redeem, you can allocate a certain percentage of your investment funds to purchasing these type of liens. Then you can allocate the rest of your funds to purchasing liens that are more likely to foreclose, and wait out the redemption period or purchase more mature liens. This is not an exact science, but it will help you to consider the following information when determining a bidding strategy.

Calculating Redemption and Risks

We mention risk here because the acceptance or avoidance of risk is a strategy in itself. If you accept the risk of investing in liens in general and on certain properties, then you must have a plan to deal with the possibility that something goes wrong. Many situations can be overcome if you have the means to deal with them, some will plainly be a loss or a write-off, a few could become nightmarish. Although the likelihood of redemption can be assessed to some extent, we will consider the advantages and disadvantages of foreclosures, since they hold the potential for the greatest profits and the greatest losses.

Vacant Residential

Potential Advantages

- You know exactly what you're getting.

- If large enough, you can divide into multiple lots, potentially increasing your investment.

- Offers a clean slate for development.

- In some areas, these resell like hotcakes.

Potential Disadvantages

- The property may represent an environmental risk if it is nearby or next to a gas station or some other potential Environmental Protection Agency (EPA) hazard. Many times, these properties are unkempt and get fines piled on them by the city.

- Zoning issues can arise if no structure is currently there and you try to build something new. If the city so desires, they can change or deny zoning for the property because of this.

Vacant Commercial

The potential advantages and disadvantages are the same as for vacant residential properties, with zoning and EPA issues being potentially larger problems.

Vacant Industrial

The potential advantages and disadvantages are the same as for vacant residential properties, with zoning and EPA issues being potentially much greater problems. Selling land zoned industrial can be very difficult because of these issues, especially since it is likely that there are EPA problems with the property itself.

Common Areas & Easements

Potential Advantages

None

Potential Disadvantages

- Impossible to develop
- Impossible to sell

Zoned Other—Usually Parks or Schools

Potential Advantages

Better have a good lawyer

Potential Disadvantages

Better have a good lawyer

However, if you are able to look further into the properties that are zoned "Other" you may find something good—something very likely to pay off or simply something strange, but marketable commercial property nonetheless. If there is good data from the county and you have the ability to dig a little, I would not necessarily discount these.

Government & University Land

Don't even think about it.

Mobile Homes

The potential advantages are not significant; either they are going to pay off or they are not. There is one potentially big disadvantage—if they are not one of the larger affixed mobile homes, they can drive off at any time.

Residential

Potential Advantages

- Large profit potential.

- Likely to pay off if "Lien-to-Value" is low.

- Can provide for good rehab opportunities, thus providing flip or income property.

Potential Disadvantages

- House burns or is destroyed in some other way and the resulting property is worth less than the lien you bought plus any priors or subs you may have to pay off to foreclose.

- Bankruptcies and other legal issues—these can pop up but are usually listed in the information with the county. They can occur between the time you buy the lien and redemption period end.

- You have to choose whether you want to take a loss or take some poor old lady's home. It's something you may have to deal with. Just the truth here, folks.

Commercial Property

Potential advantages and disadvantages are essentially the same as for residential, with EPA risks being an issue depending on the type of property. There is a higher rate of foreclosure on properties of lesser quality due to the likelihood that they may become a write-off for a corporation or individual, if the "Lien-to-Value" is higher. Remember though, it typically takes a lot more knowledge and effort to rehab a commercial property.

Industrial Property

These are always a bit risky due to zoning restrictions, potential EPA risks, and the marketability of such properties. If the business looks to be in good shape, "Lien-to-Value" is not exceptionally high, and there are no large EPA or zoning issues, these properties will likely pay off. If you end up in foreclosure and the lien has not cost you that much, as long as you can fund the asset until it sells or re-leases, you can probably make a lot of money.

Government & University Property

Don't even think about it.

Afterword

■ **Prior Taxes**. If a redemption period expires and you gain the right to file the tax deed, you may need to pay off prior years' taxes to file the deed. This then becomes another investment. The clerk's office or tax collector's office will provide this information once you claim interest in filing the deed. You must compare the property's investment cost with its market value, then decide if it is worth continuing with filing the tax deed and pursuing the subsequent foreclosure, if available. If not, you will hope that some other lien holder from another year will find it worth it to do so or that the property owner eventually pays off the lien. Otherwise, you may be stuck with your investment.

■ **Subsequent Taxes**. When property owners become delinquent in paying their taxes, these are called defaulted, delinquent, or back taxes. If taxes aren't paid the second, third, or fourth year, these are called subsequent taxes. In some states a tax purchaser is required to pay these subsequent taxes, thus resulting in an increased investment. Some states will have a subsequent tax sale and the original tax purchaser is redeemed. In others, you may lose your investment for failure to pay these taxes. All states have their peculiarities on the procedures for handling these subsequent taxes. You will earn interest on subsequent taxes.

■ **Tax Deed Process.** Tax deeds are issued by the clerk of the court. Once the redemption period has passed and all subsequent or prior taxes are satisfied, if need be, the right to file deed becomes realized. In some states, such as South Carolina, the deed is immediately issued upon filing. In other states, such as Florida, the deed is then placed on the tax sale roll to be auctioned at a tax deed sale. The actual sale may not occur for that particular property for a number of months, but in most states you will earn the maximum interest on total taxes owed during that time period. You may still be outbid at the tax deed sale by a competitive bidder, since these sales are also held as an open marketplace. They will then in turn pay everything that is owed to you. So, it's still not such a bad deal.

■ **Notices and Foreclosure.** Notices are of the utmost importance. Giving the proper notices is just as important as bidding. If you are the successful bidder on a valuable piece of property and you acquire this property, you can lose everything if you have failed to give the proper notices. In some counties, the treasurer, tax collector, or auditor will perform this task for you. However, it is your responsibility to get these procedures done, even to remind the county official to do this.

In every state code or statute there are notice requirements. Mortgagees, lien holders, creditors, heirs, and owners of record that have an interest in a property are called "interested parties." All interested parties have to be notified, either by publication, by certified mail, by personal service, by sheriff, or simply by a posting. If interested parties aren't notified as prescribed by law, then the tax buyer will not receive a deed, or the deed will be attacked at a later date.

Each state's statutes or codes always have sections pertaining to the requirements for notification of interested parties. Some of these requirements are in detail. These notices are given not only for the benefit of the property owner, but also for the interested parties. This is due process of law. These notices give the interested parties the right to not lose their property at a tax sale, or the right to redeem or recover ownership of their property or interest in property.

If all notices are given properly and you are not redeemed, then that is just too bad for the interested parties. You will receive the property. Interested parties forfeit ownership to property for a multitude of reasons.

■ **Title Issues.** Title insurance companies will not insure a tax deed. In some cases they may insure the title after the tax deed has been issued for four years, others say they will after twenty years. If you want to sell the property and offer title insurance you must file a "Quiet Title Suit." The Quiet Title process is not complicated, but it will require hiring an attorney. It is recommended that you use a company or attorney that specializes in Quiet Title Suits. The minimum fee is $300 to $500 for a noncontested suit. If the former owner files an answer, this will require more of the attorney's time and possibly an appearance in court for a hearing, thus increasing your cost.

During the tax deed process a title search is conducted on the property; you paid for it and you have a right to obtain a copy of it. Make sure you always get a copy. It will be helpful and should save you additional expense in the event you chose to file for a Quiet Title. It is also recommended that you write letters to former owners, offering to pay them a small fee ($100 to $200) in exchange for their signing a Quit-Claim Deed. This will avoid the Quiet Title Suit and their names being published in the paper. Few will take you up on your offer, but it is well worth the try, and you get to at least verify their address so your attorney can serve them with notice if you file the Quiet Title Suit. If you receive and record a Quit-Claim Deed you can offer title insurance.

For the investor who wants to benefit from the high-interest returns of real estate, but who doesn't want to get involved with property upkeep, tenants, and the daily challenges of owning real estate, the tax lien investment can be a good alternative. Understand your risks, visit your local tax lien auction, and ask the tax office plenty of questions about how the local auctions work. For more information and assistance, visit www.TaxLiens.com.

Appendix

State Housing Finance Authorities

Alabama Housing Finance Authority, Web: www.ahfa.com Phone: (800) 325-AHFA

Alaska Housing Finance Corporation, Web: www.ahfc.state .ak.us Phone: (800) 478-AHFC (outside Anchorage, but within Alaska)

Arizona Department of Housing/Arizona Housing Finance Authority, Web: www.housingaz.com Phone: (602) 771-1000 (Voice) (602) 771-1001 (TTY)

Arkansas Development Finance Authority, Web: www.state.ar .us/adfa Phone: (501) 682-5904

California Housing Finance Agency, Web: www.calhfa.ca.gov Phone: (916) 322-3991

Colorado Housing and Finance Authority, Web: www.colo hfa.org Phone: (800) 877-2432

Connecticut Housing Finance Authority, Web: www.chfa.org Phone: (860) 721-9501

Delaware State Housing Authority, Web: www2.state.de.us/dsha Phone: (302) 739-4263

District of Columbia Department of Housing and Community Development, Web: http://www.dchousing.org/ Phone: (202) 535-1000

Florida Housing Finance Corporation, Web: www.florida housing.org Phone: (850) 488-4197

Georgia Department of Community Affairs/Georgia Housing and Finance Authority, Web: www.dca.state.ga.us Phone: (404) 679-4940

Housing and Community Development Corporation of Hawaii, Web: www.hcdch.state.hi.us Phone: (808) 587-0524

Idaho Housing and Finance Association, Web: www.ihfa.org Phone: (208) 331-4882

Illinois Housing Development Authority, Web: www.ihda.org Phone: (312) 836-5200

Indiana Housing Finance Authority, Web: www.in.gov/ihfa Phone: (317) 232-7777

Iowa Finance Authority, Web: www.ifahome.com Phone: (800) 432-7230

Kansas Development Finance Authority, Web: www.kdfa.org Phone: (785) 357-4445

Kentucky Housing Corporation, Web: www.kyhousing.org Phone: (502) 564-7630

Louisiana Housing Finance Agency, Web: www.lhfa.state.la.us Phone: (225) 763-8700

Maine State Housing Authority, Web: www.mainehousing.org Phone: (207) 626-4600

Maryland Department of Housing and Community Development, Web: www.dhcd.state.md.us Phone: (410) 514-7000

Massachusetts Department of Housing & Community Development, Web: www.state.ma.us/dhcd Phone: (617) 727-7765

MassHousing, Web: www.masshousing.com Phone: (617) 854-1000

Michigan State Housing Development Authority, Web: www.mshda.org Phone: (517) 373-0011

Minnesota Housing Finance Agency, Web: www.mhfa.state.mn.us Phone: (651) 296-7608

Mississippi Home Corporation, Web: www.mshomecorp.com Phone: (601) 718-4636

Missouri Housing Development Commission, Web: www.mhdc.com Phone: (816) 759-6600

Montana Board of Housing/Housing Division, Web: www.commerce.state.mt.us/Housing/Hous_Home.html Phone: (406) 841-2700

Nebraska Investment Finance Authority, Web: www.nifa.org Phone: (402) 434-3900

Nevada Housing Division, Web: www.nvhousing.state.nv.us Phone: (702) 486-7220

New Hampshire Housing Finance Authority, Web: www.nhhfa.org Phone: (603) 472-8623

New Jersey Housing and Mortgage Finance Agency, Web: www.nj-hmfa.com Phone: (609) 278-7400

New Mexico Mortgage Finance Authority, Web: www.housingnm.org Phone: (505) 843-6880

New York City Housing Development Corporation, Web: www.nychdc.com Phone: (212) 227-5500

New York State Division of Housing and Community Renewal, Web: www.dhcr.state.ny.us Phone: (866) 275-3427

New York State Housing Finance Agency/State of New York Mortgage Agency, Web: www.nyhomes.org Phone: (212)688-4000

North Carolina Housing Finance Agency, Web: www.nchfa .com Phone: (919) 877-5700

North Dakota Housing Finance Agency, Web: www.ndhfa.org Phone: (701) 328-8080

Ohio Housing Finance Agency, Web: www.odod.state.oh.us/ ohfa Phone: (614) 466-7970

Oklahoma Housing Finance Agency, Web: www.ohfa.org Phone: (405) 848-1144

Oregon Housing and Community Services, Web: www.hcs .state.or.us Phone: (503) 986-2000

Pennsylvania Housing Finance Agency, Web: www.phfa.org Phone: (717) 780-3800

Puerto Rico Housing Finance Authority, Web: www.gdp-pur .com Phone: (787) 722-2525

Rhode Island Housing and Mortgage Finance Corporation, Web: www.rihousing.com Phone: (401) 751-5566

South Carolina State Housing Finance and Development Authority, Web: www.sha.state.sc.us Phone: (803) 734-2000

South Dakota Housing Development Authority, Web: www .sdhda.org Phone: (605) 773-3181

Tennessee Housing Development Agency, Web: www.state .tn.us/thda Phone: (615) 741-2400

Texas Department of Housing and Community Affairs, Web: www.tdhca.state.tx.us Phone: (512) 475-3800

Utah Housing Corporation, Web: www.utahhousingcorp.org Phone: (801) 521-6950

Vermont Housing Finance Agency, Web: www.vhfa.org Phone: (802) 652-3400

Virgin Islands Housing Finance Authority, Web: http://www .vihousing.org Phone: (340) 774-4481

Virginia Housing Development Authority, Web: www.vhda .com Phone: (804)782-1986

Washington State Housing Finance Commission, Web: www .wshfc.org Phone: (206) 464-7139

West Virginia Housing Development Fund, Web: www.wvhdf .com Phone: (304) 345-6475

Wisconsin Housing and Economic Development Authority, Web: www.wheda.com Phone: (800) 334-6873

Wyoming Community Development Authority, Web: www .wyomingcda.com Phone: (307) 265-0603

Index